LIBERALISING A REGULATED BANKING SYSTEM

For Clyde, Dawn and Paul

Liberalising a Regulated Banking System

The Caribbean Case

MARION V. WILLIAMS

Avebury

Aldershot • Brookfield USA • Hong Kong • Singapore • Sydney

Published by
Avebury
Ashgate Publishing Limited
Gower House
Croft Road
Aldershot
Hants GU11 3HR
England

Ashgate Publishing Company
Old Post Road
Brookfield
Vermont 05036
USA

British Library Cataloguing in Publication Data
Williams, Marion V.
  Liberalising a regulated banking system : the Caribbean case
  1.Banks and banking - State supervision 2.Banks and banking
  - Caribbean Area - State supervision
  I.Title
  332.1'09729

Library of Congress Catalog Card Number: 96-85207

ISBN 1 85972 432 9

Printed and bound by Athenaeum Press, Ltd.,
Gateshead, Tyne & Wear.

Contents

Figures and tables   viii
Appendices   xii
Questionnaire   xiii
Symbols and abbreviations   xiv
Acknowledgements   xvi
Preface   xvii

1 Introduction   1
1.1 Regulation   3
1.2 The interrelationship between structural, monetary and
    prudential regulation   6
1.3 Measures of bank performance   9
1.4 Cost-axiomatic and accommodative pricing   11
1.5 Summary of bank performance   11

2 Review of the literature   15

2.1 Monetary regulation in developing countries
    with special reference to the Caribbean   15
2.2 A review of the literature on the impact of regulation on
    commercial bank performance   30
2.3 Empirical studies: monetary and prudential regulation   55
2.4 Conclusion   60

**3 The structure and performance of the banking system
in the Caribbean**   64

3.1 Introduction   64
3.2 Structure of the banking system   65
3.3 The Caribbean experience with monetary regulation   69
3.4 Prudential concerns   80
3.5 Bank performance and regulatory costs in the Caribbean   86
3.6 Conclusion   99

**4 Regulation and commercial bank performance: evidence
from a survey of banks**   105

4.1 Introduction   105
4.2 Impact of regulatory measures on bank profitability   105
4.3 Impact of regulatory measures on bank liquidity   115
4.4 Impact of regulatory measures on bank risk   118
4.5 Impact of regulatory measures on bank solvency   121
4.6 Impact of regulatory measures on bank market share   123
4.7 Summary of views and expectations   127

**5 A model for testing the impact of regulation on
Caribbean commercial bank performance**   131

5.1 Introduction   131
5.2 Assumptions   132
5.3 The model   132
5.4 Explanation of the independent variables used   134
5.5 Profitability measures   137
5.6 Tests using other bank performance measures: dependent variables 138
5.7 Data constraints   139
5.8 Methods of testing   140
5.9 Discriminant analysis: calculating composite measures
of bank performance and regulation   146
5.10 Causality tests   148

6 Regulation and bank performance: results of empirical tests   151

6.1 Introduction   151
6.2 Regulation and bank profitability: results of regressions   152
6.3 Regulation and bank risk: results of regressions   179

6.4 Regulation and liquidity: results of regressions   184
6.5 Regulation and bank solvency: results of regressions   193
6.6 Regulation and market share: results of regressions   199
6.7 Discriminant analysis: developing a composite score   210
6.8 Granger causality tests: regulation and bank performance 224
6.9 Summary of results of empirical analysis   225

7 Conclusion and implications for the future   229

Appendices   234
Questionnaire   262
Bibliography   285
Index   302

Figures and tables

Table 1.1 Summary of structural, monetary and prudential regulation 5
Figure 1.1 The structural-monetary-prudential regulatory
    cycle 6
Figure 2.1 Savings and investment under interest rate ceilings: The
    McKinnon and Shaw view 18
Figure 2.2 Interest rates and output - the Van Wijnbergen case 19
Figure 2.3 Interest rates and output - the conventional response 19
Figure 2.4 Low risk and high risk loan markets 21
Figure 2.5 Deposit volumes under required reserve ratios 29
Figure 2.6 Deposit maximising required reserve ratio at different
    inflation rates 29
Figure 2.7 The Pelzman model of consumer surplus 33
Figure 2.8 Anonymously equitable pricing (p*) 33
Figure 2.9 Bounding insolvency risk by capital regulation 53
Table 3.1 Summary of economic statistics on Barbados, Jamaica and
    Trinidad and Tobago 65
Table 3.2 Types of structural regulation in the Caribbean 67
Table 3.3 Growth of assets of commercial banks 70
Table 3.4 Personal lending as a % of total commercial bank assets 71
Table 3.5 Foreign exchange reserves: equivalent number of months'
    imports 72
Table 3.6 Comparative reserve requirements (liquid assets ratios) 75
Table 3.7 Comparative interest rate spreads 76
Table 3.8 Differential between prime rate and 3 month deposit rate 77
Table 3.9 Tools of monetary regulation in the Caribbean 78
Table 3.10 Number of banks and non-banks 84
Table 3.11 Growth of non-banks 85
Table 3.12 Tools of prudential regulation used in the Caribbean 87

Table 3.13 Comparison of average lending rate and treasury bill yields 89
Table 3.14 Interest (% p.a.) spreads (% points) 90
Table 3.15 Cost of intermediation of Caribbean commercial banks 91
Table 3.16 Financial intermediation ratios in the Caribbean 93
Table 3.17 Comparative commercial bank profitability 94
Table 3.18 Bank performance indicators: Barbados 95
Table 3.19 Bank performance indicators: Jamaica 96
Table 3.20 Bank performance indicators: Trinidad and Tobago 97
Figure 3.1 Bank profitability (ROA): Barbados 98
Figure 3.2 Bank profitability (ROA): Jamaica 98
Figure 3.3 Bank profitability (ROA): Trinidad and Tobago 99
Figure 4.1 Primary and secondary reserve requirements: Barbados 106
Figure 4.2 Primary and secondary reserve requirements: Jamaica 107
Figure 4.3 Primary and secondary reserve requirements:
        Trinidad and Tobago 107
Figure 4.4 Comparison of credit to controlled sectors
        and treasury bill yields: Barbados 112
Figure 4.5 Liquidity and deposit rate variance: Barbados 117
Figure 4.6 Excess liquidity/manufacturing credit: Barbados 119
Figure 4.7 Capital, reserves and borrowing: comparison with
        profitability: Barbados 123
Figure 4.8 Banks' market share: Barbados 124
Figure 4.9 Banks' market share: Jamaica 124
Figure 4.10 Banks' market share: Trinidad and Tobago 125
Figure 4.11 Mortgage rates and mortgage loans: Barbados 126
Table 4.1 Expectations about regulatory changes: the Caribbean
        experience 128
Table 6.1 Dickey-Fuller (DF) and Augmented Dickey-Fuller (ADF) tests:
        part 1 153
Table 6.2 Barbados: results: cointegrating equation: profitability 156
Table 6.3 Barbados: results: error correction model: profitability 157
Table 6.4 Barbados: regulation and profitability: a cointegrating
        equation with capital 161
Table 6.5 Barbados: error correction model with capital 162
Table 6.6 Barbados: regulation and other measures of bank
        profitability 163
Table 6.7 Cointegration LR tests based on maximal eigenvalues of the
        stochastic matrix 164
Table 6.8 Maximum likelihood procedure: cointegration LR test based
        on the trace of the stochastic matrix 165
Table 6.9 Estimated long run matrix: Johansen estimation 165

ix

Table 6.10 Dickey-Fuller and Augmented Dickey-Fuller tests: part 2   167
Table 6.11 Dickey-Fuller and Augmented Dickey-Fuller tests: part 3   171
Table 6.12 Barbados: regulation and profitability:
           large, small and foreign banks   173
Table 6.13 Barbados: regulation and profitability: cointegrating
           equation: local banks   174
Table 6.14 Jamaica and Trinidad and Tobago: regulation and bank
           profitability: ECM   177
Table 6.15 Granger causality tests: (running from reserve requirements
           to bank profitability)   178
Table 6.16 Barbados: regulation and bank risk: error correction model 182
Table 6.17 Jamaica and Trinidad and Tobago: regulation and bank
           risk: ECM   183
Table 6.18 Barbados: regulation and liquidity: ECM   186
Table 6.19 Barbados: regulation and liquidity: ECM: small banks   188
Table 6.20 Barbados: regulation and liquidity: cointegrating equation
           and ECM: foreign banks   189
Table 6.21 Barbados: regulation and liquidity: local banks ECM   190
Table 6.22 Jamaica: regulation and liquidity: cointegrating equation:
           long run   191
Table 6.23 Trinidad and Tobago: regulation and liquidity: ECM   192
Table 6.24 Barbados: regulation and bank solvency (all banks)   195
Table 6.25 Barbados: regulation and solvency (local banks)   196
Table 6.26 Trinidad and Tobago: regulation and solvency   198
Table 6.27 Barbados: regulation and market share: cointegrating
           equation and ECM   200
Table 6.28 Cointegration LR tests based on maximal eigenvalues of the
           stochastic matrix   202
Table 6.29 Cointegration LR tests based on the trace of the stochastic
           matrix   203
Table 6.30 Cointegrated vector and weights   203
Figure 6.1 Market share: foreign banks: Barbados   205
Figure 6.2 Market share: local banks: Barbados   205
Figure 6.3 Market share: large banks: Barbados   206
Figure 6.4 Market share: small banks: Barbados   206
Table 6.31 Jamaica: regulation and market share: cointegrating
           equation and error correction model   208
Table 6.32 Trinidad and Tobago: regulation and market share: ECM   209
Table 6.33 Canonical discriminant functions: Barbados   210
Table 6.34 Standardised canonical discriminant function coefficients:
           Barbados   211

Table 6.35 Structure matrix   212
Table 6.36 Varimax rotation transformation matrix   212
Table 6.37 Rotated standardised discriminant function coefficients   212
Table 6.38 Correlation between canonical discriminant functions
           and discriminating variables   213
Figure 6.5 Composite index of bank performance: Barbados   214
Figure 6.6 Composite index of bank performance: Jamaica   215
Figure 6.7 Composite index of bank performance: Trinidad and
            Tobago   215
Table 6.39 Canonical discriminant functions: regulation   216
Table 6.40 Correlation between canonical discriminant functions and
           discriminating variables   217
Figure 6.8 Composite bank regulation index: Barbados   217
Figure 6.9 Composite bank regulation index: Jamaica   218
Figure 6.10 Composite bank regulation index: Trinidad and Tobago   218
Table 6.41 Index of bank performance (normalised)   219
Table 6.42 Index of bank regulation (normalised)   220
Table 6.43 Bank performance scores (non-normalised)   221
Table 6.44 Bank regulation scores (non-normalised)   222
Table 6.45 Granger causality tests: t-values and joint restrictions on
           coefficients of additional variables   224

Appendices

2.1 Solution via the method of Lagrange multipliers   234
3.1 Barbados: monetary and prudential regulatory changes:
    1972-92   237
3.2 Jamaica: monetary and prudential regulatory changes:
    1973-92   242
3.3 Trinidad and Tobago: monetary and prudential regulatory
    changes: 1972-92   247
3.4 Foreign exchange reserves in Barbados, Jamaica
    and Trinidad and Tobago   253
3.5 Total assets of commercial banks: Barbados, Jamaica
    and Trinidad and Tobago   254
3.6 Share of banks in total assets of banks and non-banks   255
3.7 Comparative bank rates: Barbados, Jamaica and Trinidad and
    Tobago   256
6.1 Results: excluding and including regulatory variables   257
6.2 Results of regression using the narrow definition of capital
    as an explanatory variable   258
6.3 Regression results with loan loss provisions (and staff expenses)   259
6.4 Loan deposit ratio: small banks: 1977-92   260
6.5 Loan deposit ratio: large banks: 1977-92   260
6.6 Loan deposit ratio: local banks: 1977-92   261

Questionnaire

Questionnaire   262

Responses to questionnaire   268

4.a   Responses on reserve requirements   269
4.b   Responses on credit controls   274
4.c   Responses on interest rate controls   278
4.d   Responses on prudential requirements   282

Symbols and abbreviations

General*

B'dos: denotes Barbados
BDS$: denotes Barbados dollars
GDP: denotes Gross Domestic Product
IFI: denotes International Financial Institutions
J'ca: denotes Jamaica
J$: denotes Jamaica dollars
n.a: denotes not available
T'dad and T'go or T & T: denotes Trinidad and Tobago
TT$: denotes Trinidad and Tobago dollars
.. denotes not applicable

Performance Measures

BTSETA: denotes Profits plus staff expenses as % of total assets
SOLV: denotes Solvency (Capital as a % of total assets)
CONSURDA: denotes Excess liquidity as a ratio of total assets
MKS: denotes Market Share
P*: denotes Performance index
ROA: denotes Before tax return on assets
ROPA: denotes Return on operating profit as a % of total assets
R*: denotes Regulation index

Dependent Variables

CAPB: denotes Capital, Reserves and Long-term borrowing as a % of total
        assets
CON: denotes Concentration ratio
DEP: denotes Deposits as a % of total assets

Dumin: denotes Dummy variable for interest rate control
Dumcr: denotes Dummy variable for credit control
ER: denotes Exchange rate
FX: denotes Foreign exchange reserves
I: denotes Interest rate spreads
Inf: denotes Inflation
LD: denotes Loan Deposits Ratio
LR: denotes Average lending rate
M: denotes Money supply
Perdis: denotes Loans outstanding to the personal and distributive sectors
Resid: denotes Residual
RR: denotes Reserve requirements as % of total assets
SAVR: denotes Weighted average savings rate
SF: denotes Staff expenses as % of total assets
s1,s2,s3: denotes seasonal dummies
TB: denotes Treasury Bill yield

Other Symbols

DW.: denotes Durbin-Watson Statistic
ECM: denotes Error Correction Model
Hetero denotes Heteroscedasticity
S.E.: denotes Standard Error
Ser.cor: denotes Serial Correlation
SSE_r: denotes Restricted sum of Squares
SSE_u : denotes Unrestricted sum of Squares
Π : denotes Profit

Prefixes

BC: denotes Local banks
J: denotes Jamaica
LA: denotes large banks
NL: denotes non-local (foreign) banks
SM: denotes small banks
TT: denotes Trinidad and Tobago

Acknowledgements

I wish to thank Dr John Mayers for the idea of embarking on this project and I am grateful to him for his initial and continual encouragement. I am indebted to Professor Graham Bird for his tremendous support and encouragement throughout the preparation of this work; his critical analysis was invaluable to its successful completion. I also wish to thank Professor Compton Bourne and Dr Andrew Downes for their support and for their insightful comments. Comments from Mr John Nankervis and Dr Roland Craigwell on my empirical work were also especially helpful. I am indebted to Miss Muriel Saunders for providing most of the voluminous statistical data for processing, and to the commercial banks for their cooperation in providing data and in completing questionnaires.

A huge debt of gratitude is owed to Mrs Arlette King for her committed assistance in providing unstinting secretarial support throughout the tedious typing of several drafts.

Lastly, my deepest thanks and appreciation go to my family, especially to my husband Clyde, whose whole-hearted support, encouragement and understanding were indispensable to the completion of this task; and to my children Dawn and Paul, who gave unstinting support and accepted with great understanding, my preoccupation during the period of preparation of this work.

Preface

It is the central hypothesis of this study that monetary controls impact adversely on commercial bank performance and on banks' market share, and that the simultaneous implementation of monetary and prudential regulation can undermine the objectives of monetary stability and the growth of the banking system. This study argues that those monetary measures most frequently applied to protect the balance of payments; primary and secondary reserve requirements, credit controls, and interest rate controls, force cost adjustments and non-optimal portfolio realignments which stymie commercial bank performance. These arguments are illustrated from the cases of Barbados, Jamaica and Trinidad and Tobago for the period 1973-92. These measures were taken in the context of structuralist models of development which still persist in the 1990s, and many developing countries continue to target macroeconomic stability through aggressive monetary controls based on structuralist assumptions. Simultaneously, prudential criteria, principally capital controls take effect through the commercial banking system.

The study discusses the rationale for regulation, analyses commercial bank performance in the Caribbean and formulates a model which includes regulatory variables for testing the impact of monetary and prudential regulation on bank performance. The model also defines the determinants of bank performance and provides the basis for deriving regulation and performance indices with global application. Results disclose that most regulatory variables are negatively associated with commercial bank performance and tentative causality is established running from regulation to bank performance. Where cost-axiomatic interest rate-setting is practised the adverse impact on bank performance is alleviated, but unevenness of monetary and prudential regulations adversely influence the performance of commercial banks, contributing to loss of market share of banks relative to non-banks. Regulation assists in achieving macroeconomic objectives, but greater liberalisation appears desirable for the development of commercial banking. However, new monetary theories are needed to identify alternative vehicles, for giving effect to monetary policy, if macroeconomic objectives are to be achieved in increasingly liberalised environments.

1 Introduction

Contemporary thinking on liberalisation of the financial system generally makes the point that liberalisation offers greater advantages for financial development. This position is usually based on the view that prices should be determined by market forces and that monetary regulation stymies the performance of the banking system. In the Caribbean context, this view has gained considerable ground but has not been supported by any empirical research.

The literature on commercial bank performance normally examines performance in terms of effectiveness and efficiency but seldom takes fully into account the impact of monetary and prudential regulation. Studies on the impact of monetary regulation on commercial banks tend to analyse particular forms of monetary regulation, such as reserve requirements, credit controls or interest rate controls, but rarely their combined impact on bank liquidity, solvency, profitability or market share.

More recently, studies on prudential regulation have analysed the impact of capital adequacy on bank performance but have tended to omit the simultaneous impact of other forms of monetary regulation, largely because concerns of capital adequacy and other forms of prudential regulation have only recently been ascribed increased importance. As a result, joint examination of monetary and prudential regulation was not viewed as a priority, even during periods when direct monetary controls were in place in Europe and North America.

In developing countries, and particularly in the highly regulated case of the Caribbean, where monetary controls continued to be employed up to the early 1990s, the macroeconomic response to monetary regulation tended to be a more critical concern. Caribbean studies therefore focused on the effectiveness of monetary regulation in bringing about expected macroeconomic outcomes, and researchers largely omitted analysis of the impact of monetary regulation on commercial banks. This study of the joint impact of monetary and prudential regulation in the Caribbean is intended to fill this gap in the literature. It is based on the view that the financial sector in general, and the banking system in particular, are important vehicles for achieving accelerated growth and development and that banks should not only be seen as conduits for monetary control; and that high levels of regulation are not long term solutions to macroeconomic management. The four main hypotheses are, firstly, that monetary regulation impacts adversely on the performance of banks, secondly, that monetary regulation when imposed conjointly with prudential regulation sometimes conflicts with the prudential objectives of regulators; thirdly, that regulators sometimes engage in cost-axiomatic or accommodative pricing, and fourthly, that even where cost axiomatic pricing is practised, that regulation still reduces the flexibility of commercial banks and depresses their market share relative to non-banks. This occurs even where banks continue to make profits.

In addition to the four main hypotheses cited above, other issues will be addressed. These include, firstly, the view that equity holders bear the cost of reserve requirements; secondly, the view that regulated credit ceilings do not affect profitability (due to the profitability of default); and thirdly that reserve requirements tend to be associated with increased bank risk. Fourthly, the study also examines whether the views of commercial banks that reserve requirements and interest rate controls are the most important factors which limit bank performance are borne out by the analysis. Fifthly, the study reveals that a model of bank performance in the Caribbean of the 1970s, 1980s and early 1990s cannot have good predictive capability unless regulatory variables are explicitly included.

Several other assertions are discussed which do not lend themselves easily to empirical testing. These include the view that 'a priori' indications suggest that entry barriers decline when oligopolistic behaviour among banks is reduced. This finds support in the observations of Spiller and Favaro (1984) and in the Caribbean, Howard (1976). The Caribbean case of few explicit barriers to entry also reflects the observation of Pastré (1981) that while some countries will allow access to the market, monetary and other controls may prevent any meaningful level of expansion within the market (a view shared by Farrell (1990) about Trinidad and Tobago).[1] Relatively high returns on assets, and the rapid rise of non-banks and their under regulation, also give credence to the observation that low failure rates and discriminatory pricing policies are a result of lack of competition, and that the converse, high failure rates, result from intense competition [Phillips (1964)]. The Trinidad and Tobago situation of the 1980s further raises the related view that bank crises are frequently caused by over-entry to the industry attracted by boom profits,

2

resulting from governmental controls which leave producers in the industry earning super-normal profits [Barclay (1978)].[2]

The first section of the introduction identifies the major issues raised in the analysis. The following section defines regulation; that is, structural, monetary and prudential regulation; and proceeds to establish the purposes for which monetary and prudential regulation are employed. It then describes the regulatory cycle as well as the interrelationships between various forms of regulation, presenting a brief summary of the theoretical context in which regulation takes place. Similarly, it provides definitions of bank performance and a brief overview of the performance of commercial banks in the Caribbean during the period reviewed.

1.1 Regulation

Regulation, defined as 'the public administrative policing of a private activity with respect to a rule prescribed in the public interest' [Mitnick (1980 p.7)], suggests a public good approach to regulation based on non-rivalry and non-excludability characteristics as described by Gowland (1992).[3] The notion that the process of regulating interferes with free market choice is conveyed in the further definition that regulation is a 'process consisting of the intentional restriction of a subject's choice of activity, by an entity not directly party to or involved in that activity' [Mitnick (1992, p.9)]. The purpose of regulation is generally the prevention of systemic failure [Bank of England (1992, p.322), Vittas (1992)].[4][5] The public interest view of regulation has however, been challenged by Posner and Stigler (1974) and others of the Chicago School who argue that this definition does not necessarily describe action taken in the public interest but rather action perceived by regulators to be in the public interest. They describe a theory which shows regulation to be undesirable, arguing that regulation can often operate in the interests of producers and that producers can manipulate (capture) the regulatory process so as to create unnecessary regulations in their own self interests. Pelzman (1976) further attempts to describe regulatory theory in terms of an equation and derivatives which in equilibrium equate the marginal costs of regulation to the marginal benefits; a position articulated earlier by Pigou (1920) and developed later by Coase (1985).

There are several other approaches to the study of regulation. An analysis of regulation as intermediation between constituents is found in Fiorina and Noll (1978) and models of bureaucratic behaviour in Downs (1957) and Tullock (1975) and as public choice theory and regulatory behaviour in Romer and Rosenthal (1985). Modern techniques of analysis of regulation are well

3

documented in Spulber (1989) and Kahn (1989). Empirically, however, the measurement of benefits and costs of regulation are not easily quantifiable and testable. A position less frequently adopted, is that regulators sometimes accommodate the regulated industry by taking costs into account so that profitability of the industry is not diminished. Such prices, when they are market clearing are referred to as anonymously equitable prices [Faulhaber and Levinson (1981)] or when they are a result of bargaining, are similar to Aumann-Shapley prices [Aumann and Shapley (1974)]. They are not unlike theories of monopoly which emphasise the impact on profits and on risks of entry. Such theories of monopoly and regulation tend however to involve the utility and communications industries, but can be made applicable to the banking system.

Commercial bank regulations are of three types: structural, monetary (or macro-monetary) and prudential. Structural regulation refers to boundaries placed on the activities of commercial banks, determining the activities in which they may become involved and those from which they are debarred. Monetary regulation,[6] sometimes termed macro-monetary regulation, refers to the process of setting monetary policy directives designed to bring about predetermined macroeconomic outcomes. In the Caribbean this covers a wide range of monetary policy tools but focuses principally on regulation of interest rates, credit controls and primary and secondary reserve requirements. Prudential regulation emphasises the control of systemic risk through, principally balance sheet constraints such as capital adequacy and permissible bank concentration ratios;[7] it establishes guidelines for banks which are intended to ensure the safety and soundness of the banking system.

Table 1.1 summarises the main regulatory tools applied to the banking system in the Caribbean and Figure 1.1 describes the cycle of interrelationships involving the three types of regulation: structural, monetary and prudential. Structural regulation sets the general parameters for the banking system [Revell (1980)]; it defines restrictions on activities of certain types of institutions and sets the context in which both prudential and monetary regulation operate. Monetary regulation impacts on the deposit-taking and lending activities of commercial banks through adjustments in price, volume, portfolio changes and in risk-taking (line CD in Figure 1.1). These influences flow through to aggregate expenditures and output and determine macroeconomic outcomes (line DE) but also impact on bank profitability, liquidity, solvency and market share (line DF).

Table 1.1
Summary of structural, monetary and prudential regulation

	Structural regulation		Prudential regulation		Monetary regulation
1.	Setting of boundaries to the business of banking.	1.	Capital requirements.	1.	Interest rate controls.
2.	Debarrment from engagement in commercial activities.	2.	Limits on customer concentration.	2.	Credit controls.
		3.	Risk-based portfolio assessment.	3.	Cash reserve requirements.
				4.	Secondary reserve requirements.

The resulting outcomes in turn influence future decisions about the need to apply further monetary measures (line EC). Simultaneously, prudential regulations, principally capital adequacy provisions, influence the availability of credit and hence prices and volumes (line BD). The outcome of these and other portfolio decisions, further impact on profitability, solvency and market share and guide the decisions of authorities about future adjustments in prudential regulation (FB). Over the longer term, macroeconomic outcomes and commercial bank performance influence decisions about the appropriate structure of the banking system and the role of banks in that system, (i.e about the need for structural regulation). However, such structural changes tend to be rather infrequent.

This classification differs somewhat from that of Vittas (1992), who places financial regulation into six categories: macro-economic, allocative, structural, prudential, organisational and protective. The classification used here combines macroeconomic and allocative into a single category called 'monetary'; and structural and organisational regulation in another termed 'structural'. Similarly, prudential and protective regulation are combined in the single category called 'prudential regulation'. The classification is not therefore essentially at odds with that used by Vittas but is a compressed form of his six-tier classification.

1.2 The interrelationship between structural, monetary and prudential regulation

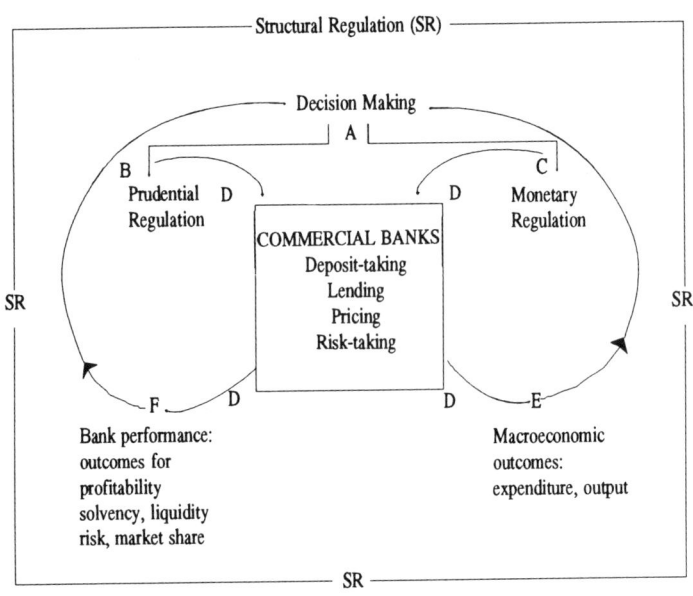

Figure 1.1 The structural-monetary-prudential regulatory cycle

Structural regulation aims to prevent excessive market power, to limit the potential for conflict of interest and to discourage financial institutions from assuming excessive risks by expanding into areas that are remote from their main focus of operations and expertise [Vittas (1992)]. This supports the generally held position that the rationale for regulation is the need to prevent market failure but adds the further objective of avoidance of conflicts of interest. Revell (1980) is of the view that it is structural regulation rather than prudential regulation that is largely responsible for inhibiting competition, and suggests that structural regulation requires some trade-off between competition and financial stability. Barriers to entry or exit, or lack of them fall largely within the category 'structural regulation' and bear on what banks (and non-banks) are permitted or debarred from doing but also include the effect of the general business environment on the banking industry.

Not unlike financial regulation in the US, which was first imposed in response to the stock market collapse of 1929, monetary regulation in the Caribbean[8] is principally a monetary response to macroeconomic forces. Where the objective of regulators is to achieve macroeconomic stability, principally protection of the balance of payments, profitability, solvency and market share are seldom explicitly taken into account in the presence of the overwhelming need for achievement of monetary goals. This is reflected in the observation by Blackman (1982) that if the nations's reserve position is 'desperate' the only relevant objective is (foreign exchange) liquidity. It is echoed by Gowland (1990 p.39) who observes that monetary authorities have always had to trade-off structural objectives against those of macro-monetary policy. While, the Caribbean has never had to choose between the extremes of systemic failure of financial institutions and macro-monetary stabilisation, it is suggested that in the process of securing balance on the external account, the goal of development of the financial system was often subordinated.

In the Caribbean of the 1970s and 1980s regulation of the banking system was heavily influenced by the theories of regional economists of the 1960s who rejected monetarist prescriptions based on the notion that the transmission of influences to expenditure and output was a direct result of changes in the money supply[9] [Beckford (1972, Thomas (1974) Best (1968]. Policy makers embraced the structuralist views of Rual Prebisch (1959), Myrdal (1951) and Hirschman (1958) and later of Lance Taylor (1983) who emphasised the need for authorities to take charge of the direction of their economies and to change their structures. They identified inappropriate structure as an explanation of slow rates of economic development in the Caribbean, and suggested that government action was required in order to achieve economic goals since market prices did not prompt the appropriate responses but merely altered prices and widened the disparity in earnings between economic groups.

The structuralist doctrine which formed the basis for macro-monetary policy in the Caribbean was not unlike the credit availability doctrine of the sixties. It placed the emphasis on activity in the market for government securities and the private sector loan market as opposed to the money and bond market of Keynesian proponents [Keynes (1936)]. The effective thrust is to induce liquidity pressure and encourage a tight bank lending policy which together lead to an absolute decrease in the supply of loanable funds to the private sector. The doctrine differs from the neoclassical view of the interest rate as

7

the price of loanable funds in that it assumes sticky interest rates on private sector loans and a locked-in effect of government securities, that is, an imperfect market for government bonds.

These arguments were given concrete form in the monetary policies in the Caribbean over the past two decades and though the process was taken further in some Caribbean countries than in others, the similarities are undisputable. Barbados, Jamaica and Trinidad and Tobago all used credit as an important tool for achieving economic development. In Jamaica and Trinidad and Tobago this included taking banks under public control. In all three countries it included encouraging institutions to lend to selected sectors and keeping interest rates low, usually below the rate of inflation. While the primary reserve requirement was the conventional fractional reserve system used in metropolitan countries and was a universally accepted monetary policy tool, it was the use of secondary reserve requirements or liquid assets ratios (principally required holdings of treasury bills or government bonds) which were most heavily relied upon in the Caribbean. This process was not peculiar to the Caribbean, but was applied in Europe and North America in the 1950s and 1960s, and in Latin America in the sixties and seventies. Vittas (1992) observed that although these policies met some of the Governments' objectives they failed to create robust financial systems. Similar views have been expressed by Brown (1990) about the Jamaica case. Neither writer specifies how the lack of robustness is reflected in commercial bank performance or more particularly how it translates into the impact on profitability, solvency, liquidity or market share.

While monetary policies in the Caribbean may have been consistent with the objectives of authorities during most of the period under study, they were facilitated by the relatively low level of internationalisation of markets and low levels of globalisation of corporate structures. However, as markets became more international and corporate structures more global, the effectiveness of these measures declined and the process of liberalisation became inevitable.

The justification for prudential regulation of the Caribbean banking system has less clear theoretical origins and greater practical justification. Prudential regulation, initiated by monetary authorities to protect the banking system, emphasises capital adequacy in order to prevent banks from operating on low levels of capital, and hence more cheaply, while leaving customers less protected. However it is rarely integrated into macro-monetary regulation, though like macro-monetary regulation, it impacts on the profitability and liquidity of banks and on market share. Prudential regulation is rooted in the view that the collapse of a single commercial bank can seriously damage the viability of the entire banking system[10] - an outcome referred to in recent

8

literature as 'infection'. It emphasises not only capital adequacy, but the dangers of concentration of both deposits and credit, both by product and by customer, and encompasses concerns about portfolio risk. It reflects in principle the views of the Basle Committee on Bank Supervision developed many years later in the 1980s and 1990s, and in the Caribbean, is based on guidelines similar to those followed by banks in Europe, the U.K. and North America.[11]

Central banks therefore have objectives of macroeconomic stability, allocative efficiency and financial sector stability, much of which is achieved through the banking system. As a result the problem reduces to one of joint determination of appropriate macroeconomic objectives as well as the safety and efficiency of the financial system, so that an important ingredient that shapes the functioning and efficiency of financial institutions is the stance of macro-financial policy [Vittas (1992)].[12] Vittas recognises the conflicting influences of macro-financial policies on financial institutions, noting that failure to maintain macroeconomic stability has adverse effects on the operations of financial institutions and that the pursuit of macroeconomic and financial stability may conflict with the process of financial innovation. The relative outcome is influenced by the type of regulatory controls employed by monetary authorities.

1.3 Measures of bank performance

The indicators employed to analyse the impact of these monetary and prudential regulations on bank performance are modifications of the conventional performance indicators. Traditionally, bank profitability is considered the most important measure of bank performance. The study therefore places relatively greater emphasis on this measure. Revell's (1980) landmark study on bank performance applies a number of profitability measures, principally interest margins, gross earnings margin, net earnings margin and profits before tax. These are similar to measures of bank performance employed by audit firms and Securities Exchanges in the Caribbean which tend to focus on net interest income, net profits, and loan losses; for example Price Waterhouse (1992). Performance scores which employ the technique of discriminant analysis, Altman (1984) and Taffler (1984) and the Bank of England (1982) tend to consider ratios which include liquid assets ratios, retained earnings, before tax earnings, some equity measure and in the case of trading companies, a sales ratio. These ratios tend to be survival ratios which focus on the short term. In the banking industry the Basle Committee of Bank Supervisors takes a longer view of survival of the industry and focuses on earnings, capital adequacy, management, liquidity and solvency.

This study does not place emphasis on the micro analysis of the components of bank profitability emphasised in the Revell study and in other accounting and audit based analyses, nor does it emphasise the full range of indicators applied by bank supervisors using their CAMEL rating,[13] since many of these ratings require some subjective micro analysis. Instead it stresses the measurable outcomes which impact the longer term viability of the institution, such as liquidity, solvency, profitability, risk, and a measure not used by bank supervisors - market share.

The main profitability measure employed is before tax return on assets, though other profitability measures are used selectively throughout the analysis. Liquidity is defined by reference to banks' holdings of cash and government securities in excess of required amounts. Insolvency is defined to exist where assets are less than liabilities; in simplified form the ratio of capital and reserves to total assets is taken as the measure of solvency. Market share is measured with reference to the share of assets of commercial banks in the combined assets of banks and non-banks. Bank risk (an outcome) as opposed to banks' attitude to risk-taking (a process) is measured by the variability of bank profitability, and is considered a subset of the bank profitability measure. It is based on the view that the high-risk lenders' profit over the planning horizon may be described as simply the difference between total interest collections and the sum of the cost of capital and defaulted principal. The lender chooses to maximise expected profits such that:

$$E\ (\Pi) = \sum_{i=1}^{n} Y_i q_i r_i - I - ZK - EPL \qquad (1.1)$$

Where:

Y_i = expected return of interest per dollar of interest due in loan category i

q_i = cash advanced in loan category i

$r_i q_i$ = demand function loans in category i;

I = interest standardised for lengths of maturity

Z = constant unit cost of capital

K = total capital

EPL = expected portfolio losses.

To the extent that major profits or major losses are made, bank profitability is either increased or decreased, so that the variability in bank profitability (σ^2_π), where σ^2 is the measure of variance, becomes a measure of bank risk.

1.4 Cost-axiomatic and accommodative pricing

Indications are that while some regulations may have restricted bank profitability, at least one regulatory measure, interest rate controls, may not have constrained bank profitability as is often assumed, but may have rather helped to offset or minimise the negative impact on bank profitability resulting from other monetary controls. The impact of interest rate regulation on bank profitability in the Caribbean may have therefore conflicted with the generally held view of bank performance under financial repression. This outcome is likely to have been the result of accommodative or cost-axiomatic price setting.

Cost-axiomatic pricing or autonomously equitable pricing is defined to exist where costs such as transactions costs, relative rates of return, default costs, insurance costs, labour costs, the cost of deposit attraction and marginal reserve costs are taken into account in the setting of regulations in order to provide banks with a return on investment which is market clearing. Where such pricing takes some of these costs into account but does not result in a market clearing rate it is termed 'accommodative'. Levels of regulation can therefore be seen on a spectrum from rigid------> to accommodative-------> to cost-axiomatic. This study asserts that authorities in the Caribbean engaged in cost-axiomatic, or at the least accommodative pricing, but that this was inadequate to prevent the loss of market share by banks and from time, the decline in bank profitability.

1.5 Summary of bank performance

An overview of bank performance in the Caribbean discloses that bank profitability appears to increase during periods of less intense regulation and to improve during periods of increasing liberalisation. This occurred in Jamaica in the post-1985 period, a period described by Brown (1991) as one which marked the shift by Jamaica to an increasingly liberalised system. Similarly, in Trinidad and Tobago bank profits increased up to 1980 and declined during the period 1980-86, a period described by Farrell (1990) as one of stabilisation and adjustment. In Barbados the period 1981-85, a period of declining bank profitability, also coincided with a period of tight monetary control, which included principally higher reserve requirements.

One of the major outcomes of the performance of commercial banks in the Caribbean has been the loss of market share to non-banks. While the rise of non-banks has been a global trend over the past 20 years, this growth was

11

assisted by the absence of regulation of non-banks in the Caribbean for most of the period. Regulation of banks in the Caribbean may have influenced the exit of banks and the absence of regulation of non-banks appears to have influenced entry of the latter. The accepted explanation of the exiting of banks was that this was a response to localisation and nationalisation rather than regulation. In Barbados where banks have tended to be rather more regulated than Trinidad and Tobago, those banks which withdrew were new banks and were all branches with small portfolios,[14] underscoring the concern for small and new banks in a regulated environment.[15] While profitability may have been at the root of their withdrawal to the extent that regulation impacts on profitability, the causes may have been inter-related.[16] The impact of regulation on small banks and on local banks will therefore be given special attention. Such an examination also permits analysis of the existence of economies of scale in the Caribbean context.

A review of the literature follows in Chapter 2. It is divided into two sections; the first reviews the literature on monetary policy in developing countries and establishes the rationale for the use of monetary controls; the second reviews the literature on the impact of monetary and prudential controls on bank performance. Chapter 3 describes the structure of the financial system in the Caribbean, particularly the composition of commercial banks' portfolios and shows how authorities imposed direct monetary controls on commercial banks in order to protect the balance of payments. It then presents the resulting outcomes for bank performance in terms of profitability, liquidity, market share, risk and solvency. Chapter 4 presents the views of commercial banks about the impact of regulation on bank performance. This evidence is provided from responses to questionnaires sent to commercial banks. A model and methodology for testing the impact of regulation on bank performance are developed in Chapter 5, which employ ordinary least squares regression analysis, cointegration, and error correction models. The maximum likelihood procedure [Johansen and Juselius (1990)] is employed to analyse the relationship between bank regulation and individual measures of bank performance and in other selected circumstances. A composite measure of performance is then developed employing the technique of discriminant analysis, to produce a composite measure of bank performance and of bank regulation. These scores are then tested for causality, employing Granger causality tests [Granger (1980, 1988)]. The results of the empirical analysis are discussed in Chapter 6. The book concludes with a summary and a commentary on the insights gained into the impact of regulation on commercial banks in the Caribbean. This includes a discussion of the implications for the development of the financial system and for the effectiveness of monetary policy in increasingly liberalised systems of the

Caribbean as well as in other developing countries, in the context of increasingly open capital markets and corporate globalisation.

Notes

1   Pastré cites the case of France where there were ceilings on overall increases in credit and suggests that new entrants to the market are condemned to an insignificant market share, even though there are barriers to entry.

2   In 1981, in Trinidad and Tobago, 20 non-banks sought to establish operations in Trinidad and Tobago (Farrell (1990), compared with eight non-banks then in operation.

3   A good is a non-rival if consumption by A does not produce the amount available for consumption by B, and is non-excludable if the good by being supplied to one person is automatically supplied to others A well functioning financial system is such a public good.

4   A market is contestable if a new firm can both enter and leave the industry without cost.

5   Increasingly, financial regulation has also become concerned with providing consumer protection and ensuring high standards of business conduct, but these aspects of bank regulation are not included in the study.

6   Some writers refer to 'macro-monetary' regulation and others to 'monetary regulation.' The terms essentially refer to the same process of using monetary tools to achieve macroeconomic outcomes. The term monetary regulation will be used in this paper.

7   The term 'concentration' ratio used in the context of a commercial banks' asset distribution, refers to the share of the bank's assets (or liabilities) held in a particular sector or by a particular individual or company. It differs from the industry concentration ratio normally used as an indicator of oligopoly in the corporate literature.

8   While the Caribbean comprises a number of other countries, because of data availability, the study is restricted to the English speaking countries of Barbados, Jamaica and Trinidad and Tobago. Central banks were in place in these countries for the entire period of the study.

9   In the Caribbean, money supply was treated as an exogenous variable and foreign exchange availability was seen as critical to economic viability.

10   The financial crisis in the 1980s in the form of the Savings and Loan debacle in the U.S. which served to underline the importance of prudential regulation and both bank and non-bank failures in the past decade have demonstrated that failure of financial institutions can have as serious macroeconomic implications for economic growth as inappropriate monetary policies.

11   Not all the criteria developed by the Basle Committee on Bank Supervision were applied in the Caribbean during the period studied. The application of the full range of prudential criteria is a more recent phenomenon. For most of the period covered by this study the principal prudential criteria used were capital adequacy and to a lesser extent the requirement to observe certain concentration ratios.

12   Vittas uses the term 'macro-financial' in the same way as the term 'macro-monetary' or 'monetary'.

13   This is reflected in 'CAMEL' rating which emphasises capital, asset quality, management, earnings and liquidity. it was considerably tightened in July 1988 when the Basle Accord was proposed by the Basle Committee on Bank Regulation and Supervisory practices and endorsed by central bank governors of the group of 10 (G-10) countries. It introduced risk-based capital standards which were to be phased in over a 4-year period ending in 1992.

14   The banks which withdrew were First National Bank of Chicago, Citi Bank, and Chase Manhattan bank. The causes of exit, of most foreign banks in Jamaica and Trinidad and Tobago were related to policies of localisation and nationalisaton.

15   In 1993 Canadian Imperial Bank of Commerce because the first major foreign owned bank in Barbados to cede any significant portion of its ownership to regional equity holders.

2 Review of the literature

2.1 Monetary regulation in developing countries with special reference to the Caribbean

2.1.1 Introduction

The first section of this chapter reviews the literature on the theory supporting monetary regulation in developing countries, and in the Caribbean in particular, and traces the development of monetary theory through the appealing Keynesian argument of expansionary monetary policy to the neo-structuralist position of the imperfection of markets, a position which facilitates an enlarged role for government, and which implicitly supports direct monetary controls. It shows how the views of the McKinnon and Shaw school which argued that price and interest rate distortions retarded economic growth were countered by the views of Cavallo (1977), Wijnbergen (1983) and Taylor (1983) that rather, it was high interest rates which retarded economic growth. It points to the twin argument for control of credit which found official support in the monetary theory of the balance of payments and shows how arguments about the inefficiencies of direct controls [Kane (1977), Fry (1988)] were countered by arguments of their effectiveness [Brown (1991)]. The second section concentrates on the narrower focus of the study, that is, the impact of these regulations on bank performance.

2.1.2 Monetary regulation in developing countries

Monetary policies in most developing countries had their root in Keynesian economic theory which argued that inadequate investment could be corrected by changing the relative returns on money and capital [Keynes (1936)] and that expansionary monetary policy could be achieved by lowering interest

15

rates while satisfying liquidity preference. This Keynesian solution had strong appeal to developing countries. Subsequent models of money and economic growth which included expansionary macroeconomic postures argued that since households allocated wealth between money and capital assets, one means of accelerating economic growth was to increase the return on capital by raising the ratio of capital to labour. It was argued that this could be achieved by reducing deposit rates and by accelerating growth of the money stock. These monetarist views were also appealing to developing countries. However, in contrast to neo-classical monetary growth theory, theories of financial liberalisation of McKinnon (1973) and Shaw (1973) strongly dominated the thinking of the international financial institutions (IFIs) during the 1970s and 1980s. McKinnon (1973) argues that real money balances are complements to, rather than substitutes for, tangible investment. His model of 'outside money', loans to government which are not available to finance private sector development, emphasises the role of deposits in encouraging self-financed investment. He advocates that high real interest rates are necessary as a means of stimulating capital accumulation. Similarly, the debt intermediation view advanced by Shaw (1973) argues that bank loans are channelled primarily into capital accumulation. It emphasizes expanding the potential of financial intermediaries, who it is argued, are able to offer attractive rates and so reduce costs of intermediation between savers and lenders. The central argument of both McKinnon and Shaw is that distortions of financial prices, including interest rates and foreign-exchange rates, reduce the real rate of growth and the real size of the financial system relative to non-financial sector and that high interest rates promote investment and economic growth.

These views are summarised in Figure 2.1. They suggest that financial repression represented by administratively fixed nominal interest rates (F) holds the real rate (r) below the equilibrium level such that actual investment is limited to (I_0), and the amount of saving forthcoming at the real interest rate r_0, since, they argue, at these low interest rates, savings will not be adequate to finance investments. If interest rates were not subject to a ceiling, equilibrium would be at E with interest rates at r_2. However, at the ceiling F, banks will make large profits (r_3 - r_0) which are likely to be used for non-price competition and conspicuous spending. They argue that relaxing (raising) the interest rate ceiling from (F) to (F') increases savings and investment and rations out the low yielding investments in the area r_0, b_0, b_1, r_1. Thus the average efficiency of savings rises, income rises to S_{y1} and the inefficiencies of rationing which result from a low interest rate regime, are reduced.

The policy prescription for the financially repressed economy in the

McKinnon (1973) and Shaw (1973) model is therefore to raise institutional interest rates or to reduce the rate of inflation. Shaw maintains that expanded financial intermediation between savers and investors resulting from financial liberalisation (high real institutional interest rates) and financial development increases incentives to save. Measures such as exchange controls, interest rate ceilings, high reserve requirements, suppression of capital markets and selective credit controls were regarded as signs of financial repression.

These views were countered by the neo-structuralists [Taylor, (1983), Cavallo (1977) and Van Wijnbergen (1983)] who identify the problem as one of low levels of economic growth and inappropriate structures, arguing that low elasticities of demand and supply in developing countries required large price changes which were socially inefficient. They argue that raising interest rates increases inflation in the short run through a cost-push effect and lowers the rate of economic growth by reducing the supply of credit (in real terms) available to finance investment. Most of these models were based on Tobin's (1969) portfolio allocation framework.

Taylor (1983) observes that the financial liberalisation theory is more likely to reduce growth since an increase in the desire to save reduces aggregate demand and makes economic contraction more likely; affecting particularly deposit flows to the banking system from controlled markets. He concludes that, in practice, financial liberalisation is likely to reduce the rate of economic growth by reducing the total real supply of credit available to business firms. Van Wijnbergen goes much further; he stresses the importance of incorporating the curb or unorganised money markets in monetary models of developing countries. He bases part of his model on the Wicksellian credit availability effect[1] an argument first used by Cavallo (1977) and supported by Diaz-Alejandro (1985).

2.1.3 Theoretical justification for interest rate controls

The views of Van Wijnbergen (1983) on the desirability of a low interest rate regime coincide to a great extent with the thinking of Caribbean policy makers. It emphasises the link between the financial sector and the supply side of the economy via the financing of working capital, and shows how higher real rates may actually push inflation up in the short run rather than slow it down and so reduce real output. He describes a model in which credit is needed to finance labour costs, and where labour and other costs depend on the real wage (w), output (y) and the cost of credit (i-p).

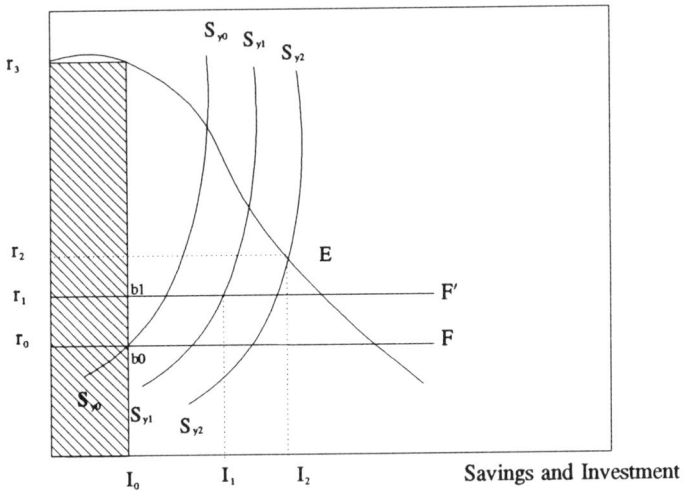

Figure 2.1 Savings and investment under interest rate ceilings: The McKinnon and Shaw view

Applying the Cobb Douglas production function with share parameter α

$$LC = wY^a K^{-(a-1)} (1+i-p) \ where \tag{2.1}$$
$$a = 1/(1-\alpha) > 1 \ and \ LC = \text{labour cost in real terms} \tag{2.2}$$

This determines output so that profits pY - LCp will be maximised, which leads to the aggregate supply function

$$1 = aY^{a-1} K^{-(a-1)} w (1+i-p)$$
$$= ay^{a-1} w (1+i-p), \ \text{where} \ y = Y/K \tag{2.3}$$

That is, output will decline if either the real wage or the real rate goes up. The real wage (w) is fixed exogenously reflecting the assumption of a Lewis-type surplus labour economy. [Lewis, (1974)] where I (fixed capital formation) depends on Y and K and a given real wage. In the contractionary case the real rate (i-p) will rise and output will decline.

The initial spurt in inflation caused by higher the higher real rate leads to a loss in competitiveness, the effects of the steady state growth rate of

18

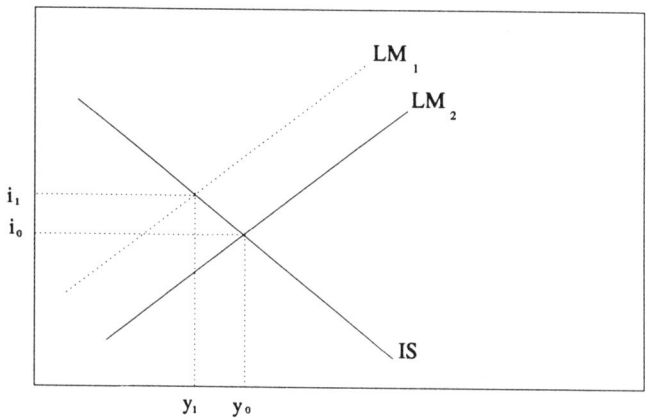

Figure 2.2 Interest rates and output - the Van Wijnbergen case

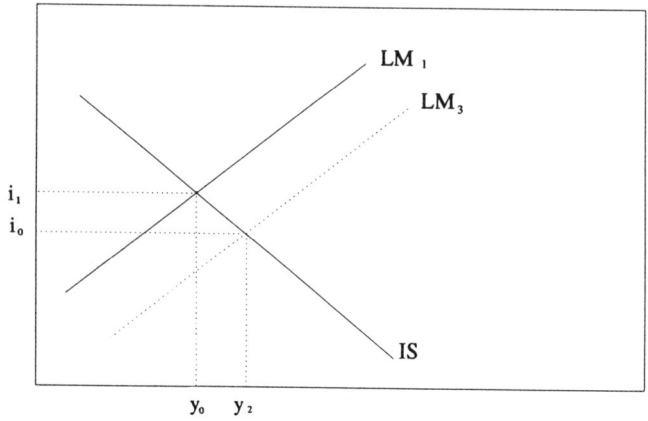

Figure 2.3 Interest rates and output - the conventional response

19

output per unit of capital are unambiguously negative as medium run profits fall and the real rate rises as demonstrated by the IS/LM curves in Figures 2.2 and 2.3. Van Wijnbergen (1983) therefore showed that shifts into time deposits will lead to reserve accumulation by banks and will be contractionary. He argues that when the banking system is constrained by direct limits on total lending then the increase in time deposits is always contractionary. If the banking system is operating under a system of direct credit limits an increase in the lending rate will induce banks to hold less free reserves and to assume more loans thus increasing the volume of credit outstanding.

Not only was it argued that higher deposit rates lead to less rather than more financial deepening and lower growth in the medium run but also that the need for the supply side of the economy to access low cost working capital for the financial sector was important. Some writers compromised on a fixed deposit rate, but a flexible loan rate [Benavie and Froyen (1982] and describe a model in which deposit rates are fixed and set exogenously below the market clearing rate. In this fixed deposit rate setting, the interest rate on loans is a function of the required reserve ratio on deposits, the discount rate, loans, central bank lending and some stochastic error term. They argue that in the fixed rate case, the increase in loan demand mitigates the upward pressure on the loan rate. Where the loan rate is flexible the new equilibrium is achieved with a higher loan rate and a higher level of deposits, but this flexibility creates uncertainty as to the effects of these instruments and the behaviour of the monetary aggregates. A more recent study, [Dutt (1991)] in examining the implications of liberalisation in a closed economy characterised by excess capacity, also agrees that it is highly likely that on balance, aggregate demand will fall in response to high interest rates and that output will decline and real investment will be reduced.

Support for this position is found in Beckerman (1988) who argues that market clearing interest rates may be non-positive and that a policy to increase nominal interest rates above the rate of inflation may be damaging and distorting; since investment demand may be very low because of depressed expectations or high uncertainty. He argues that savings may occur at negative real interest rates and wealth holders may prefer real assets, a position supported in the Barbados case by Worrell and Prescod (1983). This hypothesis is also supported by Buffie (1984) who argues that if curb loans constitute a large share of total loanable funds and are relatively good substitutes with demand deposits, the total supply of credit in the economy can contract in response to an increase in interest rates, since more funds are allocated to banks which are subject to reserve requirements in contrast to the curb market which is not.

Caribbean economists therefore argued that the effects of interest rate liberalisation in 'financially repressed' economies were not compelling and that nominal interest rates at levels intended to effect positive real rates could be burdensome to business activity [Farrell, Najjar and Marcelle (1986)]. Local authorities viewed the ability to access low cost working capital as more important and saw the financial sector as supplying this need. It was their view that via the financial sector and the supply side, higher real interest rates will reduce output if the effect on aggregate supply is stronger than the deflationary impact on aggregate demand, and that high real rates may actually push inflation up in the short run rather than slow it down[2], views similar to those of [Cavallo 1977)].

It is an empirical question whether the negative Cavallo effects of a higher real rate on output really dominate the positive effects of a higher savings rate in the short run, and that higher deposit rates will lead to less rather than more financial deepening (a lower r) and lower growth in the medium term. Empirical studies in the Caribbean are divided on whether the growth maximising rate is a low rate of interest. Worrell and Prescod (1983) found no causality, but others have found some correlation between deposit rates and economic growth but note that interest rate policy seemed more concerned with maintaining external balance rather than promoting economic growth (Craigwell 1990).

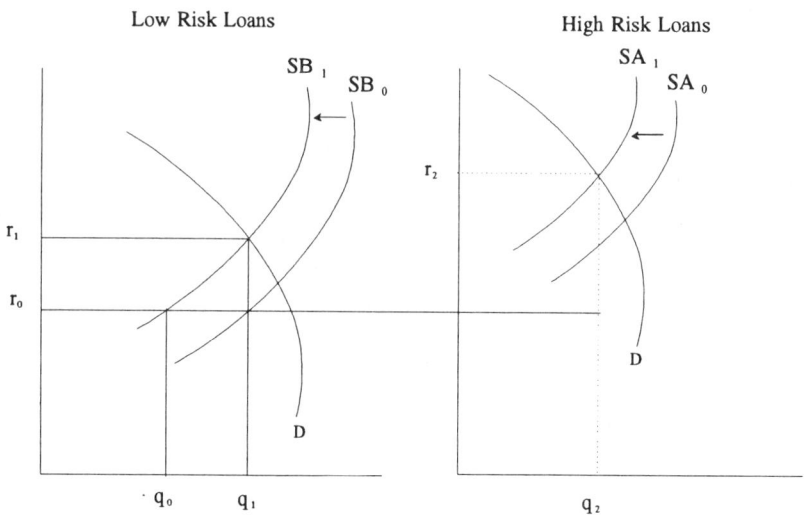

Figure 2.4 Low risk and high risk loan markets

21

Results of many empirical studies on the impact of liberalisation policies on growth in developing countries provide increasingly less support for the repressionist arguments against low interest rate regimes. Gupta's (1987) research in 22 Asian and Latin American countries led him to conclude that there is little support for the repressionists hypothesis that the positive substitution effect of real interest rates on savings dominate the negative income effect. The results of Giovanni (1983) in a study of eight Asian countries also cast doubt on the view that interest elasticity of savings is significantly positive in developing countries. Similarly, Cho and Khatkhate (1991) in a study of five Asian countries indicate that there does not seem to be any significant difference in saving and investment following new financial regimes in these now liberalised countries. Studies on Sub-Sahara Africa [Nissanke (1990)] have also shown that financial liberalisation and interest rate deregulation have had little effect on improving the size and allocation of savings. A similar study [Warman and Thirlwall (1994)] for the case of Mexico, found that while financial savings rise with higher interest rates there is no evidence that high real rates led to higher total savings investment and economic growth.

The justification for monetary controls was based not on their efficiency but on their effectiveness and arguments about inefficiency were not disputed [Brown (1991)]. Kane (1978) argues that interest rate regulation is an inefficient means of credit rationing and that credit flows through so many channels that it is virtually impossible to design an effective credit rationing system, observing that after controls are set, markets adapt, and controls are redesigned for yet another round.

The inefficiency argument as it applies to interest rate controls tends to be particularly cogent in its application to risk-taking by commercial banks. In two independent markets shown in Figure 2.4, a loan rate ceiling produces a supply curve of S_{B0} for low risk loans and S_{A0} for high risk loans. The supply of low risk loans is q_0 where the supply of risky loans is zero. Both supply curves shift as a result of the abolition of the loan rate ceiling. The supply of low risk loans is reduced at each rate of interest because of substitution into higher risk loans. A reduction in the supply of high risk loans results since abolition of loan ceilings produces a higher rate for less risky lending. In equilibrium the actual quantities of both low risk and high risk loans are increased from q_0 to q_1 for the former and from zero to q_2 for the latter (Figure 2.4).

However, policy makers in the Caribbean in the 1960s, 1970s and 1980s Thomas (1974), Beckford (1972) and Best (1968) accepted these deficiencies but argued for their macroeconomic effectiveness, observing that there was an under-development bias in the Caribbean which led to forgone linkages and

22

spread effects. They stressed the transformation role of banks and industry and felt that this called for planned implementation of a structure of domestic output consistent with domestic demand.

These views were also influential in determining monetary policy in other countries, for example in the 1970s and up to the early 1980s, in Latin America and West Africa where interestingly, macro-monetary policy differed very little from that of the Caribbean.

2.1.4 Theoretical justification for credit controls

While the financial liberalisation view focused principally on interest rate controls, other control mechanisms featuring in the arguments were credit controls and reserve requirements. Central banks in developing countries also focused on influencing the level of credit expansion, particularly where exchange rates are fixed. However, with a fixed exchange rate, monetary aggregates are difficult to control over an extended period. These demand management policies however often failed because of pressures to expand money and credit to finance government, and the latter often overrode other objectives of monetary policy [Page (1993)].

Consequently, writers like Fry (1988) advocate abolishing ceilings on institutional interest rates or raising them to levels nearer their competitive free-market equilibrium levels so as to reduce the price level by increasing money demand, arguing that deposit and loan rate ceilings tend to worsen the distribution of income. Fry observes that most of the economic rent goes to large borrowers rather than small savers/lenders when deposit and loan rates are held below their market equilibrium levels and that capital intensive production methods encouraged by low interest rates reduce the demand for labour, and wages of unskilled labour fall.

He advocates the allocation of credit on the basis of planning priorities even while observing that selective credit controls are likely to be accompanied by high reserve requirements designed to reduce commercial banks' own funds available for discretionary, non-priority lending. He cites six general inconsistencies relating to selective credit policies. Firstly, they encourage lower yielding investments through interest rate subsidies vis-a-vis higher yielding investments that are not subsidised; they typically involve a downward sloping term structure of interest rates; they lead to inversion of deposit and loan rates of interests; they reduce the demand for labour by distorting factor prices; they discourage saving and so reduce the aggregate supply of investible funds; and they provide the wrong signals to private sector institutional lenders. His arguments however tend to underplay the importance of such controls for a sustainable balance of payments and for economic stabilisation.

Fry (1988), cautiously implies some role for well administered selective credit controls. He observes that for credit controls to work financial markets must be kept segmented and that otherwise financial channels would develop for re-routing subsidised credit to uses with the highest private returns. Yet, a wide definition of financial repression would imply that segmented markets are repressive, and Fry (1988) at the same time, opposes financial repression, observing that typically, financial repression is the unintended consequence of low, fixed, nominal interest rates combined with high and rising inflation. His position on segmented markets therefore seems an uneasy compromise.

Page (1993) makes a case for the development of the financial sector in its own right as a vehicle for promoting financial intermediation and not merely because a well functioning banking system is an important vehicle for giving effect to monetary regulation. She argues that though many developing countries have generally allocated credit to priority sectors and rationed others, in the context of stabilisation these systems institutionalise government's unwillingness to sterilise the impact of flows across the exchanges on the domestic money supply.

Others argue that information failure in loan markets may lead to credit rationing because the quality of a bank's loans will be adversely affected if banks try to charge higher interest rates - because of the possibility of default. Thus, increases in interest rates will raise the overall riskiness of their portfolios [Stiglitz and Weiss (1981) and Zephirin (1990)]. They argue that a profit maximising bank will practice credit rationing and that in the presence of an excess demand for credit banks will be reluctant to raise interest rates in any market. It therefore appears that although credit rationing is potentially financially repressive, it is also a problem in liberalised markets. Evidence from developed countries as well, supports the view that liberalisation often leads to more credit for consumption rather than for industry. Evidence from France [(Melitz (1990)] suggests that liberalisation has led to a greater dependence of firms on internally generated finance, also Englund (1990), and Cho (1988) for Korea and Japan respectively, and Muelbauer and Murphy (1990) who show similar results for the U.K. case.

Support for credit controls can be found even in developed countries. Early work by Cohen (1968) and Silber (1975) support the view that credit policies were effective in altering expenditure patterns in the U.S. Their position was later supported by Glick and Plaut (1987) who argued that monetary policy becomes potent only when agents are rationed by credit ceilings. They disputed the view that credit rationing is inefficient. This position is put less strongly by Farrell (1990) who, in referring to selective credit controls, in

24

Trinidad and Tobago, observed that the maintenance of a tight credit policy was important in the achievement of the balance of payment objective in Trinidad and Tobago in the 1980s.

The monetary theory of the balance of payments which emphasises control of domestic credit expansion also offers a theoretical construct for the control of foreign exchange reserves through control of credit. In its most extreme form this approach states that central banks in open economies with fixed exchange rates have no ability to affect the nominal money stock and that the critical factor is domestic credit expansion. Leon (1988) in empirical work on the application of the monetary theory of the balance of payments found that these 'a priori' expectations were not rejected for the case of Jamaica. Similar evidence of fairly strong reserve flow mechanisms and strong patterns between foreign reserves and domestic assets were obtained by Looney (1991) for the case of Barbados, Jamaica and Trinidad and Tobago.

The model employed by monetary authorities to justify credit controls, drew much of its support either explicitly or implicitly, from the Polak (1957) model which argued that deficits in the balance of payments could persist only if accommodated by increases in credit. The model provides a theoretical framework for selecting those target variables which control credit and hence the balance of payments. The Polak model contrasts with much of the early literature on the transmission mechanism through commercial banks which saw money as the key factor in controlling economic change. This monetary approach to the balance of payments, also supported by the IMF at the time, derives a consolidated balance sheet of a simplified banking system to show that :

Reserves + domestic credit = money supply
or R+ D = H   (2.4)
Where H represented high powered money, R = reserves
and D = domestic credit.

Since a deficit on the balance of payments implied a loss of reserves, it follows that there must be a counterpart to a deficit in the form of credit creation (sterilisation) or dishoarding (i.e a fall in H). Since dishoarding is a temporary or disequilibrium phenomenon, a payments deficit could only persist if it is accompanied by credit creation. i.e. any additional credit will ultimately leak abroad. The model assumes exogenous exports and domestic credit is a policy variable and therefore is also exogenous. It assumes that demand is homogenous of degree one in prices and assumes a stable long run demand for money function. By emphasising credit, it also emphasises the importance of commercial banks in the adjustment process and helps to provide a justification for credit controls as a stabilisation tool.

The assumption of a constant velocity of money means that

$$Y_t = H_t \qquad (2.5)$$

Imports (M) are assumed to be a fixed proportion (m) of the value of the previous period's nominal income Y_{t-1}, so that

$$M_t = mY_{t-1} \qquad (2.6)$$

Money supply and balance of payments identities are added to complete the model. In equation (2.4) and (2.5) the change in H is given as

$$\Delta H_t = \Delta R_t + \Delta D_t \qquad (2.7)$$

and

$$\Delta R_t = X_t - M_t \qquad (2.8)$$

Substituting (2.6) and (2.7) into (2.5) gives

$$Y_t = H_t = H_{t-1} + \Delta H_t = Y_{t-1} + \Delta R_t + \Delta D_t \qquad (2.9)$$

This gives the basic monetary theorem already deduced at (2.4). Since $Y_t = Y_{t-1}$ in equilibrium (by definition), a payments deficit ($\Delta R < 0$) can persist only when domestic credit creation (ΔD) is positive. If initially, at time $t=0$, the economy is in equilibrium so ($\Delta D=0$) and $M=M_0$, then since this implies that $X_t = X_0 = M_0$, then

$$\Delta Y_t = \Delta D_t + \Delta R_t = \Delta D_t + X_t - M_t = \Delta D_t - (M_t - M_0) \qquad (2.10)$$

The model explains the emphasis placed on limiting domestic credit expansion and contributed to the ready acceptance by the IMF in the 1960s and 1970s of policies aimed at controlling credit.

Further theoretical underpinnings for the use of credit as a control variable are provided much later by Brunner and Meltzer (1988) who modified the Hicksian IS/LM paradigm to incorporate interaction with the credit market. Brunner and Meltzer reveal that impulses to output depend on the operation of the credit market, thus assigning an important role to credit in the determination of output.

Their analysis explains changes in monetary policy in developing countries, provides an enhanced framework for analyzing problems posed by regulation while bringing forcibly to attention the role of commercial banks in the transmission process and offers a further rationale for the use of credit as a control variable.

2.1.5 *Theoretical justification for reserve requirements*

Reserve requirements, a third monetary control tool, was viewed by the McKinnon and Shaw school as a leakage in the intermediation process which prevented banks from efficiently intermediating between savers and lenders. This negative effect does not exist in the same way in neo-structuralist models. Neo-structuralist models argue that the market determined nominal interest rate in the curb or non-institutional credit market adjusts to equate demand and supply of money and credit. Any negative effect of required reserves on financial intermediation in the neo-structuralist models comes entirely from the assumption that reserves are not available for investment finance either by the private or public sector.

The use of differential reserve requirements has been given some support by Page (1993) who suggests that this monetary control device is relevant to developing countries since banks in these economies tend to be characterised by a high degree of liquidity. She observes that a reserve base system, by giving monetary authorities control of the supply of eligible assets, permits them to achieve monetary restraint by reducing supply and that when different parts of the financial system have different degrees of liquidity, different reserve ratios may be required. She notes that proponents of the reserve base system claim that that method causes fewer distortions than would the method of applying more direct controls to each bank. Most writers tend to accept the need for reserve requirements but question the level and the cost. Tobin (1984), for example, prefers to leave the reserve tax in place and advocates payment only on excess reserves.

A less conventional view of reserve requirements is the deposit-maximising view. It is based on the premise that reserve requirements form a safety net for deposits and therefore are deposit increasing. Courakis (1984) Mathieson (1980) and Kapur (1982) show that when the banking system faces loan demand that is not perfectly interest elastic, the imposition of a required reserve ratio actually raises the profit-maximising deposit rate and hence the volume of deposits. The relationship is not, however monotonic. Whereas reserve requirements are deposit-inducing up to some level, after some threshold the advantage of higher reserve requirements declines in its impact on deposit volumes (see Figure 2.5). Also, as the inflation rate rises, deposit maximisation requires that interest- earning loans be held in order to raise the nominal deposit rate of interest above zero. This would normally involve a

27

reduction in the required reserve ratio (Figure 2.6). However in a scenario where reserve requirements are continuously increased, no positive effect on deposit volumes will be possible. The case of the rise of non-banks who are not required to hold reserve requirements tends to support this theory of diminishing impact of deposit-maximising reserve requirements.

A common argument invoked against the use of reserve requirements, the tool most frequently used by Caribbean policy makers, was perversely the very basis for its application. It is frequently argued in the literature that reserve requirements raise the marginal productivity of banks' reserve position and reduce asset and monetary multipliers and that bank credit and money stock are also reduced with corresponding repercussions in the output market [Brunner and Meltzer (1988)]. It is this very argument which prompts policy makers to view reserve requirements as a useful tool to effect rapid economic contraction or expansion and encourages its use by central banks in both developed and developing countries. However, cash reserve requirements do not address the financing problem. Governments therefore relied more heavily on secondary reserve requirements. Secondary reserves or liquid assets ratios have little justification in the literature of developed countries, but are essentially a method of transferring resources from the private to the public sector on the grounds of avoidance of the adverse balance of payments impact of increases in private spending and are therefore generally viewed as a means of compulsory government financing.

Many of the problems of developing countries relate also to vulnerability to balance of payments shocks and their inability to cope with disequilibria and the adjustment cost involved [Bird (1982)]. Policy makers tended to see the financial system as principally a vehicle for monetary policy and macroeconomic stabilisation as taking precedence over the development of the financial sector. Though the objective of authorities is to reach that phase of financial sector development evidenced by the proliferation of different financial claims issued by different financial and non-financial institutions as per Gurley and Shaw (1960)[3], such serious problems face developing countries, that the importance of developing the banking and financial sector tends to take second place in the concerns of analysts and policy-makers [Page (1993)]. Generally, however, after the disastrous results of financial liberalisation in the pre-1985 period in Latin America, World Bank Reports have been giving greater verbal recognition to macroeconomic stability as a prerequisite for financial development, following the 1989 Report which strongly advocated financial liberalisation. The fact that the theories have not produced the expected results[4] and has been strongly attacked in recent times [Dutt (1991) and Fisher (1993)].

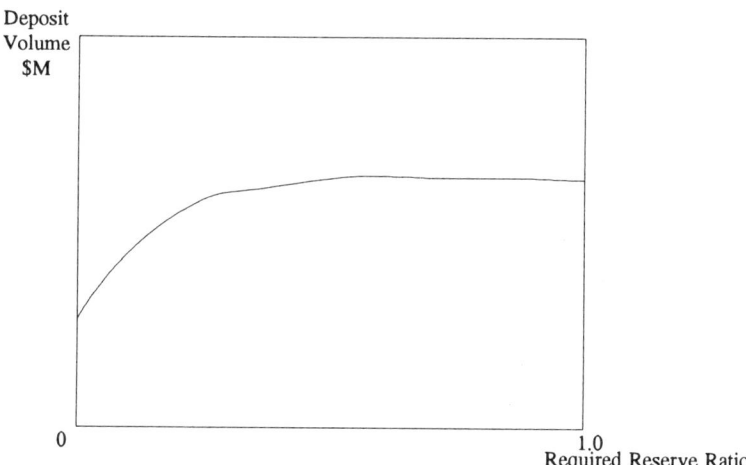

Figure 2.5 Deposit volumes under required reserve ratios

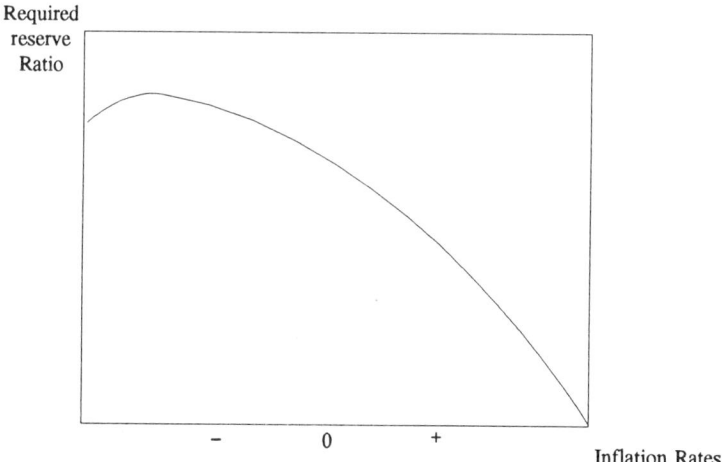

**Figure 2.6 Deposit maximising required reserve ratio
at different inflation rates**

2.1.6 Conclusion

In summary, the view that responses to changes in prices and interest rates in developing countries differed from the outcomes predicted by orthodox theory dominated the thinking of Caribbean economists and policy makers. They considered that markets were imperfect, that interest rates on private sector loans were sticky downward and there was a locked in effect of government securities. Consequently, direct controls were relied upon, principally, reserve requirements, credit limits, interest rate controls. These positions had their theoretical foundations in the views of the neo-structuralists.

2.2 A review of the literature on the impact of regulation on commercial bank performance

2.2.1 Introduction

We have so far discussed the rationale for monetary controls. This section examines the narrower focus of the study, the literature on the impact of various forms of bank regulation on bank performance. The section first discusses the literature on the theory of the firm in a regulated environment and the proceeds to examine the impact of scope and scale economies on the firm's performance. Discussion follows of the literature on bank performance as it is influenced by monetary and prudential regulation and the final section reviews empirical work on regulation and bank performance.

2.2.2 Literature on the regulation of the firm

Theories of regulation which focus on the loss of consumer surplus resulting from regulation tend to emphasize the micro rather than the macro aspect of regulation. The loss of consumer surplus can be depicted using the Peltzman (1976) model which examines the process of price setting on regulation. He refers to a majority generating function (in this context a public good objective function). He lets $S = S(p)$ represent consumer surplus and $\Pi = \pi(p)$ represent industry profits as a function of the market price (p). The political production function or public good objective function is, in this case, macroeconomic stability, and is given by $M = M(S,\pi)$, where $M_1 \equiv \delta M/\delta S > 0$ and $M_2 = \delta M/\delta \pi > 0$. Consumer surplus is greatest at the competitive

$$S = \Pi(p,(\Pi) = S(\pi^{-1}(\Pi)) \qquad (2.11)$$

30

price p^c, $\pi(p^c) = 0$, and smallest at the monopoly price (p^m), $\pi'(p^m) = 0$. He derives a political production possibilities frontier (a macroeconomic stabilisation frontier in this case) where Π takes the value between π (p^c) and $\pi(p^m)$.

Assuming that (M) exhibits diminishing marginal rate of substitution, the majority curves (or macroeconomic stabilistion curves) resemble the curves MM in Figure 2.7. The regulated price solves

$$\max_p M(S(p), \pi(p)) \qquad (2.12)$$

subject to $p \in [p^c, p^m]$. Therefore the regulated price p satisfies

$$\frac{M_2(S,\Pi)}{M_1(S,\Pi)} = \frac{-S'(p)}{\pi'(p)} \qquad (2.13)$$

where $S = S(p)$, $\Pi = \pi(p)$. This corresponds to point A in Figure 2.7.

Restrictions are also often seen in a benefit-cost framework as a transactions cost which must be covered and which can lead to higher interest rates or to lower profitability depending on the elasticity of demand for credit facing the particular financial institution. In the Caribbean case, the benefit of regulation is attainment of balance of payments equilibrium and the cost, possibly lower levels of bank performance resulting from bank regulation.

If the risk of deterioration in the balance of payments which results from unregulated banking is seen as an external diseconomy and the objective of regulators is to trade-off the cost of the externality against the benefit of the service, subject to some reasonable return to banks, this appears to combine a) the views in the literature of Coase (1960) which place emphasis on transaction costs and b) the administrative approach to allocation of Aumann and Shapley (1974) who use a value allocation approach to calculate explicitly the regulated firm's optimal pricing policy.

The Aumann-Shapley allocation is attained by discriminatory prices that are explicitly calculated from the cost function given specific weights. The resulting prices have an interesting economic interpretation. In any bargaining group, consumers marginal cost prices are given such that prices are a weighted average of the marginal cost price that the consumer would pay and hence prices allocate total costs. Since the outputs maximise welfare, the only demand compatible prices are therefore marginal cost prices. The Coase theory separates these marginal costs into marginal private costs and marginal external costs.

Marginal costs of production are the sum of marginal private costs (MPC) for the company (in this case bank), and marginal external costs MEC (used here to refer to macroeconomic instability). The marginal social benefit of production represents the marginal private benefits MPB to purchasers of the final output Q. By placing some of the burden of avoiding losses (in this case avoiding macroeconomic instability) on the company (bank) the company (bank) is required to internalise MEC as part of its marginal costs so that at market equilibrium

$$MPC\ (Q*) + MEC(Q*) = MPB(Q*) \qquad (2.14)$$

Alternatively, if we trade-off the net benefit of the banks' service activity with the cost to the economy we have at market equilibrium

$$MEC(Q*) = MPB(Q*) - MPC(Q*) \qquad (2.15)$$

Such models although intuitively clear, do not however easily lend themselves to empirical analysis because of the difficulties of measuring social and private costs. In addition special concerns of the banking firm's response to monetary and prudential regulation are not easily accommodated in traditional industrial economic theory.

The Coase theorem and Aumann-Shapley prices are not unlike cost - axiomatic pricing of Bös and Tillman and approximate the process referred to in the literature as anonymously equitable prices [Faulhaber and Levinson (1981)]. For the case of the downward sloping demand curve and decreasing average costs, the market charges average cost price which is the uniquely anonymous equitable price. A price vector is said to be anonymously equitable given the cost function C(Q) and market demand D(p) if for all Q and D(p), p ε T(Q). This is represented by price p* where p* Q' < = C(Q') for Q' < =Q*. This situation does not necessarily involve bargaining, and therefore seems to more closely approximate the Caribbean case. The anonymous equity of price p* is depicted in Figure 2.8.

This study is however, less concerned with the process of price-setting or regulation-setting and more with its impact on the performance of commercial banks, so that these aspects of the process of price-setting are only discussed in order to put in focus the analysis of the impact of regulation.

2.2.3 Literature on the effect of regulation on the firm

A study of regulation of multi-firm markets by Meyer (1980) notes that whether firms act independently or collusively the impact of regulation is to

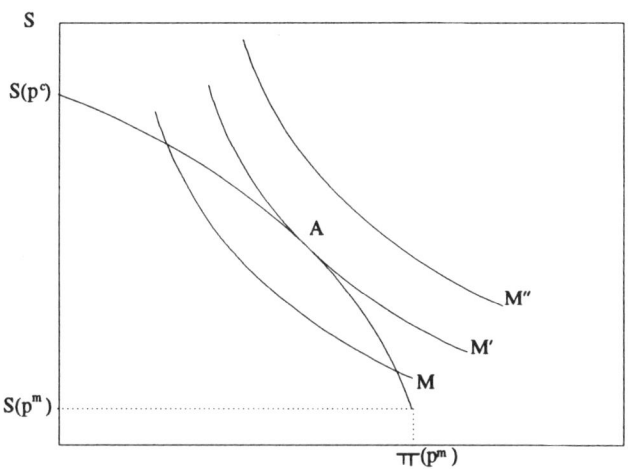

Figure 2.7 The Pelzman model of consumer surplus

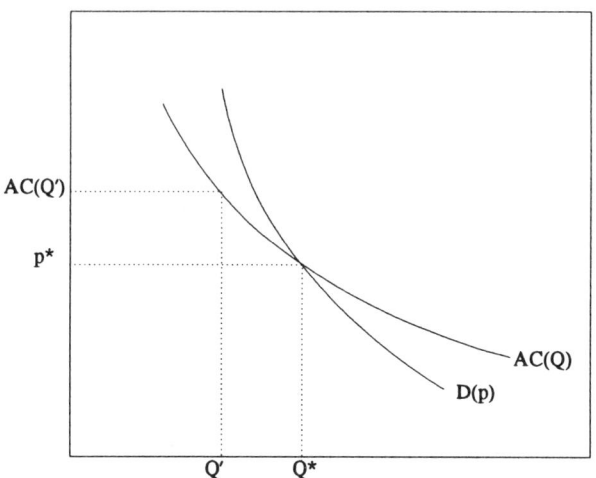

Figure 2.8 Anonymously equitable pricing (p*)

33

increase the equilibrium price, to reduce the total output of firms as a group, and to induce increased average costs and increased risks. Meyer's analysis focuses on rate-of-return regulation in competitive yet regulated settings, similar to the Caribbean banking system. He argues that there is a potential bias for greater capital usage in the non-collusive regulated firm compared with the regulated least cost production situation. These arguments have important implications for the banking firm, where capital adequacy and safety have become major concerns of policy makers.

Among the other branches of the literature which address aspects of corporate regulation and its impact on the banking firm, is the literature relating to size. One such view builds a case for differential regulations favouring small operations. It implies that the impact of uniform regulations affects small firms more so than large. The differential effect of regulation across plant size has been found to be important where there are economies of scale in regulatory compliance so that optimal regulatory policy may require imposing lighter regulatory burden on smaller than on larger plants [Pashigian (1968)]. In the U.S. this notion is captured in the Regulatory Flexibility Act of 1980 which minimised the disproportionate effect of regulatory requirements on small business. While this legislation does not apply explicitly to banks, the preferential treatment of thrifts in the U.S. and in many other countries is based on that premise. This aspect of regulation has its roots in studies of the production side of financial institutions which suggests economies of size and scope in cost structures particularly in operations under a certain size.

Economies of scale are not explicitly taken into account, though the literature does show that these affect profitability, and that there tends to be less regulation of smaller units than of large. A detailed study of multipurpose banking in developed countries by Khatkhate and Klaus-Walter (1980) claims that economies of scale and scope in rural areas particularly enhance performance and profitability.[5][6] Such economies, however, seem to vary with the size of the firm. They show that large scale economies are a decreasing function of the level of output. To that extent these studies confirm the usefulness of examining the differential impact of regulation on banks according to size.

Studies of the traditional concept of scope economies investigate the question of whether a fixed output bundle at a given point could be more cheaply produced by dividing these outputs among two or more firms which specialise in some of these products. Scope economies are said to exist in the simple case of the two-product firm if:

$$C\ (y,0) + C(0,y_2) - C(y_1,y_2) > 0 \qquad (2.16)$$

where $C(y_1, y_2)$ is the cost of joint production and where $C(y,0) + C(0,y_2)$ represents the costs of producing the same output levels at separate specialising firms. (Input prices are suppressed for convenience).

Scope economies are determined at a specific point usually at an actual data point in a mean value calculated for actual data point [Berger, Hancock and Humphrey (1992)]. They argue that the procedure does not address the important question of whether joint production versus specialised production is optimal for the firm. However, whether economies arise from scope or scale, they are reflected in the impact on bank profitability, variance of profits and market share.[7] If the cost of regulation is not covered and prices are subsidy free, and there remains for some output a set of prices that exceed their production costs, this provides an incentive to rival firms to provide those outputs at competitive prices, and may have some effect on the market share of the firm. This may partly explain the rise of non-banks in the Caribbean, but other scope economies may also exist which are unrelated to regulation [Berger, Hancock and Humphrey (1992)].

Studies on the benefits and costs of monetary and prudential regulation have not been conducted for the Caribbean. The more extensive studies on commercial bank behaviour in the Caribbean are by Bourne (1977) and Ramkissoon (1982). The Bourne (1977) study examines portfolio allocation of commercial banks' assets in Jamaica using three variants of a model of commercial bank behaviour. Ramkissoon (1982) examines commercial bank portfolio behaviour in Trinidad and Tobago with special emphasis on adjustment times. These studies are all premised on the need for a developmental role for commercial banks and do not examine the repressive aspects of regulation. Research by Zephirin (1990) addresses the question of asymmetric information and financial liberalisation in the Caribbean. While some of these writers have tended to support the view that monetary controls are important in a Caribbean setting, the impact of these regulations on commercial banks has only recently been given attention [Williams (1989), Brown (1991) and Rolle (1992)].

2.2.4 Theories of financial regulation and the banking firm

Theory assumes that the objective function of commercial banks is to maximise profits.[8] Safety and soundness are often presumed to be the responsibility of the monetary authority. Consequently, literature on the banking firm does not always explicitly accommodate analysis of the impact of monetary and prudential regulation. For example, all equilibrium models do not explicitly include the capital constraint as a factor in prudential regulation. Leverage models [Taggart and Greenbaum (1978)] which do focus on capital adequacy and include a capital constraint, do not however adopt the portfolio approach, so that areas such as sectoral credit control are not jointly accommodated. Some writers who use the portfolio approach assume a given leverage. Koehn and Santomero (1980) include some element of leverage in their analysis, so permitting the inclusion of some elements of regulation such as capital adequacy. Indeed, there does not yet exist any comprehensive theory of the banking firm which describes the behaviour of banks under any set of assumptions which can fully accommodate changes in expected outcomes given variations in the internal and external environment [Revell (1980)].

Portfolio theory deals with the pricing of assets and explicitly recognises the relationship between risk and return. Litner (1965) and Sharpe (1964) have shown that the equilibrium market value of a firm can be expressed as

$$V = (E[\pi] - \beta \rho \sigma_\pi) r_f \qquad (2.17)$$

where ρ is the correlation between the firms return and the return on a portfolio of all securities on the market, r_f denotes 1 plus the riskless rate of return, β is part of the market price of risk and $E[\pi]$ and σ_π are the expected value and standard deviation of profit.

This approach assumes the firm to have unlimited riskless ability to borrow and leverage. In the case of the banking firm this is not the case, since regulation underscores the risk-return nature of both assets and liabilities. Hence it is appropriate to describe a firm attempting to maximise profits subject to regulatory standards of bank soundness. Such approaches have been used by Mingo and Wolkowitz (1977), Meyer (1980) and Huggins and Morgan (1993).

They set the balance sheet identity

$$A + A' + C = D + K \qquad (2.18)$$

Where A = loans, A' = government securities, C = required cash reserves, D = deposits and K = capital. They define bank profits as

$$pA + rA' - gK - hD \qquad (2.19)$$

Reserves are assumed to be non-interest bearing and the constraints are interest costs, credit controls and capital adequacy; p is the loan rate where $p = p(a,A)$ where (a) is the credit worthiness of the loan customer and $p_a < 0$ and $p_A < 0$. The rate of return on government securities (r) is exogenously given and is presumed to be less than the return on loans.

g = g(K) where g is the cost of capital and $g_K > 0$; and h = h(D) where h is the cost of deposits and $h_D > 0$.

The soundness constraint is

$$\tau = aA + a'A' + cC + hK - cD \qquad (2.20)$$

(Lower case letters represent the weights associated with balance sheet entries and are all positive.) An increase in loans is therefore at the expense of a decline in cash and securities and additional bank capital (K) implies greater soundness. Greater deposits (for a given capital) imply less soundness. Thus the bank which maximises profits subject to a soundness constraint must consider the effect of all balance sheet items on soundness as well as profits.

The model is solved via the method of Lagrange multipliers. First order partial derivatives are taken with respect to each of the exogenous variables, Loans (A), loan quality (a) capital (K) and deposits (D) and the Lagrange multiplier (λ). (See Appendix 2.1).

In examining how equilibrium values change in response to a change in regulatory posture ($d\tau$), total derivatives of the first order equations are taken with respect to $d\tau$ and the results are presented below. The complete derivations can be seen in Appendix 2.1. A change in τ has several effects. The first ($dA/d\tau$) is expressed in terms of the model's parameters and equilibrium values of endogenous variables and the rest is expressed in terms of $dA/d\tau$. First, the long run absolute size of the portfolio declines. That is,

$$\frac{dA}{d\tau} = -[X + YZ]^{-1} \qquad (2.21)$$

where $= a' - a$

$$Y = \left(\frac{A - (a' + k)^2 p_{aa}}{(Kg_{KK} + 2g_K)} - \frac{((a' - c)v)^2 p_{aa}}{Dh_{DD} + 2h_D} \right)$$

$$Z = \left(\frac{AP_{AA} + 2P_A}{(a' - a)p_{aa}} \right)$$

The bank can adjust to imposed increases in soundness by improving loan

37

quality, as well as decreasing loans (in favour of securities). That is

$$\frac{da}{d\tau} = - \left[\frac{Ap_{AA} + 2P_A}{(a' - a) \, P_{aa}} \right] \frac{dA}{d\tau} \tag{2.22}$$

which is positive under the same conditions that ensure $dA/d\tau < 0$. The effect on bank capital of an increase in soundness is given by:

$$\frac{dK}{d\tau} = \frac{a'+k \left[\dfrac{Ap_{AA} + 2p_A}{(a'-a)} \right] \dfrac{dA}{d\tau}}{\left[Kg_{kk} + 2g_k \right]} \tag{2.23}$$

which is positive under the same conditions that ensure $dA/d\tau < 0$. Finally, $dD/d\tau$ is negative under the same conditions that ensured the signs of the other derivatives:

$$\frac{dD}{d\tau} = \frac{(a' - c)v}{Dh_{DD} + 2h_D} \cdot \frac{(Ap_{AA} + 2p_A) \dfrac{dA}{d\tau}}{(a'-a)} \tag{2.24}$$

Also, the sign $dA'/d\tau$ is ambiguous; that is, government securities could rise or fall in response to an increase in soundness. On the other hand, A' can be expected to rise as loans (A) are drawn down. However, the total size of the bank's balance sheet may decline (i.e. if $|dD/d\tau| \; dK/d\tau$) leading to a decline in all asset types including securities.

Among the models of the banking firm which assist in explaining adjustments to monetary measures, is that of Klein (1971). He presented a model of the banking firm which separates asset and liability management and determination by emphasising that the share of each asset in a portfolio was independent of the size and structure of deposit liabilities and thus of deposit market features. This aspect of the independence of asset structure partially accommodates the regulated environment where the volume of particular assets are determined by exogenous controls and is not a direct function of the stock of deposit liabilities. He assumes that the bank is a price-taker in government securities and a price-setter in the loans and deposits markets. His model is based on the assumption of maximisation of a rate of return on equity where W= equity invested and borrowed funds through the issue of deposits = B, and

$$F = W + \Sigma B_i \qquad (2.25)$$

Where F = total funds, E_F = expected rate of return on total funds, R_i = rate of interest on types of deposits, X_j= proportion of total funds allocated to the jth asset type, E_j= expected rate of return on that asset type and α_i represents a specified proportion of total funds (F). Funds secured from equity and issuance of deposits are allocated among n classes of assets.

$$since \quad F = W + F \sum \alpha_i \qquad (2.26)$$

and $B_i = \alpha_i F$ and $\Sigma_j X_j = 1$

$$\therefore E_F = \underset{j}{\Sigma} X_j E_j - \Sigma \alpha_i R_i \qquad (2.27)$$

$$E_w = \frac{E_r}{1 - \Sigma \alpha_i} = \frac{\Sigma X_j E_j - \Sigma \alpha_i R_E}{1 - \Sigma \alpha_i} \qquad (2.28)$$

where W = equity originally invested. Liquidity management was an important part of Klein's model. He formulated an expression for the expected loss from the banks' cash management policy:

$$n \frac{[X_r - c)^2]}{[2(c-b)]} \qquad (2.29)$$

where (b) represented the lowest deposit loss or gain and (c) the largest possible interest disbursement. He separated the rates of return on securities into private (X_L) and public (X_g); and the return on deposits into demand ($\alpha_1 R_1$) and time ($\alpha_2 R_2$); arriving at an expression for determining return on equity E_L = expected return on loans. Default risks are exogenous to the banks so that

$$E_L = h(X_L) \quad where \quad h'(X_L) < 0 \qquad (2.30)$$

His model has been heavily used in the literature because of its simplicity and easy applicability. The expected return on government securities is a random variable with density function ϕ (g) where (g) is the holding period of return and E_g the expected rate of return. The full equation was given by:

$$E_w = \frac{1}{(1-\alpha_1-\alpha_2)} X_L h(X_L) + X_g E_g - n\frac{(Xr-c)^2}{2(c-b)} - \alpha_1 R_1 - \alpha_2$$

(2.31)

The model helps to explain the process which determines the prices which banks charge for their services, but does not accommodate an environment where interest rates are prescribed and limits are placed on credit. It does not include resource costs and insolvency costs or provide a framework for the study of regulatory impact, nor does his assumption of the bank as a monopolistic price-setter accommodate examination of banks in a regulated setting.

Expanded models include the capital decision (with and without deposit insurance). In his model Dermine (1986) shows that expected insolvency costs, where no deposit insurance exists, is borne by depositors and where deposit insurance exists, it is borne by borrowers. The optimal loan rate is a function of the probability of bankruptcy and depends on the deposit rate so that indirectly insolvency costs are still borne by depositors.

Using the generalised form of utility maximisation, Pyle (1971) incorporates risk aversion, but disregards liquidity, solvency and resource cost considerations. In addition, yields are assumed to be exogenously determined and depend on yield differentials as the basis for the banks decision. The assumption of exogenous, though stochastic, net yields for all different assets and liabilities does not accommodate the case where returns are regulated.

An integrated approach to the banking firm which facilitates the study of regulation is found in Baltensperger's (1980) work. His study combines the real and financial effects of banking behaviour and allows an endogenous determination of the overall operation of the banking firm and is described in the literature as a real resource model [Bourke (1988)]. Though his own work was presented in terms of a banking firm which was subject to no particular constraint or regulation, his insights into modelling of optimal asset choice, determinants of the distribution of deposit changes and the deposit capital decision, bring to the analysis of bank behaviour an appreciation of how liability management could be integrated with the asset management. Baltensperger's analysis (1980) by explicitly incorporating costs and the capital decision facilitated the examination of commercial banks' adjustment to both monetary and prudential regulation.

He formulates a model which assumes that banking firms act to maximise

40

expected profits. Profits are determined by earnings on assets less cost of deposits, less resource costs, less liquidity costs, less the opportunity cost of equity capital.
This was expressed as :

$$E(\Pi)=rE-tD-C(D,E)-L-S-\rho W \qquad (2.32)$$

where C = resource costs of producing and maintaining deposit and credit accounts
L = liquidity costs, or expected cost due to reserve deficiency
S = expected cost of insolvency
W = equity capital
D = deposits
L = liquidity costs
ρ = the opportunity cost of equity funds

This model permits a study of the impact of regulation through an analysis of the cost of regulation because it accommodates costs which are reflected not only in the flow of inputs and outputs but also in the stock of assets and liabilities, and can be modified to accommodate the full gamut of regulatory measures which apply in the Caribbean. Since an examination of bank performance must look at the commercial bank in terms of costs and earnings, a Baltensperger type formulation is more appropriate for such purposes. Such general models are helpful in analysing the balance sheet impact of specific monetary regulations which follow in the next section.

2.2.5 Literature: reserve requirements and bank performance

Most of the literature on the response of the banking system to primary and secondary reserve requirements is quite unequivocal about the adverse implications for bank profitability resulting from imposing reserve requirements.
    Most writers, like Baltensperger, argue that primary and secondary reserve requirements force banks into portfolio adjustments as they seek to maximise a profit function (π) represented usually as:

$$\Pi=\sum_{i=1}^{m} r_i A_i - \sum_{j=1}^{n} s_j D_j - C(A_i D_j) \qquad (2.33)$$

Where A = assets, D = Deposits, C = costs
and r_t = rate of return on assets and r_i = rate of return on deposits.

41

The profit of the banking firm (II) is the return on assets, principally loans less the cost of deposits. Viewed in terms of optimum liquidity levels one can conclude that in maximising profits the optimum liquidity level is a function of the asset structure, the liability structure and the volume of assets and deposits.

Regulation limits the range of banks' choices; but within the limited scope afforded to banks, cost adjustments can be made by deriving a reserve management approach which adjusts cost functions through changes in returns on deposits and assets. If net withdrawals exceed reserves available, or if repayments are insufficient to meet withdrawals, the bank adjusts its flow of loans and deposits and their costs to restore its profit position. By implying an objective of restoring a profit position, this approach suggests that changes in profitability of banks are only temporary and tends to assume that banks will not accept lower profits in response to changes in costs consequent on changes in reserve requirements.

In the Caribbean case where both minimum deposit rates and maximum lending rates are set for much of the period under study, the bank becomes more of a price taker, so that the expected adjustment cost due to reserve deficiencies or the liquidity cost is likely to be:

$$L = \int_R^\infty \rho(X-R) \ f(X) \ dX \qquad\qquad (2.34)$$

where

X denotes the outflow of deposits and thus reserves with density function f(X).

L = liquidity costs due to reserve deficiency

R = beginning of period reserves

ρ = cost per dollar of reserve deficiency

Holding an extra dollar of reserves implies a marginal opportunity cost of r > 0 but a marginal reduction in liquidity cost such that:

$$L_R = -\rho \int_R^\infty f(X)dX < 0 \qquad\qquad (2.35)$$

where r = the loan rate.

Optimisation requires minimisation of the sum of these two cost elements. i.e - equalisation of marginal cost and marginal 'return' of holding additional

Optimisation requires minimisation of the sum of these two cost elements. i.e - equalisation of marginal cost and marginal 'return' of holding additional reserves.

$$r = \rho \int_{R}^{\infty} f(x)dX \qquad (2.36)$$

This means that the bank must choose the level of reserves such that f(x) dX = the probability of a reserve deficiency is just equal to the ratio of r/ρ. This condition defines the banks desired reserves as a function of the data of the model r, ρ and f(X), where rR = the opportunity cost of holding reserves.

If the legal requirement is that reserves at the end of the period (R-X) must be at least equal to a specified proportion k of the end of period deposits (D-X). A reserve deficiency occurs where:

$$R - X < k(D - X) \qquad (2.37)$$

or

$$X > (R - kD)/(1-k) \equiv \hat{X} \qquad (2.38)$$

If a reserve deficiency occurs its size is

$$X(1-k) - (R - kD) = (X - \hat{X})(1-k) \qquad (2.39)$$

The expected value of these costs thus is

$$L = \int_{\hat{X}}^{\infty} \rho [X(1-k) - (R + kD)]f(X)dX \qquad (2.40)$$

with derivative

$$-L_R = \rho \int_{\hat{X}}^{\infty} f(X)dX \qquad (2.41)$$

representing the marginal reduction in liquidity costs.

Thus optimality requires again that the marginal opportunity cost of holding reserves (r) if the bank is a price taker in the loan market) is equal to (ρ) multiplied by the probability of a reserve deficiency. This probability is given by the probability of X exceeding X, rather than X exceeding R. The ratio (ρ) cannot be identified simply as the discount rate but the total of all costs

43

including administration and information, so that (r) and (ρ) are functionally related to but not identical to the loan rate.

In the presence of adjustment costs, however, an adjustment to R is profitable only if the resulting gain (reduction in rR+L i.e the opportunity cost of holding reserves plus liquidity costs) more than offsets the cost of the adjustment itself. In this case there exists a range around R which the bank will let its reserves fluctuate freely, without making adjustments. Furthermore, if adjustment costs also include a fixed element which is independent of the size of the adjustment, an adjustment is profitable only if the resulting gain covers all adjustment costs, including the fixed element.

For this to be the case, the total gain (i.e reduction in rR +L) resulting from bringing reserves up to the optimum levels, must be at least as large as the fixed adjustment cost plus the proportional cost term fixed element multiplied by the size of the adjustment. Thus, the range within which active adjustments are profitable is further increased.

Writers are however, uncertain about the relative impact of reserve requirements on depositors and bank borrowers. Black (1975) and Fama (1980), found that reserve requirements had an observable adverse impact on the market valuation of commercial banks. They saw reserve requirements as a direct tax on deposit returns which lowers the return on deposits by the fraction of deposits that must be held in reserves, so that deposits involve an opportunity cost, providing lower returns than non-deposit based assets with the same risk. Fama, in a later work (1985) develops a model which shows that such costs are borne by bank borrowers depending on the elasticity of demand for loans and deposits. The results taken together suggest that the incidence of the cost of reserve requirements can be shifted to depositors or to borrowers depending on the structure of the market.

Increases in reserve requirements therefore raises bank costs and artificially constrain the size of the banking firm. [Ramakhrisnan and Thakor (1984)] and [Boyd and Prescott (1986)] also argue that a set of marginal customers is lost to the banking sector because it is non-optimal for these firms to deal with banks, an argument that is consistent with the rise of non-banks in a regulated environment of the Caribbean, where open market operations are not fully developed and where most of the adjustment has to be in loans and deposits.

Further examination of the incidence of reserve requirements was undertaken by Osborne and Zaher (1992) who used classical event studies methods and conclude that reserve requirements are a tax on depositors, but that shareholders bear part of the tax. Romer (1985) splits the cost of reserve requirements between bank borrowers and banks themselves by showing how increased reserve requirements not only raise loan rates but reduce bank lending. Some writers question the need for reserve requirements altogether and others have suggested that to provide compensation to banks, reserve requirements should be retained but interest should be paid on reserves [Friedman (1984)].

More important to the focus of this study, they conclude that reserve requirements impact on the size of the banking industry, but are not specific about the kind of circumstances in which equity holders as opposed to depositors bear the cost. The arguments are also open to the possible inference that firm industry size can be reduced without profitability being affected. This argument suggests that banks may not permit changes in reserve requirements to impact on profitability, but may prefer to make the required accommodation in terms of bank size while maintaining or even sacrificing profitability levels. They suggest that a set of customers at the margin are lost to the banking system as a result of higher costs of services to customers as banks seek to recover income lost from higher reserve requirements. To the extent however, that banks in Barbados operate in an oligopolistic environment, and where non-banks offer services which are not fully substitutable for commercial bank services, it is possible that additional costs may be borne by customers in an oligopolistic environment without loss to business.

Reserve requirements have been shown to have significant adverse implications for bank shareholder wealth. Slovin, Sushka and Bendeck (1990) show that this adverse impact is uniform across banks and that changes in reserve requirements have no significant effect on treasury securities. Their work also implies that reserve requirements contribute to reduced profitability of commercial banks and to the rise of non-banks.

Generally, most writers conclude that reserve requirements impact negatively on bank profitability and bank market share. However, a pure accounting interpretation would suggest that bank risks are improved since the additional assets held in cash or government securities requirements are risk-free.

2.2.6 Literature: credit controls and bank performance

Analysis of the effect of regulatory changes suggests that attention be centred on the impacts borne by customers, creditors and equity owners and requires a framework for integrating these multiple facets of the operations of financial institutions. Meyer (1980) asserts that the study of aggregate credit system expansion or contraction relevant to macroeconomic policy models should logically proceed from a macroeconomic model of financial regulatory impact. While studies have not provided us with a framework for analysis of the full regulatory impact of all bank regulations, studies of the impact of individual

45

regulatory measures are instructive.

Distinguishing between the impact of credit limits on the solvency of healthy and unhealthy banks, White (1981) suggests that the impact of credit limits on solvency will depend on the existing net asset situation of each bank. He suggests that banks which are already experiencing solvency problems are however likely to suffer further deterioration in net assets through reduced profitability and that credit restrictions will reduce the solvency of all banks through the effect on profitability but are unlikely to have more than an interim impact on healthy banks during the period of adjustment to the controls.

He suggests that the adjustment of one portfolio item is influenced by all other portfolio adjustments at a particular time and that portfolio adjustments are constrained by changes in net worth. He suggests that the inability to accumulate income earning assets adversely affects net worth and hence solvency over the medium term and that if liabilities continue to grow banks must find new areas of investment or negative net worth can result.

The effectiveness of credit ceilings is challenged by Ducca and Vanhoose (1990) who trace the transmission mechanism with special reference to the effect of loan contracts on monetary policy and conclude that changes in loan contract type towards committed loan arrangements influence how monetary policy disturbances alter intended results. They suggest that loan commitments can undermine the effectiveness of credit ceilings.

Ceilings on lending rates effectively place limits on the extent to which banks can charge customers higher rates in compensation for higher risks, so reducing the effectiveness of the loan rate. Indeed by reducing the effectiveness of the loan rate as a control device the credit rationing hypothesis by implication, assigns greater importance to credit controls, since equilibrium rationing predicts that the market will be in equilibrium in a state of excess demand and that loan supply will not depend positively on the loan rate.

This position differs slightly from that of Bester (1985) who argues that in an environment of credit controls banks will choose a rate of return to screen investors' riskiness. He argues that collateral and interest rates are determined simultaneously and that banks adjust to limited supply by raising collateral requirements for high risk customers. This point is also made by Zepherin (1990) who however places the emphasis on the impact of information on rationing and concluded that asymmetric information of borrowers led to increases in reservation service prices and to credit rationing. The non-market clearing views of Stiglitz and Weiss (1981) tend to be non-committal on the effectiveness of credit and interest rate controls.[9] They argue that once one moves beyond the IS/LM analysis of incorporating credit and introduces a general substitution process, loan rationing supplements interest rate rationing and other responses to relative price changes as part of the monetary transmission process. Stiglitz and Weiss (1981) argue that banks trade-off profitability against the risk of default but they do not throw any light on rationing which arises from regulation, nor do they indicate whether there is a different impact on profitability arising from regulation induced rationing compared with voluntary rationing. If banks do ration credit in an environment where credit limits are exogenous to the firm the inference is that the high-profit low-risk controlled sector would first be satisfied and that banks would withhold credit from the high risk, usually the productive sectors, which authorities wish to promote.

Fry (1988) is much more explicit on the question of allocation but less so on the question of the impact on profitability. He concludes that where credit ceilings exist credit is not advanced according to expected productivity but according to transactions costs and perceived risk of default, thus suggesting that commercial banks' main concern in a credit controlled environment is not the viability of the project but the impact on costs and risk. (See also Williams (1989)). An indirect reference to the impact of credit controls on profitability is found in King (1986) who develops a model which implies that for a given level of core deposits, the marginal cost of issuing loans rises with the volume of loans made as the bank becomes less liquid. However liquidity increases the probability that the bank will have to borrow on the open market, which increases the marginal cost of funds. Since credit controls tend to increase bank liquidity thus reducing the marginal cost of funds the implication is that such controls could possibly improve the profitability of banks.

2.2.7 Literature: interest rate regulation and bank performance

Conclusions about credit controls often need to be modified in the presence of interest rate controls. Early work on interest rate regulation [Mingo (1978)] found that deposit rate ceilings which limit banks' ability to compete via payment of interest may be counter-productive if the aim of deposit rate ceilings is to reduce risk. He argues that since banks rely on interest rate payment to attract funds, where this option is precluded, then interest rate controls can lead to increased risk. However, subsequent literature has tended to focus less on whether controls achieve their objective and more on who bears the cost of controls.

The literature on interest rate controls in the U.S., tends also to focus on

47

controls on deposit rates rather than lending rates.[10] Meyer (1986) argues that deposit interest rate ceilings, by limiting price competition confer a subsidy on bank equity holders and a cost to depositors. His comments were, however, made in the context of a ceiling on deposit rates but would need to be modified for the Caribbean case where there were floors on deposit rates and ceilings on lending rates. He finds that in a regulated environment risk adjusted returns are lower. This implies either that returns to equity are lower than they would otherwise be or that in a cost constrained portfolio, loan prices (as opposed to strict interest rates) may be lower or services fewer than would otherwise occur without restrictions. If equity owners do not bear the impact through lower yields or lower market prices of their stock, then higher revenues are needed to compensate for the higher portfolio risk in order to provide the same risk adjusted return.

In a model of uncertain rates of return, Pyle (1971) suggests that for a profit maximising firm the covariance between loans and deposits leads to intermediation by encouraging the risk averse profit maximiser to transform deposits into loans. That position is developed by Sealy (1977) who sees a scenario where rates are set by the intermediary rather than by the open market. He suggests that ceilings on lending rates prompt commercial banks to voluntarily set ceilings on their own deposit rates and concedes that the ability of the bank to subsidise banking activity such as check cashing, funds transfer and account variance costs may encourage deposit values. He found that the covariance reduces the uncertainty around expected profits and encourages intermediation.

An extreme position is, however, taken by Barro and Santomero (1972) who cite the case in which production and operating costs rise due to regulatory constraints. This argument is also made by Mitchell (1986) who examines the case where production and operating costs due to regulatory constraints were incapable of rewarding the depositor sufficiently. He applies a utility function defined over the mean and variance of portfolio return to examine how bank risk is affected by both deposit rates paid by the central bank on reserves and the required reserve ratio. He concluded that bank risk, however measured is affected partly by the interest rate on bank loans and separately by the reserve requirement.

Greater disaggregation of the costs involved in the adjustment of banks to monetary changes can be found in the contributions of Sealy and Lindley (1977) who also examined aspects such as implicit payments and embedded costs and identified other operational costs such as insurance costs, labour costs, and default costs. This is not an area which has been greatly examined as much of the literature tends to merge all costs into a single parameter representative of all operational costs or separates only liquidity and

48

insolvency costs.

The model of a quasi-fixed production developed by Flannery (1989) comes close to the approach of the regulated environment and is closer to conventional views of shared costs. He assumes that the cost function relates to changes in deposit balances rather than on, or in addition to, the level itself. He assumed that customer specific costs are shared by the customer and the bank. The model demonstrates how deposit rate variation may be reduced relative to open market movements. He argues that such a production process can explain both the long run customer relation and the tendency for deposit rates sometimes to lag behind open market rates both on the up and the down side of the market. He suggests that such quasi- fixed production technology explains the concept of core deposits.

The objective of stimulating the productive sectors through a low interest rate regime is generally not supported by later economists. Stiglitz and Weiss (1981) for example argue that monetary policies which seek to increase investment by lowering interest rates will not have the desired effect since there is no shortage of willing borrowers, and that policies that increase the availability of loanable funds will increase investment. Their view implies that profits may be maximised at lower interest rates and hence that ceilings on lending rates need not adversely affect bank profitability. However, if one assumes that rationing behaviour of commercial banks occurs whether or not there is central bank regulation, unless it occurs to a greater extent when there is regulation, then we can take rationing as given in all situations and proceed to analyze the effect of regulation by monetary authorities on bank profitability in a situation where voluntary credit rationing can be described as almost profit-neutral. Their analysis infers that regulated ceilings on lending rates do not necessarily adversely affect bank profitability since higher rates may be accompanied by higher risks and consequently higher losses with adverse implications for profitability.

To the extent that banks observe loan rate ceilings Fry (1988) agrees that non-price rationing will occur, but suggests that credit rationing caused by administratively imposed loan rate ceilings differs from credit rationing identified by Stiglitz and Weiss (1981). However, he observes that loan rate ceilings discourage risk-taking on the part of financial institutions, since risk premia cannot be charged when ceilings bind profitability.

Both types of credit rationing, induced and voluntary, are analyzed by Cho (1986) who concludes that abolishing interest rate controls will be insufficient to maximise investment efficiency, since banks may hold lending rates below the rate at which funds could be lent in order to reduce the probability of default and that credit rationing will persist even in the presence of financial liberalisation.

by limiting the opportunity set of banks such controls impact adversely on bank profitability and bank market share - but the implications for liquidity and solvency are often left undetermined.

2.2.8 Literature: prudential regulation and bank performance

The literature on prudential regulation focuses more on bank performance than does the literature on monetary regulation. Until very recently, writers were ambivalent about the form prudential regulation should take, particularly with regard to capital adequacy, risk and the probability of failure, e.g., Flannery (1989) and Kim and Santomero (1988). It is often argued, for example, Flannery (1989), that the combination of loan examination procedures and capital adequacy regulation lead insured banks to prefer relatively low risk individual loans, even while they pursue high portfolio risk in order to maximise their deposit insurance put option value. He argues that as a result of capital adequacy guidelines, banks will increasingly securitise loans that they cannot effectively finance from their own portfolios. Kim and Santomero (1988) agree that capital regulation via a simple capital asset ratio gives banks an incentive to increase their business risk by portfolio realignment and is an ineffective way to bound the insolvency of banks, but that the recent move to risk-related capital regulation in the U.S. and in many other countries which are part of the Basle agreement, is potentially more effective but is in danger of putting serious restrictions on bank activities and on product pricing. However, writers are unnanimous on the impact of capital adequacy on profitability, and to a lesser extent on market share, arguing that capital regulation bounds insolvency risk with adverse implications for return (see Figure 2.9).

Defining bank solvency as an event where the bank's capital is completely eliminated, that is, the return on capital E $\leq$ -1, then if return on equity is normally distributed the probability of insolvency denoted by (p), can be specified for any (E,σ) where σ, is the standard deviation of return per unit of capital.

Thus

$$prob[E \leq -1] \quad = prob \frac{\hat{E}-E}{\sigma} \leq \frac{-1-E}{\sigma} = p \qquad (2.42)$$

$$E = 1 - \phi(p).\sigma \qquad (2.43)$$

and

$$-\phi(p) = \frac{E+1}{\sigma} \qquad (2.44)$$

where $\phi(.)$ is the inverse of the cumulative standard normal distribution function. The value of $\phi(.)$ is always negative since the probability of failure considers only the lower end of the distribution. A larger absolute value of corresponds to a lower insolvency risk for a chosen portfolio.

The introduction of risk-based capital criteria (K^R) forces greater adjustment on banks and lowers the scope for trading-off risk and return. Using the expression in equation (2.38), regulators want to make sure that banks operate in the region to the left of the line LR (see Figure 2.9). LR is the regulation preference line and G_0 G_1 G_2 is the bank's global efficient frontier. The necessary and sufficient condition for the success of the banks' risk management through capital regulation is to eliminate the area between G_1 G_2 and G_1 G_3 for the opportunity set. Risk weights imposed by regulators achieve this. R_0 G_1 R_2 is now the efficient frontier conditional on capital ratio K^R, and E^R G_3 is the upward bound on the expected return associated with the solvency constraint. In the absence of capital regulation the global frontier becomes feasible to the bank. With capital regulation the bank can no longer make the normal trade-off between risk and return.

In the Caribbean, capital adequacy criteria are not explicitly risk-based and formal systems of assigning risk levels to assets did not apply; authorities, in assessing the adequacy of capital of individual banks took risk into account, so that insolvency risks, though not bound by the global frontier, were nevertheless bound by a frontier conditional on a capital constraint, albeit not fully risk-weighted.

Risk-based capital systems also have their disadvantages for the customer. Flannery (1989) examined the impact of capital adequacy criteria for insured banks in the U.S. under the risk-based scheme and found that the combination of loan examination procedures and capital adequacy regulations lead insured banks to prefer relatively low risk individual loans through the impact on permissible leverage (D/K), thus reducing the probability of failure but points out the consequences for profitability. He represented that:

$$E(R_E) = R_f + \int_{-\infty}^{R_L^*} [R_f(D/K) - \tilde{R}_L(D+K)/K]f(\tilde{R}_L) \, .dRr_L \qquad (2.45)$$

51

where:

K = an exogenously fixed amount of equity

W = end of period wealth and $W/K = R_E$ = return on capital and $E(R_E)$ expected

return to shareholders

$R_L = 1+$ the realised loan rate

$R_f = 1+$ the risk free rate

D = deposits

D/K = financial leverage

$R*_L = R_f /(D+K)$ is the lowest loan return for which depositors can be fully repaid and

$f(R) =$ the density function for R_L (which depends on the portfolio's riskiness θ_p).

Expressing deposit insurance as a put option written on the banks asset portfolio with an exercise price equal to end-of-period face value of outstanding deposits, he rewrites the above expression in terms of a put option with value (V). So that the attainable option value is:

$$E(R_E) = R_f + V(\theta_p, R_f(D/K)) \qquad (2.46)$$

Where: $R_f(D/K)$ is the exercise price.

The put option is increasing in both the asset variance and the exercise price : i.e.

$$V_1 > 0$$
$$V_2 > 0$$

where V_1 = asset variance and V_2 the exercise price.

Accordingly, in the absence of restrictive regulations, expected bank profits will be maximised by selecting the greatest feasible level of asset risk (Θp) and financial leverage (D/K). However, regulators attempt to influence Θp and D/K in ways that reduce the attainable option value, forcing banks into holding low risk portfolios. This could therefore largely explain the observed tendency of insured banks to specialise in low risk assets. While this confirms the impact of capital adequacy and leverage regulations on insured banks, insured banks compete with unregulated lenders in making

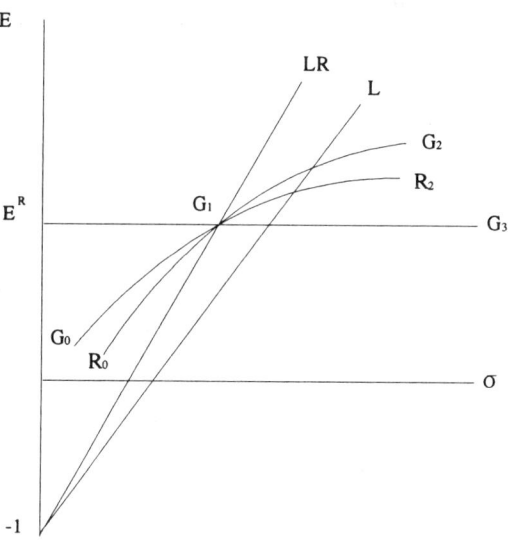

Figure 2.9 Bounding insolvency risk by capital regulation

loans, so that regulations partly determine which loans bankers have a comparative advantage in financing. The increasing practice of loan sales and loan securitisation have been identified as attempts by banks to recover profitability resulting from the constraints on capital sufficiency associated with risk weighted capital.

Most writers agree that adequate capital increases the soundness of financial institutions but suggest caution in the structuring of such requirements because of the impact on solvency. Heggestad (1979) notes that where financial regulators set rules for portfolios that it has the potential for reducing the probability of bank failure. These writers saw banks as choosing an asset portfolio to maximise expected utility of uncertain profits and that these choices were characterised by risk aversion. They defined failure as a situation where banks' losses exceeded capital.

They noted that where regulators focus solely on a relatively high variance and ignore the pooling effect of a regulatory change they may be misled into regarding the desirability of high-risk high-return assets. They do not recommend that portfolio regulation restrict high-risk, high-return assets as

53

this may increase the probability of bank failure. They argue that where regulations force banks to inefficient frontiers, regulators are likely to increase the probability that losses will exceed capital.

Later writings on the effect of capital adequacy criteria on commercial banks continue to be ambiguous with regard to risk but suggest a threshold at which the impact of increased capital requirements differs among banks. Koehn and Santomero (1980) showed that banks altered the composition of their asset portfolio with the imposition of higher capital requirements and according to the riskiness of the portfolio different results obtained. They showed that there existed some risk aversion coefficient below which any increase in capital will increase the probability of bankruptcy rather than decrease it.

Essentially therefore, safe banks became safer and risky institutions increased their risk position. Their writings have tended to support capital criteria based on asset quality as an improvement on uniform ratios. Representing insolvency risks by [E $\leq$ -1], that is, where the bank's equity capital is completely eliminated, they argue that when solvency standards are not based on asset quality banks reshuffle their portfolios toward riskier ones, thus increasing business risk in order to offset the impact of forced lower leverage, (lower financial risk) so that regulators fail to bound the insolvency risk. While such uniform capital ratios fail to bound bankruptcy risks, a risk related capital plan, by placing bank assets into risk categories and assigning a risk weight to each category bounds insolvency risks.

Assuming banks have a generally risk averse utility function in end-of-period capital, capital adequacy criteria in the presence of leveraging capability meant that banks efficiency frontier falls downward and to the left for any given value of increase in capital [Koehn and Santomero (1980)]. Their results implied unambiguously that over the entire permissible efficient frontier the total value of the portfolio falls and the returns of each set declines.

Some writers claim that because of the problem of moral hazard, deposit insurance reduces the role of the Central Bank in ensuring monetary stability in the operation of the banking system since it is claimed that banks exercise less care in credit selection in the presence of deposit insurance. Buser, Chen and Kane (1981) show that this problem can be minimised through the use of capital adequacy criteria since such criteria protect the insurance fund. They interpret the cost of regulatory restrictions as an implicit insurance premium. Without such regulations (of which capital adequacy is a part), deposit insurance schemes would not be viable. This found support in arguments that adequate capital was that which made the insurance premium actuarially fair [Sharpe (1978) and (1991)].

Regulators of commercial banks rarely see themselves as setting prices when imposing prudential regulations. Bös and Tillman (1983), using a cost-axiomatic approach to pricing in regulated firms, questioned whether prices determined by regulation are always demand compatible. It is often assumed that financial institutions will adjust prices to changes in regulations and that the changes are demand compatible. They suggest that cost adjustments may not always be passed on in terms of price adjustments and that cost-axiomatic pricing is only market clearing where firms' profits are explicitly taken into account.

The need for a model of capital regulation that takes both monetary and prudential measures into account is advocated by Mitchell (1986). This is particularly relevant to the Caribbean where there is a high level of dependence on monetary policy. Recent trends in the Caribbean to review the regulatory framework conform to the global trend in tightening prudential regulation and include some measure of regulation of non-banks. For the most part these capital adequacy measures are not explicitly risk-based, although there is the intention to introduce explicitly risk-based capital adequacy measures in some Caribbean countries.

2.3 Empirical studies: monetary and prudential regulation

In the past decade there has been little monetary regulation in most developed countries, so that there is a dearth of current empirical literature on the impact of regulation on commercial banks. Work on the impact of regulation on banks in the U.S. has tended to examine the impact of regulation on bank risk, but very few studies have examined impact on bank profitability and shareholder wealth. The latter can be divided into empirical studies on efficiency, e.g Smirlock (1985), and studies which examine the impact of some particular economic or monetary development on bank profitability. Theories such as the relative efficiency hypothesis [Smirlock (1985)] use optimising conditions to equate marginal cost of output (MC) with marginal revenue from input (MR). The objective of Smirlock's relative efficiency hypothesis is not to derive relative efficiency for the firm but to determine how the industry responds to each type of regulation. Later writers, Berger, Hancock and Humphrey (1992) derive efficiency estimates from the profit function and apply this methodology to data on U.S. banking. By using the profit function in place of the cost function they are able to examine output inefficiencies. These approaches differ somewhat from studies on regulatory impact. The only Caribbean study of which the writer is aware which examines bank profitability is an article by Rolle (1992) which examined the impact of monetary policy on bank profitability in the Bahamas. That study adopted an efficiency approach and did not include prudential regulation.

Most econometric studies which examine the impact of a single aspect of regulation employ either 'event studies' methods or regression analysis but tend to analyze the impact mostly on shareholder wealth. The work of Slovin, Sushka and Bendeck (1990) tests the impact of changes in reserve requirements on bank shareholder wealth. They use the prices of banks listed stocks in pooled cross sectional regression analysis using changes in reserve requirements as the dependent variable. A dummy variable is used which takes on the value of unity in the week of the regulation change and the value of zero at other times when there is a decrease. A second dummy variable takes on the value of unity when reserve requirements are increased and zero otherwise. The market index is used as a proxy for the return on the portfolio of all risky assets. His findings show that reserve requirements reduce bank shareholder wealth and shift resources from the regulated banking sector to the non-bank financial system.

Osborne and Zaher (1992) also examine the impact of reserve requirements on large banks' stock returns. They employ classical event study methods which allow examination of relationships between the size of tax changes and the size of associated abnormal returns. They examine changes in tax on demand deposits and time deposits and impose rigorous controls for developments in banking or in monetary policy that could be expected to affect bank shareholders' returns, thus ruling out contamination of the events as causing the observed abnormal returns.

First, following the approach used by Dann and James (1982) they test abnormal returns using the t-statistic to ensure that abnormal returns were not influenced by a change in risk structure. Separate regressions were run on the market model for the pre-event estimation period (pre-event day 85 through pre-event day 5) and the post event estimation period (days 6 through 85) and for the pooled estimation period (pre-event plus post event periods). This was followed by a Chow test for equality of the betas for pre-event and post-event periods [Chow (1960)]. Their findings were consistent with the notion that reserve requirements are a tax on deposits. They indicate, however, that shareholders bear at least part of the tax, suggesting a view contrary to the hypothesis advanced by some authors that the tax on deposits falls exclusively on borrowers.

2.3.1 Empirical studies: interest rates and bank performance

In early work on corporate finance Grove (1974) argued that conditions under which interest rate changes affect net worth of a financial institution occur if the weighted duration of assets is greater (smaller) than the weighted duration of liabilities. In these circumstances an increase in interest rates will decrease (increase) net worth. In recent writings [Akella and Greenbaum (1992)] have developed this idea in a study which examines its impact on stock returns. They show that in the U.S. when the duration of assets exceeds that of liabilities, repricing of assets in response to innovations is slower, and that since revenues adjust more slowly than costs, stock returns are affected. They impound the duration effects in the speeds of adjustment to revenues and costs and found that the difference in adjustment speeds proxies for the duration mismatch and influences the sensitivity of bank stock returns to interest rate innovations.

Their results suggest that bank stocks respond to short term interest rates. The duration of assets exceeds that of liabilities, supporting the hypothesis that the sensitivity of bank stocks is replaced by the relative speeds of adjustment of revenues and costs; so that the implication is that banks are not hedged against interest rate risk as reflected in the stock return sensitivity to unexpected changes in short term interest rates.

2.3.2 Empirical studies: deposit rate ceilings and bank performance

Other studies of the impact of monetary regulation on market values test the impact of deposit rate ceilings in France on the market value of banks' stocks [Dermine and Hillion. (1992)]. Their objective was to assess the relationship between the market value and the asset and liability structure of banks. Tests are based on the assumption that ceilings on savings and term deposit interest rates produce regulatory rents. The study tests both the effect of corporate taxation and the effect of regulatory rents on stock market prices.

Their paper contrasts sharply with traditional 'event' studies. These studies evaluate abnormal returns associated with a change in the economic environment and analyse bank-specific sources of wealth. The methodology used is compared to that proposed by Kane and Unal (1990) who regressed the market value of banks on the book value of equity. While they impose a constant cross-sectional valuation factor for the book value of equity in a given year, the accounting net worth is disaggregated in the Dermine-Hillion model into detailed assets and liabilities. A simple bank valuation model is developed to predict the relationship between asset and liability structure and market value. The goal of the empirical analysis is to estimate and draw inferences from the coefficients $\{(1-t)p/b^*, (1-t)b/b^*$ and $(1-t)d/b^*\}$ associated with the loans, bonds, and deposits respectively, where p,d and b are historical returns and p^*,b^* and d^* are current market returns. Their findings suggest that assets and liabilities subject to taxation are priced at a lower value for part of the period, and that demand deposits provided rents.

2.3.3 Empirical studies: deregulation of interest rates and bank performance

The techniques used by Cornett and Tehranian (1990) to estimate stock market reaction to the Depository institutions Deregulation and Monetary Control Act of 1980 also provide useful approaches to the examination of regulatory impact. The approach adopted was an event study methodology used to determine the expected effect of regulatory reform on future profits.

The study employed a simultaneous equations multivariate regression approach based on Zellner's (1962) seemingly unrelated regression model (SUR). The system of equations explicitly conditions the return-generating process on the occurrence or the non-occurrence of an event. This is accompanied by appending zero/one dummy variable to market model equations. The variable is set to equal one if the event occurred and zero if it did not. The coefficients multiplying the event dummy variable measures the impact on stock returns. The extended market model is used to measure returns for securities, the abnormal returns associated with a regulatory event is the residual from the model. Results of the tests were able to identify which event affected stock prices abnormally, and whether positively or negatively.

The problem in measuring the regulatory change is that unrelated events occur which affect the targeted industry during the period of regulatory reform. Cornett and Tehranain note that 'in particular the need for regulation as a solution to market failure is measured with comparison of costs imposed on society by market imperfections which exist in the absence of regulation' and that there is an indirect cost to society resulting from regulatory reform.

Other approaches to the study of regulatory impact include those of Binder (1985) who uses stock returns to measure tax effects of 20 regulatory changes which occurred since 1987 and Schreft (1992) who suggests the use of market data to measure the effects of regulation. Schreft argues that market data are more powerful than other measures because asset price movements incorporate all relevant information as soon as it becomes available. While this conclusion is accepted, in the Caribbean where stock data are either not available (as in Barbados) or are available at only long discrete intervals or in very short series (as in Jamaica and Trinidad and Tobago) this approach is not possible and profit data are used instead.

2.3.4 Empirical studies: deposit rate ceilings and bank profits

Tests on the impact on bank profitability as opposed to the impact on shareholder wealth have not been as frequently attempted and the impact of bank regulation on bank profitability is usually inferred from results using stock returns. The profit function has been used in banking to study scale economies, [Mullineaux (1978) and Hancock (1992), price elasticities of demand and substitution, Humphrey (1981) Hancock (1985) market power, Kim (1985) Berger (1991), Timme and Yang (1991), and the relationship of profits to cost based efficiency estimates, Berger and Humphrey (1991), Berger (1991) and Timme and Yang (1991)], but studies on the impact of regulation on bank profits are few.

Mingo (1978) was among the early economists to test the impact of regulation on earnings variance using return on assets as the measure of earnings. His objective was to test the effect of deposit rate ceilings in the U.S. on bank risk using linear least squares regression analysis. His data consisted of a combination of cross section and time series information for insured commercial banks in the U.S. his independent variables were;

- mean total assets for the bank over the period
- mean ratio over the period of equity to total assets
- the Herfindahl index[11] (computed on total assets for banks in SMSA[12]
- the banks market share
- per capita income in SMSA (average over the period)
- % growth in SMSA personal income
- average ratio of interest expense/total expense for the bank

The riskiness of the banks portfolio is reflected in the variance of stock prices or in the variance of profits. He chose the latter approach; an approach which is particularly useful where bank stocks are not listed on the stock exchanges. This is represented by:

$$var\frac{NI}{\overline{NI}} = \int (TA, K/TA, H, MS, Y/L, GR, I) \tag{2.47}$$

Where:

NI = net income
Var NI/N̄I = coefficient of variance of net income
TA = total assets for the bank
K/TA = mean ratio over the period of equity to total assets
Y/L = per capita income
H = index of total deposits
GR = growth in personal incomes
I = average ratio of interest expense/total expense for the bank
MS = money supply

The results of the regression provided support for the view that non-price means of competing for deposit funds can increase bank risk.

2.3.5 *Empirical studies: determinants of bank profitability*

Bourke (1988) and (1989) observes that barriers to entry may enhance profitability but other regulatory interventions may depress it. His research however, focuses more on bank performance generally than on the impact of regulation on bank performance. He tests the internal and external determinants of profitability across ten countries. Different forms of profitability are tested but only the results for profitability defined as return on assets are displayed. He used linear least squares regression equations, where the independent variables used were; a dummy variable representing government ownership; three bank concentration ratios; the long term bond rate for each country; growth of the money supply; capital and reserves as a percentage of total assets; cash, bank deposits and investments; securities as a percentage of total assets; the percentage change in the CPI for each country; and staff expenses as a percentage of total assets.

The results generally showed that capital ratios, liquidity ratios and interest rates are positively related to profitability. The results relating to liquidity ratios were less expected, as conventional wisdom is that liquidity holdings (particularly imposed by Government) represent an expense to banks. Higher levels of concentration were found to be associated with lower loan losses.

2.4 Conclusion

A review of the literature tends to suggest that regulation impacts on equity holders more so than on depositors and that it is often possible for production and operating costs due to regulatory constraints to fail to compensate depositors. The covariance between deposits and loans will voluntarily encourage banks to set their own ceilings, but where there are both ceilings and floors, banks become hostage to regulators. However, where regulators engage in cost-axiomatic pricing quasi-market prices are likely to obtain.

The review reveals that theories of the banking firm are divided into two groups, equilibrium models and leverage models. Models which include the capital constraint and which can accommodate analysis of the adjustment processes of commercial banks to various costs, such as, liquidity, solvency, and resource costs, facilitate analysis of bank performance which include prudential considerations. Empirical studies have tended to focus on who bears the cost and have mostly concluded that equity holders bear the full cost of regulation, though some argue for split costs or suggest that depositors bear the cost. The literature on the impact of capital adequacy on risk suggests that where capital provisions are not risk-based that banks will increase risk to cover return from additional capital outlays. In such cases, capital does not bound insolvency risk, but where capital adequacy is risk-based the contrary position occurs, banks will finance only low risk portfolios.

Several of these hypotheses will be tested in the course of the empirical investigation; among them, the observation that reserve requirements artificially constrain the size of the banking firm [Ramakhrisnan and Thakor (1984], and that part of the tax imposed by reserve requirements is borne by shareholders [Romer (1985)] and Osborne and Zaher (1992)]. The impact of reserve requirements on profits will be substituted in the analysis for the impact on shareholder wealth [Slovin, Sushka and Bendeck (1990)], and Arkella and Greenbaum (1992)]. More importantly, the general point made by Bourke (1988) that regulatory interventions may depress profitability will be examined.

The observation that credit limits impact the solvency of banks adversely through their impact on profitability will be among the hypotheses to be tested as well as the Stiglitz and Weiss (1981) view that banks trade-off profitability against the risk of default, that is, that a negative relationship exists between risk and bank profitability. The observation of King (1986) that credit controls increase the liquidity of banks will be tested. Mingo's (1978) observation that interest rate controls tend to increase risk due to reliance on non-price rationing will also be tested as will Mitchell's (1986) observation that interest rate controls influence bank risk. The Stiglitz and Weiss (1981) argument that regulated ceilings on lending rates do not necessarily affect bank profitability since higher rates may be accompanied by higher risks and therefore higher losses, with adverse implications for profitability will be examined with a view to observing whether a negative relationship exists between risk and interest rate regulation. Fry's (1988) observation that loan rate ceilings discourage risk-taking since risk premiums cannot be charged will be among the hypotheses tested.

In the course of the study, several observations related to bank performance and not necessarily to regulation will have the opportunity to be analysed. These include the Galbraith-Caves hypothesis that higher concentration leads to lower risks and Benston's (1972) observation that large banks are not necessarily more profitable than small banks. Many of these hypotheses will be tested in the empirical section while others which do not require econometric testing will be analysed in the course of reviewing the structure and performance of the banking system in Chapter 3.

61

Notes

1   Wicksell argued that through the supply side, price increases generate an internal drain on credit availability which leads an increase in interest rates or to a decrease in the supply of loans.

2   Interest rate policies in the Caribbean supported the views of Mckinnon (1973) and Shaw (1973) which suggest that higher time deposit rates will lead to increased savings, but differed from that branch of their thinking which suggests that time deposits will lead to higher economic growth.

3   Gurley and Shaw (1960) observe that in the first phase of financial development, outside money, commodity money or money backed entirely by Government debt is the norm, while in the second stage, direct claims and inside money backed by private debt are introduced.

4   Some econometric studies on Latin America, for example [Diaz Alejandro(1985)], do not support the view that financial liberalisation has substantial impact on the level of savings.

5   Research performed in the U.S.,[Youn Kim (1986)] found economies of both scale and scope in the growth of credit unions.

6   In Barbados, tax incentives offered to depositors who invest in credit unions are an example of that type of preferential treatment. Further parallels can be found in the U.S. in the long history of Regulation Q which was intended to protect small deposit-taking institutions from being pushed by competition from large banks into paying high interest rates to attract funds.

7   Arguments similar to those of size and scope are cast in terms of materiality; suggesting that since small operations are not material then they should not be regulated. This was the approach taken to cooperatives in Barbados until they grew to a sufficiently significant size where their failure could affect the system. In the case of banks, regulations apply to all banks irrespective of size.

8   The approach to the bank as a profit maximiser starts with a model of a wealth maximising firm in financial markets with uncertain return. Other approaches emphasising agency and utility maximisation have added to the literature but take second place to the view of the commercial bank as a profit maximiser or objective function maximiser. A summary of this literature is offered by Santomero (1989).

9 The non-market clearing hypothesis states that excess demand is handled by credit rationing and that when supply increases, loans increase even with the same demand level. It predicts that the market will be in equilibrium in a state of excess demand and that loan supply will not depend positively on the loan rate. This view was given great prominence through the work of Stiglitz and Weiss (1981).

10 In the Caribbean, however, there were both floors on deposit rates and ceilings on lending rates, unlike Regulation Q in the U.S. which set a maximum rate on deposits only.

11 The Herfindahl index or Herfindahl-Hirschman index (H-index) is the sum of squares of market shares of the firms in the relevant market.

12 SMSA denotes Standard Metropolitan Statistical area. Data refer to banks in the metropolitan area.

3 The structure and performance of the banking system in the Caribbean

3.1 Introduction

This chapter discusses the structure and performance of the banking system in the Caribbean and elaborates on the regulation of non-banks in so far as it relates to the performance of banks. It indicates the range and sequence of monetary measures and, demonstrates how the tools of monetary policy were given effect through commercial banks. It explains how monetary controls on commercial banks facilitated the growth of non-banks and suggests that the lack of adequate prudential regulation of non-banks led to their collapse. The second part of the chapter analyses the cost of financial intermediation and traces the trend in intermediation ratios in the Caribbean, particularly during periods of intense regulation. The final section of the chapter discusses the actual performance of commercial banks specifically in terms of bank profitability, risk, liquidity, solvency and market share.

The Caribbean economies of Barbados, Jamaica and Trinidad and Tobago are principally British in origin.[1] They are small economies, the largest being Jamaica with a population of 2.37 million and the smallest Barbados with a population of 0.27 million.[2] Per capita incomes were relatively high in Barbados (US$6,686) and Trinidad and Tobago (US$4,068) for most of the period of the study but were much lower in Jamaica (US$738) and declined further during the decade of the eighties (data are for the year 1991, see Table 3.1). Commercial banks were initially established to facilitate trade with the metropole.

64

Table 3.1
Summary of economic statistics on
Barbados, Jamaica and Trinidad and Tobago

Data at December 1991	Barbados	Jamaica	Trinidad & Tobago
Population	0.26 mill	2.37 mill	1.25 mill
GDP ($million) local currency	3,393	44,128	21,760
Foreign exchange reserves (US$million)	87.5	106.1	338.6
Foreign exchange reserves. Equivalent months of imports	1.2 months	0.8 months	1.7 months
BOP (overall bal)local cur	-39.9	-115.5	-2,765
BOP C/A local currency	-79.8	1,113.3	-631.5
Per capita GDP (US$)	6,686	738	4,068
Exchange rate (per US$)	2.00	21.49	4.125

Source: International Financial Statistics IMF February 1993 and Annual Reports of Regional Central Banks.

3.2 Structure of the banking system

Legislation governing commercial banks was enacted in 1961 in Jamaica,[3] in 1964 in Trinidad and Tobago and in 1963 in Barbados. It was mostly structural in its setting of parameters for commercial banks and prudential in its emphasis on capital requirements and customer concentration ratios but did not include powers of monetary regulation.[4] It identified licensing requirements, detailed the activities in which banks could or could not become involved and set minimum capital requirements. Other areas which were later to assume importance in the prudential regulation of banks were omitted from the original Banking Acts.[5] Regulations governing the financial system tended to be put in place after financial institutions had already been established.

Banking legislation was based on the U.K. model. Despite the British orientation of the Caribbean banking legislation, commercial banking in some islands (in Barbados for example) was, and still is, dominated by Canadian banks, but the presence of American banks tended to be short-lived.[6] There was no equivalent in the Caribbean of the McFadden Act of the U.S. which prohibited branching across state lines. Indeed banks with head offices in the U.S. and Canada were able to set up branch offices simultaneously in Barbados, Trinidad and Tobago and Jamaica.

Historical and cultural characteristics also influenced the structure of the banking system even where there was no explicit regulation. In the Caribbean, regulation of commercial banks is grounded in the view that commercial banks have an important fiduciary responsibility (greater than other financial institutions), should be closely regulated and supervised and should be debarred from direct involvement in commercial undertakings.[7] In this structural framework banks are differentiated from non-banks by their monopoly on the ability to offer chequing facilities and by their ability to accept demand deposits from the public. Their fiduciary responsibilities are emphasised in the requirement to hold minimum amounts of capital which are considerably higher than levels prescribed for non-banks. Specific regulations tend to be used for specific purposes but most regulations have effects that cut across different purposes. For example credit ceilings are mainly applied for macroeconomic purposes, but by preventing uncontrolled and imprudent expansion of credit, also serve to fulfil a prudential objective [Vittas (1992)].

As in most developing countries, monetary distinctions have tended to be preserved for longer periods in the Caribbean than in North America and Europe. Commercial banks, however, remain the dominant means of transmission of monetary policy and the structure of the financial system is based on the view that banks are the most important institutions in the financial system. Universal banking and the functional view of regulation have not characterised these markets. Although there is increasing recognition of the need to view non-banks as an increasingly important part of the monetary and financial environment, this latter development has so far been extended to include only a slightly greater degree of regulation of non-banks.

The predominance of Canadian banks (they distinguish between banking and investment broking and dealing activity) tended to influence the culture of commercial banking in the Caribbean. This is inferred from the case of Jamaica where most Canadian banks withdrew at an early stage, and where there was relatively more active and aggressive development of traditionally non-banking activity.

3.2.1 Areas of structural regulation in the Caribbean

Table 3.2 lists the areas of structural regulation in the Caribbean which form the background against which other forms of bank regulation - monetary and prudential- are implemented.

Table 3.2
Types of structural regulation in the Caribbean

Banks(BK) and non-banks(NB)	BK			NB		
Country	B	J	T	B	J	T
-Licensing of commercial banks	*	*	*		*	*
-Prohibition from engaging in commercial activity	*	*	*			
-Debarrment from offering chequing accounts				*	*	*
-No restriction on branching	*	*	*	*	*	*
-No restriction on investment broking or dealing	*	*	*	*	*	*

BK - banks
NB - non-banks
B - applicable to Barbados
J - applicable to Jamaica
T- applicable to Trinidad and Tobago
* = in effect

3.2.2 Growth of the banking system

Until the mid-1960s most commercial banks in the region were foreign. Localisation occurred first in Jamaica and almost immediately afterward in

Trinidad and Tobago, following a wave of structuralist economic thought of the 1960s and 1970s. Some economists, among them Beckford (1972), explicitly recommended the nationalisation of commercial banks, and by the mid-1970s most banks in both Jamaica and Trinidad and Tobago were either locally or government owned.

The Barbados case differed. Branches of foreign banks continued to operate until 1978 when the first local bank was established. The second was not established until 1984.[8] This contrasts with Jamaica and Trinidad and Tobago where most banks were local and their shares were publicly quoted.[9] By 1992, of the seven commercial banks operating in Barbados, five were branches of foreign banks. By 1992 there were six commercial banks in Barbados, eight in Trinidad and Tobago and eleven in Jamaica,[10] and their combined assets amounted to approximately US$5 billion at December 1992. Commercial banks' assets grew rapidly during the seventies and the mid eighties, but slowed considerably towards the end of the eighties and into the early nineties as the economies of Barbados and Trinidad and Tobago experienced macroeconomic difficulties. The Jamaica case differed, asset growth continued at an accelerated pace despite protracted macroeconomic problems (see Table 3.3).

Following the establishment of Central Banks, first in Jamaica in 1961, in Trinidad and Tobago in 1965, and in Barbados in 1972, much greater emphasis was placed on monetary policy. Central banks determined monetary policy and their concerns encompassed matters of macroeconomic stabilisation and accelerated economic growth. Financial systems became increasingly diversified in the 1970s and 1980s; non-banking activity increased rapidly, particularly in Jamaica where merchant banks, stock exchanges, and other specialist financial institutions were established in response to competitive opportunities and the range and scope of financial services widened [Williams (1989)]. As distinctions between commercial banks and other financial institutions narrowed and as financial assets became more accessible for transactions purposes there was a greater need to increase the scope of monetary control. In Jamaica, legislation extending control to non-banks was passed in 1974 through the Protection of Depositors Act and the Central Bank subsequently extended credit controls to trust companies and merchant banks in 1975. In Trinidad and Tobago the Non-Bank Financial Institutions (NFIs) Act was passed in 1981 and revised in 1986. This Act extended monetary and prudential control to NFIs. Legal capacity for monetary control was not extended to non-banks in Barbados until 1993.

As deposit growth increased, insufficient demand from the productive sectors such as manufacturing and agriculture, pushed banks into lending to the consuming sectors. The resulting large proportion of the assets of the banking system which was devoted to the financing of trade, principally imports, became a major concern of authorities because of the serious implications for foreign exchange sufficiency. Increased nominal incomes also contributed to the sharp rise in the level of personal loans and this sector became a major beneficiary of new credit in the 1970s. Personal loans, consumer loans and hire-purchase instalment credit rose rapidly and by the early 1970s central banks (who deemed these to be non-priority sectors) moved to control their growth; particularly in Barbados and Jamaica (Table 3.4). The impact on foreign exchange reserves of credit expansion in the distribution and personal sectors evident in Barbados and Jamaica was masked in the Trinidad and Tobago case by buoyant earnings from petroleum exports, where by 1972, the manufacturing sector had replaced distribution as the major recipient of credit. Credit controls there were mild and short-lived.[11] Controls were imposed on non-business loans in 1979 and limited new credit for consumer lending to 25% of total new credit. The policy was described as gradual but reasonably successful [Farrell (1990)]. To a large extent therefore the degree of credit regulation experienced by individual countries reflected the macroeconomic imperatives of each country and was influenced by existing production structures. Problems of foreign exchange adequacy were further magnified for Barbados and Jamaica as central banks, in support of the goal of accelerated economic growth, departed from the practice of backing local currency issues with foreign exchange holdings and provided substantial credit to the public sector.

3.3 The Caribbean experience with monetary regulation

There was a commonality in the monetary policy measures adopted. Controls on credit, interest rate controls and reserve requirements formed the core of monetary policy instruments. Regulation ranged from limited monetary control in Trinidad and Tobago, to moderately high levels in Barbados, to rigorous and complex systems of monetary control in Jamaica. (See Appendix 3.1, 3.2 and 3.3 for details of the monetary measures used). The extent of foreign exchange insufficiency which prompted authorities to put monetary restrictions in place is demonstrated in Table 3.5.

Primary and secondary reserve requirements (liquid assets ratios) were employed to absorb excess liquidity in the system and to control consumption expenditure. Interest rate controls were also frequently applied to improve the affordability of credit to the productive sectors, to defend the balance of payments and to pre-empt capital flight, and interest rates were regulated to keep the cost of operation of business to affordable levels.

69

Table 3.3
Growth of assets of commercial banks
(Local currency $million)

Period	Barbados % p.a.	Jamaica % p.a.	Trinidad and Tobago % p.a.
1972-77	12.5%	22.4%	50.3%
1977-82	21.2%	33.2%	38.7%
1982-87	12.1%	40.5%	5.1%
1987-92	5.4%	216%	4.4%

Source: Monthly Digests of Statistics, Central Banks of Barbados, Jamaica and Trinidad and Tobago.

At the same time authorities sought to restrict credit to foreign exchange-absorbing sectors and to redirect credit to foreign exchange-earning activities, applying both global and selective credit controls. Where credit limits evoked the desired response, authorities avoided imposing reserve requirements, particularly if the targeted adjustment was not significant, but as balance of payments problems intensified in the 1980s secondary reserve requirements were applied with increasing frequency.

3.3.1 The experience of the Caribbean with reserve requirements

The case of Barbados between 1973-91 vividly illustrates the use of reserve requirements in response to changes in the balance on external account [Williams (1994)]. In a series of movements, primary and secondary reserve requirements were raised from 3% of deposits in 1973 to 20% by 1978 and again by 5 percentage points to 27 percent of deposits as the balance of payments drifted into deficit in 1980. They remained there until 1986 when the securities component was increased by three percentage points and again in 1991 following two years of successive balance of payments deficits.

70

Table 3.4
Personal lending as a % of total commercial bank assets

Period	Barbados	Jamaica	Trinidad and Tobago
1972	n.a	13.49	35.4
1975	16.48	13.05	15.26
1976	18.13	10.76	29.83
1977	17.35	9.88	32.09
1978	16.53	7.76	28.41
1979	16.22	10.69	24.81
1980	15.27	8.61	24.55
1981	13.77	7.31	24.70
1982	11.80	5.35	21.35
1983	12.61	4.01	20.82
1984	12.24	2.63	24.41
1985	12.28	1.99	23.16
1986	13.10	2.25	20.0
1987	12.98	2.44	18.50
1988	15.34	2.16	19.37
1989	14.7	2.67	23.09
1990	12.99	3.2	23.09
1991	12.95	4.8	23.77
1992	11.66	4.4	23.36

Source: Monthly Digests of Statistics, Central Banks of Barbados, Jamaica and Trinidad and Tobago.

Table 3.5
Foreign exchange reserves: equivalent number of months' imports

Period	Barbados	Jamaica	Trinidad and Tobago
1972	2.2	1.8	8.4
1977	1.7	-3.4	18.6
1982	2.0	-19.5	10.4
1987	3.4	-5.2	0.7
1992	2.7	-1.9	-0.2

Source: Monthly Digest of Statistics of the Central Banks of Barbados, Jamaica and Trinidad and Tobago.

Though banking legislation placed a statutory limit on permissible increases in cash reserve requirements, (in Barbados the legal limit was reached as early as 1978) this was substituted for by greater reliance on securities requirements (secondary reserves).

The escalation of liquidity ratios (primary and secondary reserve requirements) was as rapid in Jamaica as in Barbados, rising from 15 % in early 1973 to as high as 40% in the early 1980s, and to 48% in 1985 before it was reduced to 36% in 1986 when the non-cash portion was eliminated. While the range and frequency of policy changes varied, reserve and securities requirements remained in place for most of the 20 year period and secondary reserve requirements were a continuing feature of monetary policy in both Barbados and Jamaica[12] (see Appendix 3.1 and 3.2). The vast proportion of secondary requirements was held in government securities.

Authorities in Trinidad and Tobago kept a low and relatively steady liquid assets ratio of 5%-7% throughout the 1970s and early 1980s when only cash reserve requirements were mandatory. This ratio grew to 15% by 1987 and included secondary reserves; principally treasury bills and other Government securities.[13] At its highest it compared with levels of 40% in Jamaica and 30% in Barbados. Increases in reserve requirements followed the end of the oil boom, and in the post-1983 period reserve requirements were largely relied upon to respond to balance of payments difficulties. Authorities in Trinidad and Tobago and Jamaica raised reserve requirements up to mid-1985 and thereafter lowered them as adjustments in the exchange rates permitted some ease in monetary policy (Appendix 3.3). Reserve requirements ratios are shown in Table 3.6. Data are reported as a percentage of total assets in order to achieve comparability, since different items are excluded from deposits in each jurisdiction. However, for compliance purposes reserve requirements are usually calculated as a percentage of deposits.

3.3.2 The experience of the Caribbean with credit controls

Three types of credit regulations were employed in the Caribbean: (1) selective credit controls imposed through the setting of credit limits, (2) ceilings on the total level of credit permitted to be outstanding by commercial banks[14] and (3) interest rate controls on credit outstanding to selected sectors.[15] [16] (see Appendix 3.1, 3.2 and 3.3 for details). Selective credit controls were consistently applied throughout the period and therefore form the main focus of the analysis of credit controls.

Controls on credit to the personal sector were more actively applied in Jamaica and Barbados.[17] In Barbados the share of personal lending in commercial banks' total assets was pushed gradually from 16.2% of total credit in 1974 (prior to restrictions) to 11.7% in 1992. This compares with a decline in the case of Jamaica from 11.9%, in the period prior to imposition of controls, to 2.67 % in 1989.[18] In contrast, personal lending absorbed 21% of total commercial bank assets in Trinidad and Tobago in 1974 and by 1992 absorbed slightly more, 23.4% (Table 3.4), confirming that selective credit controls in Trinidad and Tobago were used less vigorously than in Jamaica or Barbados.

Normally, credit controls on banks distribute wealth away from banks toward non-banks. In the Caribbean this was moderated by the lack of sophistication in Caribbean markets, so that controls had a greater probability of being more effective since the techniques of circumvention were not as readily implementable. It is suggested that the faster growth of non-banks in Jamaica and Trinidad and Tobago may have been associated with different levels of sophistication in these markets.[19]

3.3.3 The experience of the Caribbean with interest rate controls

One of the first monetary measures put in place by central banks in the region was the control of interest rates on deposits. In Barbados floors on the savings deposit rates, ceilings on the average lending rate, and ceilings on the residential mortgage rate, remained in force at different levels until 1991 when the ceiling on the average lending rate was removed.[20] These examples

73

typified rate-setting regimes in Barbados and Jamaica in the late 1970s and 1980s where direct controls were placed on deposits and lending rates[21](see Appendix 3.1, 3.2 and 3.3). This technique was never used in Trinidad and Tobago where there was little attempt overtly to control rates of interest. The Central Bank there depended principally on manipulation of the bank rate.[22] and control of interest rates was not a prerequisite for balance of payments equilibrium until the late 1980s.

The experience with setting of interest rates in Jamaica was very similar.[23] If one separates the highly restrictive pre-1985 period and the less restrictive post-1985 period of monetary control, the former appears highly comparable to the Barbados situation for most of the period (Table 3.7). In both Jamaica and Barbados the minimum savings rate was used as a monetary and demand management tool. When slow deposit growth and rapid growth of credit combined to create liquidity and foreign exchange difficulties, authorities raised interest rates to slow the rate of credit expansion, to improve commercial bank liquidity and to protect the balance of payments through the dampening effect of higher interest rates on the real sector.

Floors on deposit rates were from time to time adjusted relative to foreign interest rates in order to pre-empt capital flight. As the banking system became more international this became an increasingly important consideration and partly explains why deposit rates were raised during the IMF Stand-by programme of 1981-83 and 1991-93. Periods in which international rates exceeded local rates tended to coincide with periods of foreign exchange difficulties. Normally, however, the interest rate differential between local and foreign rates reflects transactions costs, unwillingness to flout Exchange Control regulations, the probability of future cash shortages and the inability to access funds at short notice. Consequently, when low or negative economic growth recommend that interest rates be kept low, international interest rates sometimes prompt otherwise undesirable increases in regulated deposit and lending rates.

Interest rate spreads were much wider in the Caribbean than in North America, reflecting possibly the need to compensate banks for higher levels of secondary reserve requirements. Spreads were much wider in Jamaica and Trinidad and Tobago than in Barbados (Table 3.8). This may reflect the position of Revell (1980) that gross margins of banks in countries where local banks predominate, tend to be wider than in countries with mainly foreign banks. (Most banks in Barbados were branches of foreign banks, while in Jamaica and Trinidad and Tobago, banks were mostly local.)

Table 3.6
Comparative reserve requirements (liquid assets ratios)
(% of total assets)

Period	Barbados	Jamaica	Trinidad and Tobago
1972	0.0	13.13	8.49
1975	11.94	16.96	11.26
1976	14.32	17.48	12.26
1977	15.73	21.72	11.86
1978	16.06	19.43	11.36
1979	18.67	21.09	12.07
1980	16.81	19.93	13.22
1981	20.31	21.19	15.33
1982	21.18	23.44	15.54
1983	20.77	26.59	16.07
1984	21.03	30.0	16.28
1985	24.42	34.82	16.02
1986	23.15	26.63	14.58
1987	21.86	25.71	13.88
1988	23.59	14.46	14.15
1989	23.35	13.11	12.21
1990	23.63	22.27	11.70
1991	25.48	10.69	10.45
1992	24.80	27.21	10.8

Source: Central Banks of Barbados, Jamaica and Trinidad and Tobago.

Table 3.7
Comparative interest rate spreads
(Average lending rate minus minimum savings rate %)

Period	Barbados	Jamaica *	Trinidad and Tobago*
1972	5.75	4.59	4.3
1975	4.25	5.5	4.5
1976	4.25	6.5	3.3
1977	4.0	6.65	6.85
1978	4.5	6.60	7.50
1979	3.12	6.96	5.96
1980	3.63	7.68	5.0
1981	5.50	7.25	4.85
1982	5.87	7.43	5.03
1983	5.50	8.02	4.42
1984	5.50	7.10	2.90
1985	4.87	9.20	9.60
1986	5.50	10.60	10.80
1987	5.50	10.20	9.70
1988	5.25	11.90	10.60
1989	5.25	10.90	8.87
1990	5.25	13.59	11.01
1991	7.25	16.03	10.87
1992	7.38	26.04	11.54

Source: Monthly Digests of Statistics, Central Banks of Barbados, Jamaica and Trinidad and Tobago.

Table 3.8
Differential between prime rate and 3 month deposit rate

Period	U.S.	Barbados	Jamaica	T'dad & T'go
1975-80	1.39%	4.375%	6.6	5.51
1981-85	2.3%	4.25%	7.2	5.36
1986-90	1.2%	4.81%	11.4	10.2

Source: Central Banks of Barbados, Jamaica and Trinidad and Tobago.

Interest rate controls assume an important role in the context of exchange rate adjustment, serving to stabilise the exchange rate. In the Jamaica case this role was assigned to the minimum savings rate, which, because of its direct impact on lending rates was an important support for demand management programmes. Between 1985 and 1990 the savings deposit rate was increased as the exchange rate came under pressure and assumed the role of a major policy instrument. Interest rate policy was used to indirectly influence the demand for cash balances.[24]

Failure to adhere to incomes policies which were essential for the success of monetary policy contributed to continued crises in the balance of payments in the Caribbean [Blackman (1991)]. By the turn of the 1990s, as pressure on the balance of payments mounted, policy makers were unable to defend the role of monetary regulation as a prescription for macroeconomic stability or as a sustainable policy over the long term. The arguments for liberalisation therefore gained ground and the Caribbean was caught in the wave of financial liberalisation sweeping the developing world. In 1991 Jamaica embarked on a programme of virtual complete liberalisation. Tentative steps toward limited financial liberalisation were also observed in Trinidad and Tobago in 1990 as reflected in the relaxation of reserve requirements and later of credit controls. In Barbados cautious steps toward liberalisation became evident in 1992 with the removal of selective credit controls and reduced interest rate regulation.[25] However, for most of the period tight monetary controls were in place and commercial banks were highly regulated.

Table 3.9 lists the tools of monetary policy applied in the Caribbean. Though the types of controls described appear to be wide, many are modifications of the same control mechanism. Controls are not easily quantifiable or ranked by intensity since they are to a large extent qualitative and differ in degree of intensity among countries (Appendix 3.1, 3.2 and 3.3).

Table 3.9
Tools of monetary regulation in the Caribbean

Banks (BK) and non-banks (NB)	BK			NB		
Country	B	J	T	B	J	T
-Cash reserve requirements (non-interest bearing)	*	*	*		*	*
-Cash reserve requirements (interest bearing)		*				
-Secondary reserve requirements - Government securities only	*					
-Liquid assets ratio - cash and specified securities (J.T.)	*	*	*	*	*	
-Voluntary liquid assets ratio		*				
-Limits on bank lending to the personal and distributive sectors	*	*				
-Global credit limits (B.J.)	*	*				
-Minimum downpayments and maximum repayment period for consumer credit	*	*		*	*	
-Limits on consumer credit outstanding by commercial banks	*	*		*	*	
-Limits on new non-business loans as a percent of incremental credit			*			
-Certificates of deposit held with the Central Bank		*				

Tools of monetary regulation in the Caribbean (cont'd)

Banks (BK) and non-banks (NB)	BK			NB		
Country	B	J	T	B	J	T
-Ceilings on mortgage interest rate	*	*		*	*	
-Floor on interest rates on savings deposits	*	*				
-Ceiling on the prime lending rate	*	*				
-Ceiling on the weighted average lending rate	*	*				
-Discount rate/bank rate-borrowing rate for banks experiencing difficulties	*	*	*			

BK - banks
NB - non-banks
B - applicable to Barbados
B - applicable to Jamaica
T - applicable to Trinidad and Tobago
* = in effect

The above table does not indicate the periods during which these monetary tools were in place. For these details see Appendix 3.1, 3.2 and 3.3.

3.3.4 Exchange rate changes - liberalisation or regulation?

Decisions to adjust the exchange rate were deferred for as long as possible. Financial liberalisation was avoided and attempts were made to change demand and supply directly through regulation. In the Jamaica case, even though there was considerable exchange rate adjustment it was heavily supplemented by monetary controls.[26] In many cases monetary controls were more intense in Jamaica where the exchange rate was a more frequently used adjustment measure than in Barbados and Trinidad and Tobago where it was not.

Jamaica's experiments with exchange rate adjustments far pre-dated those of its neighbours.[27] First floating with the pound sterling in 1972, Jamaica devalued its currency in 1973 and since then made frequent exchange rate adjustments. These include devaluations, the floating of its currency and the implementation of a two-tier exchange rate system. During this period authorities kept monetary controls in place. Frequent modifications were however made to controls on interest rates and on credit. The year 1985 was a turning point in the liberalisation process for Jamaica [Brown (1991)] and since that time Jamaica tended toward an increasingly less regulated system and announced virtual total liberalisation of the financial system in 1991. In that year Jamaica abolished exchange controls, dramatically reducing interest rate controls with a view to their eventual removal, and completely removed credit controls. Secondary reserve requirements were abolished but cash reserve requirements remained. Commercial banks were expected to satisfy all foreign currency requirements including those of Government through the forces of demand and supply. The exchange rate which had been freed for some time remained liberalised.

Exchange rate liberalisation in Jamaica permitted banks to earn substantial sums in the foreign exchange markets. The Jamaica case where deregulation exerted a positive influence on bank profitability tends 'a priori' to suggest valid grounds for the view that the reverse situation, regulation, is likely to have impacted adversely on bank profitability.

Even though Trinidad and Tobago twice devalued its currency (in December of 1985 and June of 1988) for most of the period Trinidad and Tobago kept a fixed and unchanged exchange rate.[28] Exchange rates in Barbados remained unchanged throughout the period.

3.4 Prudential concerns

Prudential concerns of Central Banks increased in importance simultaneously with heightened monetary regulation. As control formerly exerted by head offices declined and ownership became more localised, the vast resources of the overseas parent were no longer accessible to local banks. Responsibility shifted to local authorities and increased regulatory measures were put in place to maintain and improve the efficiency and stability of the system. There was growing implicit recognition that foreign ownership carried a significant benefit in respect of providing an implicit guarantee of the solvency and liquidity of banks operating in the local economy [Farrell (1990)]. Capital criteria, customer concentration ratios and audit and supervision were the main areas of prudential regulation. Levels of capital ranged from US$1 million to US$5 million and seemed to be adequate in the case of Barbados and Jamaica.

The level of concentration as well as the method of decision making in Caribbean banking systems prompted several writers to describe the banking system as oligopolistic, for example, Farrell (1990), Howard (1976), Bourne (1977) and Blackman (1982). Their views tend to confirm the observation of Fry (1988) that financial markets in developing countries not only tend to be oligopolistic but that detailed regulations concerning financial transactions are enforced more consistently and effectively. Conclusions about the oligopolistic nature of the banking system in the Caribbean are to a large extent influenced by the level of bank concentration which remains relatively high. At the beginning of the 1990s in Jamaica three banks controlled 70% of the market, while in Barbados three banks controlled 60% of the market and the same number controlled 58% of the market in Trinidad and Tobago. It is however postulated that despite high levels of concentration, in the 1980s markets were less oligopolistic than in the 1960s and 1970s. The past and to a lesser extent present oligopolistic nature of markets in the Caribbean present an interesting case for testing Jordan's (1972) hypothesis that in markets with a poor oligopolistic structure, regulation causes prices to rise and that evidence relating higher levels of regulation to lower rates of return on profit is much weaker.

The deposit aspect of concentration was not officially controlled and was managed at the level of the individual bank. Credit concentration was applied in the form of ceilings on lending to a single customer and was either related to bank capital or to total assets and applied with varying degrees of flexibility in the three countries.[29] Many of these issues of concentration were not however, problems of developing countries but problems of size and are mirrored in the operations of small banks in developed countries and were not specific to the Caribbean. However, flexibility in applying rules relating to concentration tends to become more important in small economies where the financing options of large businesses are few.

Most regulations apply to banks uniformly but impact differently on small banks than on large, and on local banks differently from foreign. Distinctions between local and foreign banks became more important in the post 1970 period following the collusive rate-setting environment of the pre-1970s.[30] Access of branch banks to international support systems and to international finance available to foreign branch banks became the critical difference separating local and foreign banks as they sought to adjust to monetary and prudential regulations simultaneously.

For example, prudential regulations relating to capital requirements tend to affect local banks more than foreign.[31] Central Banks have full authority to require indigenous banks to increase their capital but in some jurisdictions (Barbados and Trinidad and Tobago), branch banks are allowed to rely on global capital.[32] [33] Capital criteria therefore theoretically apply to overseas branches, but branch assets represent so small a percentage of total global portfolios that on the basis of materiality, head offices do not voluntarily assign capital specifically to individual branch locations.[34]

Procedures for the audit and supervision of banks were put in place from the establishment of central banks in the Caribbean and gradually improved in depth and coverage. Despite delays in implementing regulations to correct problems created by product diversification, the banking system in Barbados remained relatively free of prudential problems[35] [(Williams (1989)]. This is possibly explained by the role of moral suasion in the regulatory process and an agreed 'cooperative ethos' in the market and illustrates the benefit of small size. Many of the older banks remain bound by common customs and traditions and frown on all out competitive behaviour, preferring the signalling of policy intentions through informal channels. (The exception to this might be Jamaica where competition is more intense). This cooperative ethos makes it possible for the emerging process of financial liberalisation to be put into effect through moral suasion and the informal signalling of required targets in a cooperative approach to monetary control.[36]

Some Caribbean countries elected to deal with the question of depositor protection through the establishment of deposit insurance schemes, on the principle that by contributing small amounts to a fund, one is protected from large catastrophes. In Trinidad and Tobago where a scheme was implemented following the collapse there of several non-banking institutions, deposit insurance was quite costly. Both commercial banks and finance companies contribute to a deposit insurance fund in Trinidad and Tobago, but in Barbados to date there is no deposit insurance, despite the collapse of Trade Confirmers Ltd in 1987 and the shut-down of the Bank of Credit and Commerce in 1990. In Jamaica there is no deposit insurance.

If capital criteria are intended to protect the insurance fund and hence the system, the need for deposit insurance may be reduced if capital adequacy and other regulatory controls are adequate. One solution is to implement risk-based capital criteria, but the disadvantage is that banks are likely to avoid risky investments and could leave the financing of high risk projects in the Caribbean unsatisfied, thus resulting in costs in terms of social efficiency.

It is sometimes argued that the better option might be to increase capital requirements instead of requiring deposit insurance. This view ignores the pooling effect of resources, since in the deposit insurance case contributions of several institutions provide support to the failing bank, while in the latter, that institution relies only on its own capital, a more costly alternative. The result of either capital adequacy criteria or deposit insurance, or both, is to reduce the profitability of banks in the short term.

Indeed the implication might be that since the greatest number of bank and non-bank failures occurred in Trinidad and Tobago, the only country which offered deposit insurance, there might instead be some moral hazard associated with deposit insurance, particularly where no risk-based capital adequacy criteria exist. This is possibly explained by the fact that the presence of deposit insurance is not sufficient to assure security of deposits, but that deposit insurance needs to be accompanied by a risk based measurement of capital with constraints on leverage.

Off-balance sheet liabilities, contingent liabilities, guarantees and exchange rate exposures arising from risks originating in the Caribbean are another prudential concern.[37] Since these liabilities attract no reserve requirements, are fee-earning and in the Caribbean to date do not require supporting capital;[38] they form a cushion against loss of profitability associated with regulation, both prudential and monetary.

Whereas in a market without capital regulation the choice of the capital asset ratio is determined endogenously by portfolio composition, the stability of cash flows, the skill of management and the competitive environment, in the highly regulated case of the Caribbean the scope for adjustment in these areas is reduced. Not only are they now exogenously determined but it is argued [Tobin (1969)] that, in such environments, at the general equilibrium level, increases in the ratio of the marginal product of physical capital and the clearing rate now alter the equilibrium stock of physical capital. Tobin further suggests that regulators tend to set optimum capital at levels higher than the social optimum, largely because it is their responsibility to minimise the social cost of bank failure. He implies that the market clearing process may take place at rates which impact adversely on profitability because of higher levels of required capital. It is however virtually impossible to test this hypothesis for the case of the Caribbean and, if relevant, could have application only to locally incorporated banks who are required to hold local capital to support their operations. However, the difficulties experienced by local banks, at least in Trinidad and Tobago, do not tend to support this hypothesis for the Caribbean case.

3.4.1 Non-banks: a structural or a prudential concern?

The growth of non-banks in Jamaica and Trinidad and Tobago has been one of the most significant developments in the financial system in the 1980s. Growth of non-banks outstripped that of banks up to the mid-eighties and, with the exception of Trinidad and Tobago where significant non-bank failures slowed non-bank growth beginning in the late 1980s, this growth continued into the late 1980s and early nineties (Tables 3.10 and 3.11). The number of non-banks in Jamaica rose from six in 1972 to twenty nine in 1992. In Trinidad and Tobago twenty-one non-banks were established by 1982 at the height of the expansion compared with eight previously in operation.

The rapid rise of non-banks in the 1970s and early 1980s in Trinidad and Tobago was followed by several non-bank failures in the mid-1980s. Between 1981-86 five non-banks collapsed in Trinidad and Tobago and one was restructured. The implementation of the Financial Institutions (Non-Banking) Act which came into effect in 1981 was too late to prevent the problems of insolvency inherent within the finance companies. A revised Act which improved on many of the features of the earlier legislation was put in place in February 1986, but by that time the Central Bank of Trinidad and Tobago had committed itself to substantial support of non-bank financial intermediaries (NFIs) [Farrell (1990)].[39] In the Barbados case one non-banking institution collapsed in 1987 but [40] Jamaica was virtually free of either bank or non-bank failures.

Table 3.10
Number of banks and non-banks[41]

	Number of banks			Number of non-banks		
	1972	1982	1992	1972	1982	1992
Barbados	5	7	6	1	4	7
T'dad & T'go	8	8	8	8	21	16
Jamaica	6	9	11	9	27	29

Source: Central Banks of Jamaica, Trinidad and Tobago and Barbados.

The degree of regulation of non-banks differed as did the degree of monetary control but in all cases non-banks were less closely regulated.[42] Non-financial institutions in some jurisdictions were not required to hold legal reserves. This shifted more transactions balances to non-bank financial institutions, and less total reserves were required to be held with the result that the money multiplier process was significantly increased. Though the proliferation of non-banks, particularly in Trinidad and Tobago, is partly explained by their virtual exclusion from regulation up to 1986,[43] non-banks relied on commercial banks' lines of credit to supplement liquidity so that increasingly banks had greater responsibility as virtual lenders of last resort. Though some jurisdictions have imposed primary reserve requirements on non-banks (Jamaica in 1986) authorities did not generally require non-banks to hold secondary reserves.[44] In other jurisdictions commercial banks created non-banking arms which were able to accept deposits not subject to secondary reserve requirements so increasing their flexibility in portfolio management and enhancing profitability of the group.[45]

Table 3.11
Growth of non-banks
(Local currency $million)

Period	Barbados growth % p.a.	Jamaica % p.a.	Trinidad and Tobago % p.a.
1972- 77	88.0	6.0[p]	n.a
1977- 82	70.8	6.0	72.2
1982- 87	82.7	87.8	8.4
1988- 92	66.7	49.0	2.9

Source: Annual Reports of monthly Economic Digest of Statistics - Barbados, Jamaica and Trinidad and Tobago.
p.a. = per annum
n.a. = not available
Figures are in the currency of each country

The virtual exclusion of non-banks from regulation by authorities was based partly on small size and materiality but was also influenced by social considerations which had their genesis in the objective of encouraging institutions which provide services to small savers. In addition, since commercial banks, rather than non-banks influenced the level of high powered money, monetary authorities were more concerned with the regulation of banks and less concerned with non-banks. More recent attempts to require non-banks to hold reserves are, however, likely to bring them more closely under the control of monetary authorities.

A list of the tools of prudential regulation applied in the Caribbean is set out in Table 3.12.

3.5 Bank performance and regulatory costs in the Caribbean

3.5.1 Cost of regulation

Returns on government securities in Barbados and Jamaica were lower relative to returns on credit to the private sector. Interest on Government treasury bills ranged from 3-5% in Trinidad and Tobago and from 3-16% in Barbados. The differentials between treasury bill yields and lending rates for Barbados (See Table 3.13) were typical of the lower returns on government securities. Using the Barbados example, simple calculations which assume away other costs other than interest costs, show that increases in cash reserve requirements lead to increases in net costs (measured by alternative earnings at the weighted average lending rate), of 0.6 percentage points. The cost of holding required Government securities of (on average) 25% over the period is calculated to be equivalent to an interest rate of 1.5 percentage points when the differential between average treasury bill yields and weighted average lending rates is taken into account. The total cost of cash and securities regulation was therefore 2.1% points as compared with interest spreads which were widened by 1.1 percentage points, resulting in an overall net loss to equity holders of 1% point in equivalent interest (see Table 3.14).

86

Table 3.12
Tools of prudential regulation used in the Caribbean

Banks (BK) and non-banks (NB)	BK			NB		
-Country	B	J	T	B	J	T
-Minimum capital requirements.	*	*	*		*	*
-Powers of inspection.	*	*	*	*	*	*
-Requirement to report annual profit and loss and balance sheet results.	*	*	*		*	*
-Limits on loans to a single borrower or group.	*	*	*			
-#Provision for doubtful loans.	*	*	*			
-#Minimum solvency standards.	*	*	*			
-#Measurement of capital.	*	*	*			
-#Strict provisions concerning action/sanctions as a result of audits/inspections.	*	*	*			
-#Cease and desist orders.	*	*	*			

Bk - banks
NB - non-banks
B - applicable to Barbados
J - applicable to Jamaica
T - applicable to Trinidad and Tobago
* = in effect

#These features have been included in very recent legislation and did not form part of the original Banking Acts of Barbados, Jamaica and Trinidad and Tobago. The first four features mentioned were however in place from the inception of the Banking Acts in each jurisdiction.

3.5.2 Cost of financial intermediation

Evidence suggests that intense regulation raised the cost of financial intermediation. Using methods employed by Revell (1980), now the accepted yardstick for measuring cost comparisons of commercial banks; operating costs as a ratio of total assets in the Caribbean averaged (11%) in Jamaica, in Trinidad and Tobago (9%) and Barbados (8.5%) (Table 3.15). This compares with an average ratio of operational costs to earning assets 3.39% of U.S. insured banks in 1976 [Fry (1988)]. Such high costs may have stymied domestic resource mobilisation and tend to support the view of Terrell (1986) that banks in countries which exclude foreign banks have higher operating costs than countries that permit foreign banks.[46]

However, Hanson Roberto de Rezende Rocha (1985) in a comparative study of developed and developing countries found no evidence that banking is necessarily more costly in developing countries than in the OECD countries. However, his measure of efficiency, the spread between the gross costs of borrowing and the net returns on lending, concentrates on spreads rather than costs and so minimises the importance of domestic resource mobilisation which can result from lower operating costs.

Table 3.13
Comparison of average lending rate and treasury bill yields
Barbados

	Lending rate (actual)	Treasury bill yields
1973	12.0	8.1
1974	12.0	8.08
1975	11.3	4.0
1976	10.3	4.5
1977	10.0	5.0
1978	10.0	4.79
1979	10.1	4.95
1980	11.0	6.19
1981	13.9	13.82
1982	13.7	11.34
1983	11.9	6.81
1984	11.9	7.19
1985	10.9	4.58
1986	10.3	4.34
1987	10.3	4.99
1988	11.1	4.71
1989	12.7	5.82
1990	12.1	8.06
1991	15.0	11.30
1992	12.6	6.6

Source: Monthly Digest of Statistics, Central Banks of Barbados, Jamaica and Trinidad and Tobago.

Table 3.14
Interest (% p.a.) spreads (% points)

Barbados

Period	Cash reserve requirement	Interest cost of cash reserve requirements	Securities require-ments	Interest cost of securities require-ments	Interest cost
Averages (1966-77)	2% voluntary	(0.2%)	0%	(0%)	(0.2%)
After regulation	8%	(0.8%)	25%	(1.5%)	(2.3%)
Difference	6%	(0.6%)	25%	(1.5%)	1%

Source: Monthly Digest of Statistics, Central Banks of Barbados.

3.5.3 Regulation and financial intermediation

Financial intermediation ratios averaged 47% in Barbados, 43% in Jamaica and 35% in Trinidad and Tobago over the period but when these ratios measured by broad money to GDP are applied to Barbados they indicate a tendency to decline or stagnate during periods of intense regulation (Table 3.16). This occurred in Barbados between 1978-87[47]. In 1991, for example, the financial intermediation ratio for Barbados was 7.2 percentage points lower than in 1972. Despite a sharp increase in financial intermediation ratios in 1992 following liberalisation of credit controls and reductions in interest rate controls, the financial intermediation ratio had risen by only 1 percentage point over the past twenty years.

The trend for Jamaica was similar. Financial intermediation stagnated up to 1985, registering zero growth in 1972-85, a period of intense regulation, but increased by 10.2 percentage points following the gradual liberalisation of the system between 1985 and 1992. In Trinidad and Tobago where the level of bank regulation was considerably lower, this ratio rose slowly but gradually over the period. These trends tend to support the view that banks in highly regulated economies are asphyxiated by regulation as observed by Clarke (1986).

Table 3.15
Cost of intermediation of Caribbean commercial banks
(Operating costs as a % of total assets)

Period	Barbados	Jamaica	Trinidad and Tobago
1972	n.a.	n.a.	6.3
1975	8.9	n.a.	6.9
1976	8.1	n.a.	6.3
1977	8.4	n.a.	6.3
1978	7.9	n.a.	6.7
1979	7.3	10.0	6.9
1980	7.8	11.7	8.0
1981	9.7	9.1	12.5
1982	11.3	11.0	9.0
1983	9.7	9.6	3.9
1984	9.7	14.5	3.3
1985	9.4	17.9	2.4
1986	8.4	16.7	8.9
1987	7.2	15.7	9.7
1988	7.4	11.4	10.2
1989	8.1	14.4	10.1
1990	8.9	17.8	9.0
1991	9.3	17.0	9.1
1992	9.7	19.5	10.8

Source: Central Banks of Barbados, Jamaica and Trinidad and Tobago.

However, this measure of financial intermediation does not take fully take into account the quality of financial assets or the variety of financial instruments, factors which have become important criteria in assessing the extent of financial development. It is therefore only a proximate indicator of financial development. However, it remains a frequently used measure and its application to the Caribbean discloses stagnation of financial intermediation levels in periods of intense regulation and, in the Barbados case, for the entire period.

3.5.4 The outturn for bank performance

Figures 3.1, 3.2, and 3.3 plot trends in commercial bank profitability in Barbados, Jamaica and Trinidad and Tobago. In the Barbados case, the declining trend in 1982 followed a series of steep increases in reserve requirements and slightly improved returns in 1987 coincided with the removal of credit controls in that year (Table 3.17 and Appendix 3.1). In the case of Trinidad and Tobago where controls were very limited a change in trend was evident in the period 1980-84 and seems associated with the difficulties being experienced by non-banks and a possible shift back to commercial banks (Figure 3.2). In the Jamaica case, banks experienced improved profitability from 1983 onward, a period of increasing monetary and exchange rate liberalisation. In all cases, changes in the profitability of banks seemed associated with some form of structural, monetary or prudential regulation, mostly the former (Figure 3.3).

Commercial banks in Barbados tended to be more liquid than in Jamaica and banks in Trinidad and Tobago appeared to suffer periodic illiquidity, particularly in the post 1985 period, a period of monetary tightening in Trinidad and Tobago (Table 3.20). Banks in Trinidad and Tobago were more heavily capitalised while in Barbados solvency levels were low, partly because of predominantly branch type operations. Solvency levels in Jamaica were relatively higher and this was reflected in an enviable record of avoidance of bank failures. Banks in Barbados and Trinidad and Tobago, where economies were liberalised more slowly, lost more market share to non-banks compared with Jamaica, where commercial banks benefitted from liberalisation of the banking system at a much earlier stage (Tables 3.18, 3.19 and 3.20).

92

Table 3.16
Financial intermediation ratios in the Caribbean
(Broad money as a % of GDP)

Period	Barbados	Jamaica	Trinidad and Tobago
1972	58.1	36.7	34.7
1975	40.9	31.8	26.2
1976	40.9	33.2	30.6
1977	44.0	35.3	31.3
1978	48.8	32.9	34.4
1979	45.1	33.1	34.5
1980	40.1	35.9	31.3
1981	41.5	41.4	33.4
1982	42.2	47.3	38.6
1983	44.0	50.4	42.4
1984	43.4	44.8	44.8
1985	45.3	36.8	47.4
1986	45.7	49.9	47.6
1987	46.8	47.3	49.2
1988	49.1	53.1	49.5
1989	44.8	47.6	49.5
1990	50.7	43.2	44.4
1991	50.9	46.0	44.2
1992	59.1	47.0	39.8

Source: Digests of statistics and annual reports of regional Central Banks and various IMF statistical reports. (See page 33 for methodology for computing ratios.)

Table 3.17
Comparative commercial bank profitability
(Barbados, Jamaica and Trinidad and Tobago)
%

Period	Barbados	Jamaica	Trinidad and Tobago
1975	1.07	1.01^P	1.02
1976	1.17	1.03^P	1.43
1977	1.47	1.23^P	1.72
1978	2.19	1.06^P	1.56
1979	2.47	0.86	1.45
1980	2.50	0.79	1.60
1981	2.67	1.35	3.12
1982	2.21	2.21	2.86
1983	1.50	3.15	2.77
1984	1.15	3.22	2.49
1985	0.90	1.92	1.72
1986	1.51	2.60	0.64
1987	1.97	2.44	0.57
1988	2.11	2.79	0.49
1989	2.81	3.26	0.76
1990	2.15	0.90	0.72
1991	2.01	3.75	1.07
1992	1.78	7.40	1.43

Source: Central banks of Barbados, Jamaica and Trinidad and
Tobago. (Data on Jamaica for 1975-78 were based on 75% of reporting
banks and are provisional (p).* Returns are measured on profits before tax.)

Table 3.18
Bank performance indicators: Barbados

Year	Profita bility	Liquid -ity	Risk	Solvency	Market share
1977	1.47	0.95	0.008	0.00	94.4
1978	2.19	9.01	0.046	1.23	92.7
1979	2.46	7.06	0.080	1.24	91.2
1980	2.50	6.34	0.036	1.01	90.5
1981	2.67	2.39	0.018	1.11	88.7
1982	2.21	2.91	0.013	0.84	87.7
1983	1.50	1.03	0.038	0.72	87.5
1984	1.15	3.05	0.066	0.66	86.7
1985	0.90	2.67	0.140	1.75	87.5
1986	1.51	3.21	0.038	1.63	86.1
1987	1.97	3.90	0.040	1.89	86.1
1988	2.11	4.38	0.064	1.83	83.6
1989	2.81	1.25	0.012	1.34	82.6
1990	2.15	1.84	0.016	1.15	83.2
1991	2.01	1.26	0.014	1.26	82.1
1992	1.78	1.22	0.011	1.22	82.6

Source: Central Bank of Barbados Annual Digests of Statistics various issues and statistics supplied by the Central Bank. (See page 10 for methodology for computing ratios.)

Table 3.19
Bank performance indicators: Jamaica

Period	Profit ability	Liquid -ity	Risk	Solvency	Market share
1977	1.01	7.61	0.07	4.83	84.72
1978	1.03	6.96	0.00	4.10	85.69
1979	0.86	6.62	0.01	3.68	86.65
1980	0.79	6.10	0.06	3.41	90.64
1981	1.35	7.95	0.00	2.28	93.62
1982	2.21	4.91	0.06	3.43	92.50
1983	3.15	5.64	0.14	3.72	89.64
1984	3.22	-0.06	0.00	3.81	89.49
1985	1.92	1.12	0.00	0.70	86.83
1986	2.60	5.76	0.01	3.91	81.39
1987	2.44	4.61	0.01	5.13	84.25
1988	2.79	20.89	0.04	3.76	81.91
1989	3.26	10.42	0.29	4.34	80.14
1990	0.90	1.18	0.00	5.15	80.00
1991	3.75	5.98	0.17	4.62	81.84
1992	7.40	6.44	3.68	5.06	81.24

Source: Central Bank of Jamaica and Jamaica Stock Exchange.
(See page 10 for methodology for computing ratios.)

Table 3.20
Bank performance indicators: Trinidad and Tobago

Period	Profita-bility	Liquid-ity	Risk	Solvency	Market share
1975	1.01	14.12	0.01	13.68	87.2
1976	1.43	14.94	0.04	17.56	85.3
1977	1.71	7.74	0.16	15.90	84.7
1978	1.55	2.95	0.01	12.85	82.1
1979	1.44	8.83	0.01	10.90	83.7
1980	1.59	5.68	0.00	10.21	80.9
1981	3.11	2.74	1.37	8.69	79.8
1982	2.85	5.54	0.24	6.00	82.0
1983	2.76	1.63	0.03	6.98	78.3
1984	2.48	-0.27	0.18	7.76	76.3
1985	1.72	2.04	0.56	8.76	75.8
1986	0.64	-0.08	1.58	6.73	75.6
1987	0.57	-0.05	0.61	6.15	77.7
1988	0.49	0.13	0.13	6.31	74.1
1989	0.76	0.65	0.02	6.75	76.1
1990	0.72	1.45	0.04	6.89	81.3
1991	1.06	-0.47	0.11	6.43	81.5
1992	1.43	-0.13	0.21	7.24	78.8

Source: Central Bank of Trinidad and Tobago and Trinidad and Tobago Stock Exchange. (See page 10 for methodology for computing ratios.)

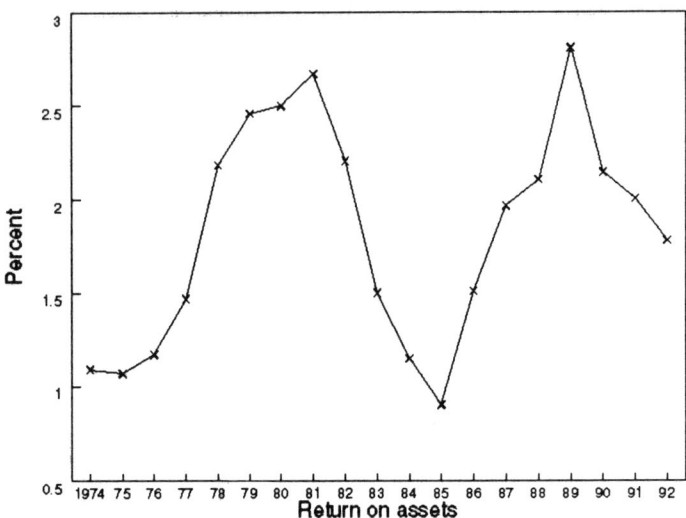

Figure 3.1 Bank profitability (ROA): Barbados

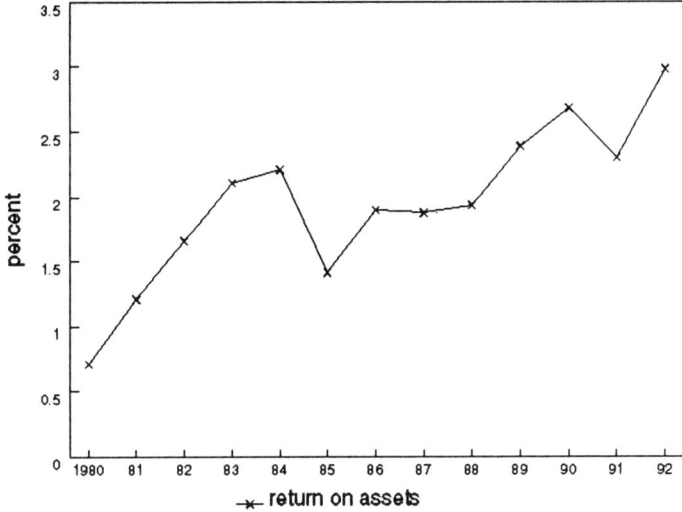

Figure 3.2 Bank profitability (ROA): Jamaica

98

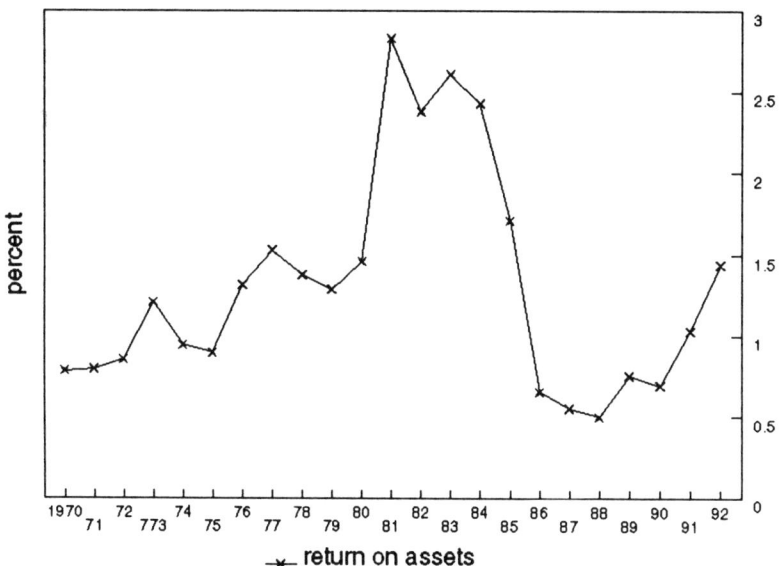

Figure 3.3 Bank profitability (ROA): Trinidad and Tobago

3.6 Conclusion

In summary, monetary regulation was intense for most of the period, particularly in Barbados and Jamaica where fractional reserve ratios, particularly secondary reserve requirements, were very high and credit and interest rate controls were in place. Simultaneously, financial intermediation costs rose and financial intermediation ratios declined. While some of this decline may be attributable to the diversification of the financial system which is expected to occur as financial systems mature [Goldsmith (1969)], these periods of declining intermediation coincided with high levels of bank regulation, suggesting that the loss of market share was attributable to more than simply a maturing system. Bank performance measures point to increasing bank profitability in periods of deregulation in Jamaica and to a lesser extent in Barbados despite the short period of time during which these systems benefitted from deregulation, and to a loss of bank market share throughout the region, suggesting that the decline in financial intermediation was greater than otherwise would have been the case in the absence of regulation.

99

Notes

1   These islands became politically independent in the 1960s; Jamaica and Trinidad and Tobago in 1962 and Barbados in 1966.
2   In Barbados the main export was sugar; in Jamaica, bauxite and in Trinidad and Tobago, oil.
3   The first commercial bank was established in Trinidad and Tobago in 1806, in Jamaica in 1836, and in Barbados, in 1838. They were administered under the British Caribbean Currency Board - the note issuing authority.
4   Criteria for monetary regulation formed part of the Central Bank Acts in the three jurisdictions.
5   Areas omitted from the three Banking Acts included, for example, bad debt provisioning and limitations on risk-taking.
6   Canadian banks still exist in Barbados, Jamaica and Trinidad and Tobago. For part of the period there were three American banks in Barbados, two in Jamaica, and two in Trinidad and Tobago, but by 1992 there were few American banks in the Caribbean.
7   This differs from the structure of other financial systems such as Germany and Japan where commercial bank have traditionally been directly involved in corporate ventures.
8   Since December 1992 a third local bank has been established.
9   Up to 1992 the shares of banks in Barbados were not publicly quoted. However, from 1988, shares of publicly quoted banks in Trinidad and Tobago and Jamaica were permitted to cross-list on other stock exchanges.
10   A local cooperative bank was established in the early 20th century but was not operated on a full commercial basis.
11   Controls imposed on non-business loans in 1979 limited new credit for consumer lending to 25% of total new credit.
12   In Barbados, secondary reserve requirements include only government guaranteed securities, while in Jamaica and Trinidad and Tobago these requirements (referred to as liquidity ratios) include investments in public companies and other specified assets, as well as government securities. In Jamaica Certificates of Deposits issued by the Central bank were included.

13   The cash portion was raised to 12% in 1989 and secondary reserve requirements were increased from 5% to 11% and reduced in the same year to 7% (see Appendix 1.c).

14   Ceilings on total credit outstanding were set in 1989 in Trinidad and Tobago, and in 1991 in Barbados, both in the context of IMF Stand-by arrangements with the IMF.

15   Controls on interest rates are usually considered an interest rate measure but are as much a credit control measure.

16   Real estate and mortgage loans were excluded. Several other minor modifications were made from time to time both in Barbados and Jamaica.

17   Unlike Barbados, the distributive sector was not subject to direct credit controls either in Jamaica or in Trinidad and Tobago.

18   No attempt is made here to identify modifications to credit controls. The analysis concerns itself with whether credit controls were or were not in place.

19   Whereas credit limits were introduced in Barbados in 1977, it was over ten years later before the corporate sector adopted the facility of leasing on any significant scale to circumvent these controls. This technique was commonly used in Trinidad and Tobago from the early 1980s.

20   Ceilings were placed on the maximum deposit rate in 1973 in Barbados, on the prime and average lending rates in 1976 and on the mortgage rate in the same year. The ceiling on deposit rates was changed to a floor in 1978 and floors on savings continued in force since that time.

21   Eighty percent of banks felt that the minimum savings rate did not help to encourage savings and suggest that savings were not interest rate responsive.

22   The bank rate was also a heavily used monetary tool in Jamaica but in Barbados it was seldom set at highly punitive levels. This occurred only in 1981 and 1991, both years of intense balance of payments difficulties.

23   Deposit rates in Jamaica were regulated for most of the 1960s until 1970 when they were temporarily deregulated. In 1972, prime rates and deposit rates were again controlled but were raised appreciably in 1985. In 1990, the savings rate was deregulated, this time as part of a general programme of deregulation.

24   In Jamaica, between 1985 and 1990 the savings deposit rate was increased as the exchange rate came under pressure. Certificates of deposits were market determined for most of the period 1985-90. Ceilings on the average lending rate were no longer set by the Bank of Jamaica after 1990.

25   In 1992 authorities in Barbados ceased to set the ceiling on the average lending rate but continued to set the minimum savings rate.

26   For most of this period Jamaica's exchange rate was not a market rate but a managed rate.

27   Devaluations and exchange rate depreciation are not included in the study as areas of regulatory control since they are usually seen by authorities and by the International Financial Institutions (IFIs) as indicators of liberalisation rather than regulation. However, for completeness, in the empirical analysis, the exchange rate is included among the independent variables influencing bank profitability.

28   Trinidad and Tobago floated its exchange rate in 1993.

29   The question of whether concentration ratios should be modified depending on asset risk has not been resolved. The Jamaica legislation offers the flexibility of examining individual cases. The Barbados legislation did not.

30   Prior to the establishment of Central Banks in the Caribbean, interest rates were set by agreement among banks operating in each Caribbean country.

31   Authorities refrained from restricting banks' involvement in leasing activity because of concerns of social efficiency and accelerated economic development. However, high levels of exposure of non-banks on leasing activities contributed to the failure of some non-banks in Trinidad and Tobago in the mid 1980s.

32   In the Caribbean the assignment of capital was not in place up to 1992 but it is included in the new Financial Intermediaries Regulatory Act of Barbados (which came into operation in 1992) and applies to new banks only.

33   Five of the seven banks in Barbados are branches of international banks which are signatories to the Basle Accord and are obligated to impose on internationally active banks minimum risk-based Tier 1 and total capital ratio requirements of 4% and 8% respectively.

34   Net long term borrowing is sometimes used as a proxy for the capital of branch banks. However, to the extent that these liabilities can be repaid at the option of the local branch, they cannot be relied upon as protection for depositors in the event of a crisis.

35   In Barbados the deposit-taking activities of commercial houses - some with commercial connections- partly prompted the implementation of new legislation in 1992.

36   In Barbados, new legislation, passed in 1992, and made effective from 1993, put in place a system of licensing for commercial houses, requiring them to seek permission to take deposits from the public, and requiring that their deposit-taking be supported by bank guarantees, collateral securities or deposit insurance and otherwise placing their financial standing under scrutiny.

37   Regional currencies are aligned to the U.S. dollar.

38   Regulatory authorities in the U.S., for example in assigning exchange rate risk against portfolios where exchange rates are volatile assign a (β) of 1, i.e. they require that the exposure must be fully covered by capital. The character (β) measures the degree of risk on a scale from 0 to 1.

39   By 1986 the Central Bank of Trinidad and Tobago had committed itself to TT$142 million in support of NFIs.

40   The collapse of the Bank of Credit and Commerce in 1992 was unrelated to the domestic environment and is not included in the count.

41   Non-banks include merchant banks, trust companies and finance companies but exclude credit unions, insurance companies and government mortgage banks.

42   Credit unions also increased their share of the market; partly in response to official encouragement and partly due to a competitive edge arising from their exemption from limits on lending for consumer credit and from tax privileges enjoyed by their members.

43   In 1981 monetary authorities in Trinidad and Tobago imposed a 3% reserve requirement on non-banks. This did not appear to halt the rise of non-banks. It compared with a ratio of 9% for commercial banks.

44   In Barbados, non-banks were required to hold neither primary nor secondary reserves.

45   Many non-banks, though not empowered to open chequing account drawn on themselves, did so through commercial banks.

46   In Jamaica and Trinidad and Tobago foreign commercial banks were not excluded but were expected to cede majority control to local ownership. This was not the case in Barbados.

47   Credit controls were abolished in Barbados in 1987 and were introduced in 1989 and were abolished again four years later.

4 Regulation and commercial bank performance: evidence from a survey of banks

4.1 Introduction

This chapter presents the views of commercial banks about the impact of bank regulation on the five measures of bank performance used in the study, bank profitability, bank liquidity, bank risk, bank solvency and bank market share. The analysis is based on responses to questionnaires sent to commercial banks in Barbados, Jamaica and Trinidad and Tobago. Response rates were considerably higher in Barbados (83%) than in Jamaica (50%) and Trinidad and Tobago (75%). (See Appendix 4 for questionnaires and summary of responses.) Each review section ends with a brief summary of expectations and these views are summarised in Table 4.1 at the end of the chapter based on whether the impact on bank performance is expected by banks to be positive or negative. This exercise assists in choosing the relevant variables for testing in the empirical chapter and offers the opportunity of empirically testing some of the views of commercial banks about regulation and its impact on bank performance, many of which are based on casual empiricism. Responses are illustrated by graphical representation of data trends.

4.2 Impact of regulatory measures on bank profitability

4.2.1 Impact of reserve requirements on bank profitability

Banks observe that of the monetary control tools applied in the Caribbean, reserve requirements was the most heavily used (Figures 4.1, 4.2 and 4.3) and represented a significant opportunity cost to banks. Unsatisfied demand for credit to the private sector (for which higher rates could be charged) would have impacted adversely on profitability given the high levels of

105

compulsory credit. In the Barbados case, authorities appeared to attempt to deliberately compensate banks by bidding up interest rates on treasury bills so as to retain commercial bank financing. Since limits on credit to non-priority sectors effectively reduced banks investment options, the bidding up of treasury bill yields may have constituted an element of cost-axiomatic or accommodative pricing in the regulatory process.

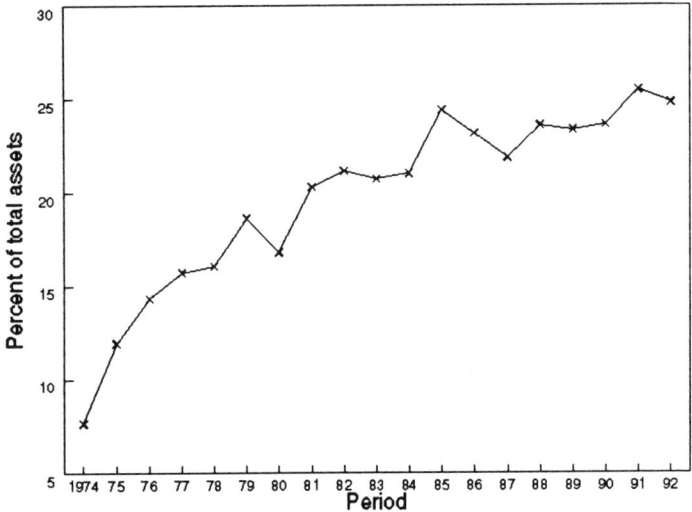

Figure 4.1 Primary and secondary reserve requirements: Barbados

Banks offer that a purely mathematical calculation shows that reserve requirements reduce bank profitability in the absence of adjustment and that they will attempt to adjust since it is their aim to maintain some profit level represented as:

$$\Pi = r_A(D-R) - \int_R^x C(\bar{X}-R)f(X)dX \qquad (4.1)$$

106

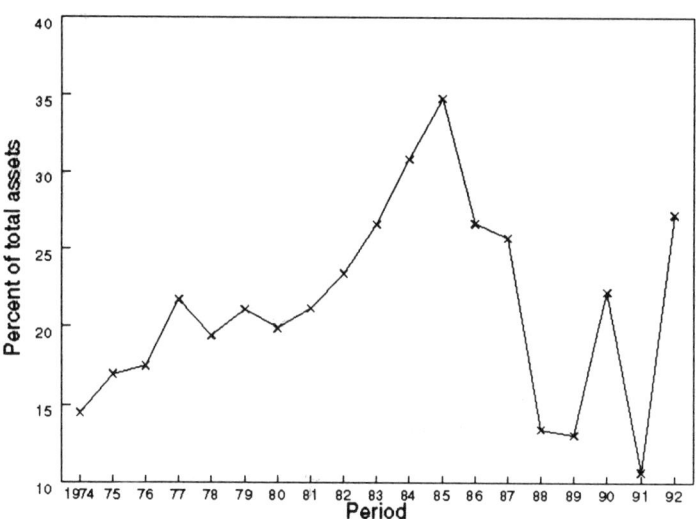

Figure 4.2 Primary and secondary reserve requirements: Jamaica

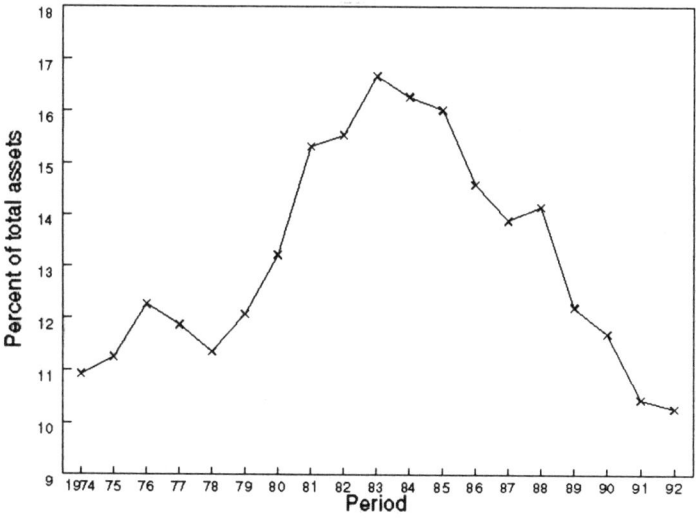

Figure 4.3 Primary and secondary reserve requirements: Trinidad and Tobago

107

The first order condition for this problem results in some reserve quantity that satisfies the condition:

$$r_A = C \int_R^X f(X) dX \qquad (4.2)$$

where:
D = deposits
R = reserves
X = a density function
r_A = return on assets

The overall return is specified in a single return r_A. The expression for a single return is an oversimplified form of the adjustment process as there are several adjustments which banks make simultaneously to their portfolios to accommodate the reserve requirement change.

Based on the responses of commercial banks to questionnaires, the adjustment of banks to changes in secondary reserve requirements is modelled below:

$$A = D - (R + G) \qquad (4.3)$$

where:
A = assets of commercial banks net of government securities
D = deposits
R = cash reserve requirements
G = Government securities

It is assumed that over some finite period commercial banks will adjust their portfolios to accommodate increased reserve requirements. Responses of commercial banks to questionnaires indicate that all banks responded to increased reserve requirements by attempting to increase deposits. In Barbados 83% of banks stated that they would also restrict credit generally, 50% stated they would also increase interest rates and 33% would reduce credit lines.

Commercial banks indicate that changes in reserve requirements prompt first a volume adjustment which implies changes in cost and profits. For simplicity we assume that the cash reserve portion of reserve requirements is non interest bearing[1] and that commercial banks do not aim to hold excess securities. Eighty three percent of banks in Barbados confirmed the latter response as did all banks in Jamaica and Trinidad and Tobago. Seventeen percent of banks in Barbados indicated that they had a predetermined policy of holding excess reserves. The relationships described below reflect the views of the majority of banks.

The cost to the bank of a change in reserve requirements can therefore be

108

represented by:

$$(Gi-Gr) \qquad\qquad (4.4)$$

where:
r = the yield on Government securities.
i = the current return on assets.
G = the volume of government securities acquired through each process.

The first expression represents the opportunity cost of buying Government bonds over offering new loans to customers and the second the cost of servicing additional business. It is assumed that the cost of managing new loans is the same as managing Government securities and that $r < i$. While other securities are included in the secondary reserve requirements, treasury bills tend to predominate. A brief comparison of treasury bill rates and the average rate on commercial bank loans discloses that commercial banks' average lending rates have been consistently in excess of treasury bill rates for most of the period so that each increase in secondary reserve requirements is a cost to banks.[2]

Banks seek to recover profitability levels by raising interest rates, adjusting other costs until the resulting increase in profit is equivalent to the loss represented by the expression at (4.3) and may be expressed as

$$(\overline{Ri}-C) = (Gi-Gr) \qquad\qquad (4.5)$$

where Ri = the return on additional business and C = the cost of obtaining additional business.

In the Barbados case, however, the scope for increasing interest rates is limited by the restrictions on the minimum lending rate and the ceiling on the average lending rate. Fifty percent of banks indicated they would offer higher interest rates and eighty three percent that they would immediately restrict lending. This assumes that banks are able to satisfy cash reserve requirements by selling excess securities in their portfolios or by liquidating other investments. These adjustments are now decomposed into the major changes affecting costs and profits.

Where banks are illiquid prior to the imposition of increased reserve requirements they will first try to borrow on the interbank market. For the system as a whole this is not a means of obtaining additional finance. Extensive use of the interbank market bids up interbank rates and leads to a general increase in interest rates. Where banks borrow on the interbank market or from non-banks to meet reserve requirements the cost to them can be represented by:

$$(Rb) \qquad (4.6)$$

where b = the interbank rate.
The opportunity cost of borrowing on the interbank to satisfy securities requirements can be represented as:

$$(Gb-C) \qquad (4.7)$$

where $r > b < i$.
While commercial banks' costs tend to be covered by the yield on Government securities, returns are less than could be earned had borrowed funds been on-lent to the private sector. Efforts to bid up the rate on treasury bills improve the profitability of buying government securities but worsen the deficit (through higher debt charges) and increase the reliance on bank financing.

Where neither option is available banks must wait for the proceeds of loan repayments or must compete aggressively for deposits. Most banks in Barbados indicate that the time frame taken to respond to increased in reserve requirements was between two weeks and two months (see Appendix 4.a.) depending on the existing liquidity situation. The time frame for adjustment by banks in Trinidad and Tobago was much shorter and in Jamaica it was almost immediate and seems to reflect the varying depth of the capital and money markets in each country.

Responses of commercial banks suggest that increases in reserve requirements push deposit rates up and lead to general interest rate increases. Also, the premium for loss of customer satisfaction in preferring bonds over loans may not be sufficiently high to attract commercial banks into holding more than the statutory amount of securities. If banks are unable to borrow on the interbank most banks will in the interim borrow at the central bank's discount window. The cost of doing so can be represented in the case of cash reserve requirements by the expression (Gd) where d = the central bank discount rate.

In the case of securities requirements the total cost to commercial banks of borrowing at the discount rate is

$$(Gd-C) \qquad (4.8)$$

where $d > r$.
A possible conclusion is that banks will increase deposit and lending rates, widening the spread between them and effecting other cost adjustments to

110

compensate for the losses incurred at (4.4) through (4.8). Summing the changes in costs over time the bank will aim to increase earnings until the lost profit (II) is recovered. Since banks may use each of these approaches to partly recover part of its profitability the terms α_1, α_2, α_3 are used to represent the partial use of each technique, so that

$$\Pi=(Gi-Gr)=[\alpha_1(\bar{R}i-C)+\alpha_2(Gb-C)+\alpha_3(Gd-C)] \qquad (4.9)$$

where $d > r$.

The three separate effects on the interest rate structure are triggered depending on the size of the adjustment. The adjustments in the expression at (4.4) always occurs. The additional pressure on costs and hence on interest rates represented by the expressions at (4.6),(4.7) and (4.8) will occur when banks are illiquid at the time of the imposition of the requirements. All banks indicated in the questionnaire that the adjustments to increases in reserve requirements often entailed increases in interest rates offered on deposits. To the extent that the Central Bank increases interest rates at the discount window the adjustment costs represented by the expression at (4.7) will rise. This adjustment process described by commercial banks and outlined here informs the variables to be included in empirical testing of the impact of regulation on bank profitability.

4.2.2 Impact of credit controls on bank profitability

Banks report that the limits on credit to the low priority sectors has two dimensions, one is the profitability impact and another is the liquidity impact. They represent that credit controls restrict the scope for decision- making over part of their portfolio and the scope for internally determined levels of profit. In Barbados the real interest rate on consumer loans was approximately 6-8 percentage points above other quoted rates because they are calculated on the original principal and not the amortised balance.[3] 'A priori' indications would therefore suggest that the impact on bank profitability resulting from credit controls would have been significant and would have been greater in Barbados where a) controls were more strict b) where consumer credit was relatively more attractive and c) this type of credit represented a significant share of banks' portfolio.

A comparison of yields on government securities and the share of credit to the non-priority (restricted) sectors shows that as banks' share in credit to these sectors fell, treasury bill yields rose, suggesting that banks turned to government securities to absorb liquidity rather than to priority (high-risk/high return) sectors.

111

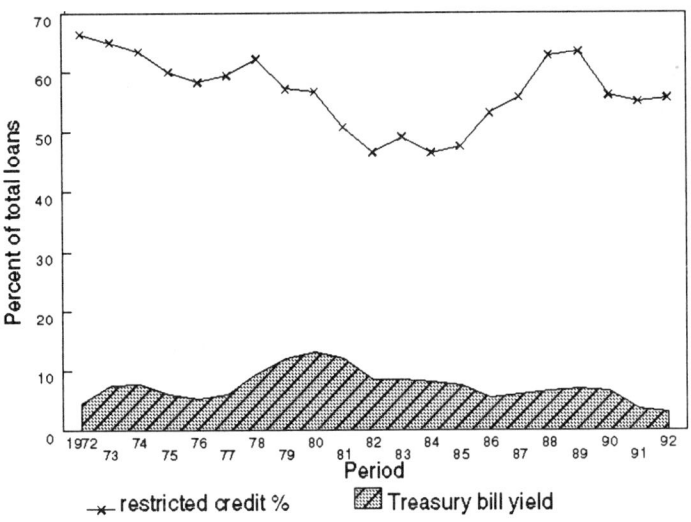

**Figure 4.4 Comparison of credit to controlled sectors
and treasury bill yields: Barbados**

Results of questionnaires suggest that some banks will risk failure to meet primary and secondary reserve requirements in order to satisfy borrowing requirements of prime customers at low or unchanged rates for fear of loss of large accounts and possibly market share. Smaller and less preferred customers are therefore either deprived of funds or obtain them at a cost which covers the loss on funding provided to prime customers, suggesting a possible trade-off between profitability and market share. Banks in Barbados indicate that credit controls restricted profitability more during periods of surplus liquidity. Eighty percent of all banks in Barbados agreed that in periods of positive growth there was considerable pent-up demand for credit to the controlled sectors, suggesting potentially higher earnings from credit to these sectors and supporting the view that in Barbados controls on credit to the non-priority sectors reduced bank profitability and that increases in credit to these sectors tended to improve profitability.

In Trinidad and Tobago and Jamaica indications are that returns on lending to the non-priority sectors (personal, consumer and distribution) are not necessarily higher than returns on credit to priority sectors (see Appendix 4.6) and thirty percent of respondents in Trinidad and Tobago indicted that they were lower. The case of Trinidad and Tobago where credit to the higher risk priority sectors (for example, manufacturing) surpassed both credit to the distributive and the personal sectors, tends to reject the notion that selective controls in themselves, (i.e. in the absence of interest rate controls), deter banks from lending to the high priority (high-return) sectors. The critical factor determining the impact of such controls on bank profitability appears to be whether selective credit controls are also accompanied by strict interest rate controls on lending.

While selective credit controls tend to encourage loan rationing, to the extent that there is pent-up demand in the higher yielding sectors, profitability can be adversely affected. Rationing, in the absence of credit controls, would appear to lead to a different portfolio allocation than exists under a regime of limits on selective credit, particularly where unsatisfied demand exists among good credit risk customers. Also, large outstanding unused loan commitments to the distributive sector tend to reduce the effect of credit controls, hence the period for compliance tends to be longer and the impact on profitability milder. The result in the Barbados case was evident in continued extensions in the period given for compliance and, by implication, a milder impact on bank performance.

In cases where broad lending guidelines were indicated by head offices on preferred areas for granting of credit, these often differed from the areas being promoted by local authorities. This coincides with the widely held view that Caribbean branch banks are viewed firstly by head offices as profit centres and that managers are judged on returns in the short term and possibly that profitability is more important than market share. The lack of correspondence between head office guidelines and actual portfolio distribution further suggests that monetary controls which influence banks' selection of the optimum profit maximising portfolio often conflict with the goals of the parent bank and that credit controls are considered by head offices to result in a less than optimum profit maximising portfolio.

4.2.3 Impact of interest rate regulation on bank profitability

Where the loan rate is also fixed, as in the highly regulated case of Barbados, and controlled as in the case of Jamaica in the 1980s, profitability is determined by absolute levels, by interest rate spreads and by other structural parameters such as elasticities of loan demand and supply and marginal costs attached to increases in both loans and deposits.[4] Where there are both floors and ceilings on interest rates the impact on bank profitability is through the interest rate spread. In responses to questionnaires banks indicated that constraints on the spread between the weighted average on deposits and the weighted average on loans were the main difficulty in adjusting to interest rate ceilings on lending.[5] (See Appendix 4.c.) The reasonableness of spreads can be judged by the record of compliance. The record shows that in some cases commercial banks will breach the regulations on interest rates if prescribed interest rates are likely to limit loan profitability more than they find acceptable. [6][7]

Despite the assumption that controlled interest rates are likely to lead to narrower interest spreads, spreads in Barbados actually widened during the period when regulations were in place, particularly between 1981-91. This was so in both Barbados and Jamaica in Jamaica and conflicts with the generally held view that interest rate regulation impacts adversely on bank profitability.

In a scenario with a binding cap on the loan rate the implication is that operating costs force greater efficiencies on banks unless rate-setting is accommodative. The extent to which banks are able to adjust to regulations while maintaining profitability will depend on such efficiencies and on the level of cost-axiomatic pricing. There is evidence to suggest that in the Caribbean case cost-axiomatic pricing was employed on an informal basis even though specific formulae may not have been explicitly used in formal calculations of appropriate rate-setting. Wider spreads between deposit and lending rates in the Caribbean relative to metropolitan countries evident in the period 1981-91 in Barbados, may be attributable to such compensatory margins permitted by regulators due to the cost of regulation.[8]

However, while spreads tended to widen with increasing regulation, this may not necessarily indicate greater profitability unless spreads were sufficiently wide to compensate for lost margins on forgone profit at higher yields. This introduces the question of whether pricing was cost-axiomatic or merely accommodative. Even if accommodative, the evidence suggests that commercial banks did not always consider spreads to be satisfactory. In 1991, in Barbados, for example, commercial banks increased spreads sharply immediately following the removal of the ceiling on the average lending rate, immediately exceeding for the first time pre-1973 spreads (i.e. pre-regulation spreads).

4.2.4 Impact of prudential regulation on bank profitability

Responses to questionnaires sent to commercial banks showed uncertainty among banks about the impact of prudential requirements on bank profitability. Forty percent of respondents felt that prudential regulation adversely impacted commercial bank profitability. A plot of consolidated capital, reserves and net long term borrowing as a ratio of total assets shows a distinct negative relationship of capital and bank profitability with some lag[9] (see Figure 4.7).

However, logically, since deposit costs tend to show a positive covariance with asset return, the implication is that deposit rates are likely to fall with increases in capital requirements. The trade-off in terms of safety may require that other costs resulting from regulation are modified in order to accommodate a plan of increased capital adequacy criteria with leveraging constraints.[10] However, banks were careful to make the distinction between the effect of capital adequacy provisions on short term profitability, which they saw as unfavourable, compared with the impact on long term profitability which was seen as favourable. Eighty percent of banks saw capital requirements as generally favourable for bank profitability.[11]

4.2.5 Summary of impact of credit controls on bank profitability

In summary, the expectation is that bank profitability suffers primarily as a result of monetary regulation, principally, reserve requirements, credit controls as well as interest rate controls, despite possible cost-axiomatic or accommodative pricing, and that capital regulation adversely impacts on profitability in the short run. The overall impact on profitability is expected to be negative.

4.3 Impact of regulatory measures on bank liquidity

4.3.1 Bank regulation and bank liquidity

While there is always a cost to the holding of excess liquidity and a greater cost when this exceeds normal precautionary levels, because of the continued availability of income earning government securities, a reserve deficiency carries an even greater cost in terms of borrowing at the central bank's discount window at punitive rates. The relative cost of a reserve deficiency is therefore more likely to have an adverse impact on bank performance than the cost of reserve excesses. The discussion below makes this point.

4.3.2 Impact of reserve requirements on bank liquidity

Initial conditions are important in evaluating the impact of reserve requirements. Where banks hold no surplus liquidity at the time of increases in reserve requirements the proceeds of loan repayments are used to buy required securities. Commercial banks report that higher reserve requirements

115

generally lead to a drawdown of deposits, reduce bank liquidity, prompt increases in deposit rates and push lending rates up. Higher reserve requirements therefore tighten both the loan market and lead to tighter liquidity as cash is withdrawn. Where banks hold surplus liquidity at the time of increases in statutory reserve requirements, the immediate cost of compliance is reduced but the problem of narrower flexibility in portfolio management remains.

The underdeveloped state of the stock market and the consequent illiquidity of securities in the Caribbean assists banks in preventing possible loss of deposits to the Government securities market. This lowers the effective cost to the banks of holding reserve requirements, as the thinness of the market reduces the risk of a movement out of deposits into bonds even where returns on government securities exceed deposit rates of comparable maturities.

Growing internationalisation of the banking system permits banks to alleviate liquidity difficulties arising from regulation by borrowing abroad, yet only twenty-five percent of foreign branches in Barbados indicate that they would borrow from head offices to satisfy increases in primary or secondary reserve requirements.[12][13] While this depends on risk and return relative to domestic interest rates, uncertainty resulting from frequent exchange rate changes in Jamaica especially, tended to raise risk premiums on foreign borrowing to exorbitantly high levels, increasing the cost of adjustment for banks in a liquidity squeeze.

The holding of liquidity cushions above normal levels also increased costs and reduced bank profitability in Barbados. Twenty percent of commercial banks in Barbados indicated that they held liquidity cushions against expectations of future increases in reserve requirements. This seemed related to the inability of authorities to reverse increases in cash and security requirements. Banks in Jamaica or Trinidad and Tobago did not factor expectations about future increases in reserve requirements into their holding of liquid assets.

4.3.3 Impact of credit controls on bank liquidity

Though credit controls are aimed at selected sectors they may also affect asset yields and prices in other markets, since increased liquidity resulting from unplaced funds can depress the price of credit generally. Overall, bank profitability may be affected and not simply earnings on credit advanced to the restricted sectors. Low levels of liquidity prevent banks from investing sufficiently large amounts in alternative areas to compensate for loss of higher return assets, as larger volumes of new credit are required to produce the same return. Higher levels of unplaced funds resulting from credit limits may

116

have been offset by greater cash withdrawals of deposits, at least in the short term, as customers try to maintain spending patterns.

4.3.4 Impact of interest rate regulation on bank liquidity

A plot of the relationship between excess liquidity (or liquidity shortages) and the 12 month deposit rate displays a lack of correlation between deposit rates and liquidity shortages (Figure 4.5).

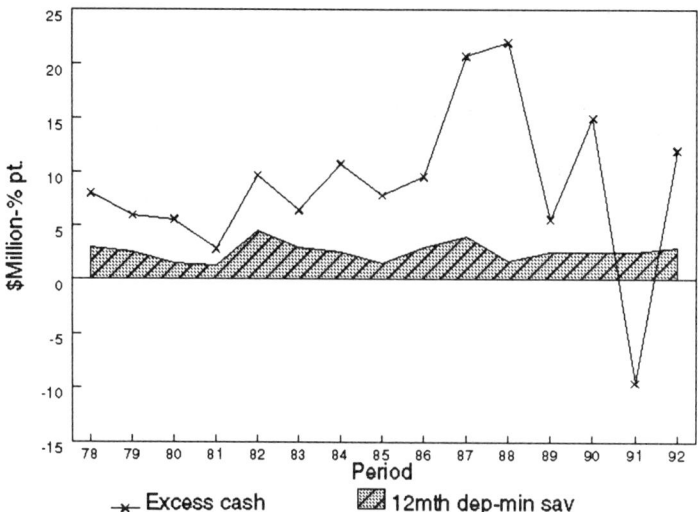

Figure 4.5 Liquidity and deposit rate variance:
             Barbados

For example in 1991 when the system experienced considerable liquidity shortages there was no interest rate response. This lack of correlation was reflected as well in uncertainty in the responses of commercial banks to the question of the impact of interest rate controls on liquidity.

Twenty percent of banks in Barbados observed that controls on savings deposit rates adversely affect the ability of banks to compete for fixed deposits during periods of illiquidity. Commercial banks tended to adopt a strategy of keeping the basic rate on savings low to offset lower earnings on higher levels of required secondary reserves, so allowing them to offer more attractive

117

returns on term deposits.[14] [15] Hesitancy of individuals to move funds out of the country in search of higher returns reduced the likelihood of withdrawal of liquidity from the system. This was less applicable in Jamaica where movements of capital abroad were compounded not only by interest rate changes but by exchange rate volatility.

4.3.5 Impact of prudential regulation on bank liquidity

Capital adequacy requirements are expected unequivocally to improve liquidity of commercial banks. The result can be derived from the simple balance sheet movements.

4.3.6 Summary of impact of controls on bank liquidity

In summary the impact of monetary regulation on bank liquidity is expected to vary with initial conditions but in general tends to tighten the loan and deposit markets. Capital adequacy requirements tend to impact on liquidity positively.

4.4 Impact of regulatory measures on bank risk

4.4.1 Impact of reserve requirements on bank risk

While regulators tend to view the regulatory aspect of reserve requirements as an additional safeguard, and depositors see reserve requirements as providing some protection in the event that banks experience financial difficulties, bankers suggest that for the deposit quantity-constrained bank, risk (however measured) is affected negatively by reserve requirements.

Volatility in the level of reserve requirements affects the degree of confidence which banks place on their ability to deliver on commitments and banks have been known to opt out of commitments following increases in reserve requirements.[16] Forty percent of banks responding to questionnaires indicate a policy of reducing credit lines in response to increased reserve requirements. Banks in Jamaica and Trinidad and Tobago indicated that they would neither cut credit lines nor cancel loan commitments, while 17% of banks in Barbados indicated they would cancel loan commitments. This suggests that the level of regulation in each country influences the loan commitment process in each jurisdiction but foregone credit and cancelled loan commitments impact adversely on banks in all jurisdictions.

4.4.2 Impact of credit controls on bank risk

Selective credit controls are more likely to reduce than increase risk. The view that selective credit controls increase risk works through the uncontrolled portion of the bank's portfolio rather than through the controlled portion. However, responses to questionnaires suggest that controls on credit to the foreign exchange-using (non-priority) sectors did not lead to increases in credit to the foreign exchange earning (higher risk) sectors. Two-thirds of banks in Barbados observed that there was no increase in the number of applications from the productive sectors when credit controls were in place and one-third were not sure.

A plot of credit outstanding to the manufacturing sector in Barbados relative to excess liquidity tends to confirm the observation of banks there that in the presence of credit controls excess liquidity did not lead to increases in credit to the priority sectors (Figure 4.6).

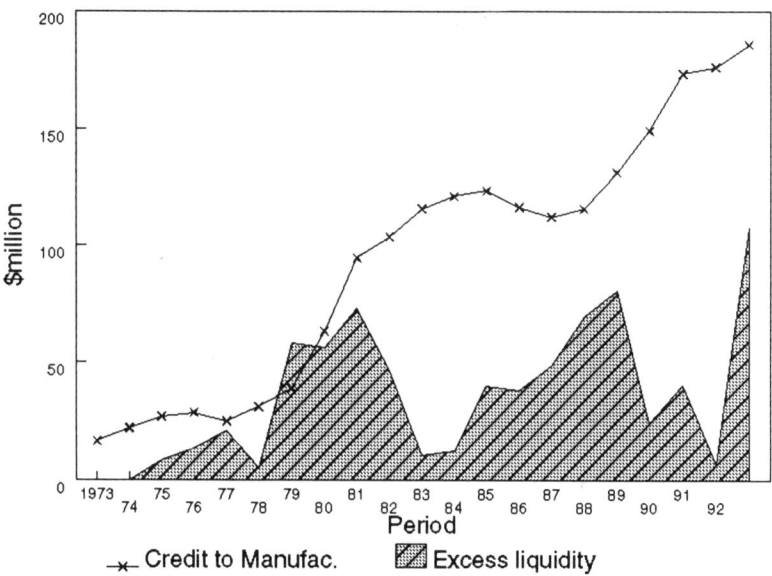

Figure 4.6 Excess liquidity/manufacturing credit: Barbados

Responses of banks suggest that those banks (one-third) who indicated that controls on credit led to increased credit to high risk sectors (priority sectors) tended to be the smaller and newer banks.

119

In Barbados, the failure of the productive sectors to benefit substantially from reductions in credit to the non-priority sectors illustrates the limited scope for appropriate risk-return trade-off resulting from regulation. Banks claim that ceilings on lending rates discourage lending to high-risk sectors and suggest that increased lending to the priority (high-risk) sectors would have improved commercial bank profitability had banks been able to charge appropriate risk premiums. Premiums charged seemed more related to risk in Trinidad and Tobago and Jamaica and stem from the absence of interest rate controls in Trinidad and Tobago, and in the case of Jamaica, from the absence of an interest rate ceiling. Credit controls were therefore more likely to have adversely affected banks' risk-taking in the Barbados case where interest rate ceilings exist.

4.4.3 Impact of interest rate controls on bank risk

A consequence of higher yields on Government securities in Barbados relative to other Caribbean countries is that it increases the interest rate premium which banks require in order to invest in higher-risk credit to the foreign exchange earning sectors. In the Jamaica case where returns on government securities tend to be lower, this lower risk-free rate permits greater scope for risk premiums charged to higher-risk customers, but in Barbados higher rates were not at the complete discretion of the bank. Two-thirds of banks thought the minimum savings rate helped to keep interest rates down.

Where spreads are too narrow financial intermediation may be reduced if deposit-taking is discouraged. The case of time and savings deposits attracting identical rates without recognition of time to maturity suggests that commercial banks took action from time to time to discourage deposit-taking. This occurred in Barbados in 1991 and was a clear sign of disintermediation triggered by prescribed interest rates which were out of line with the market expectations.

4.4.4 Impact of prudential regulation on bank risk

In an environment where prudential capital adequacy guidelines are risk-based banks have an incentive to avoid risky claims. Thus where banks must hold different capitalization rates for different assets, as is suggested by the Basle Committee of Bank Supervisors, banks will hesitate to extend credit to high risk customers. This has been observed in the reduced willingness of U.S. banks to lend to developing countries consequent on the introduction of risk-based capital criteria by authorities. Though risk-based capital criteria were not explicitly implemented in the Caribbean up to 1992, there might

120

have been a tendency for risk reduction by banks arising from the informal application of capital adequacy ratios, and in such cases this may have helped to reduce bank risk.

Where banks are controlled by large conglomerates or where they specialise in particular types of lending,[17] over-exposure increases risk.[18] However, responses from banks in Jamaica and Trinidad and Tobago differed markedly from Barbados on the question of concentration by customer. In Barbados eighty percent of respondents did not think that limits on customer concentration ratios affected banks adversely.[19] However, in Jamaica and Trinidad and Tobago all banks saw this as a major problem affecting profitability. This reflects the fact that banks in Jamaica and Trinidad and Tobago are mostly local banks and are not as highly capitalised as large international banks in Barbados (who are permitted to rely on global capital). In addition, firms in Jamaica and Trinidad and Tobago tend to be larger and a greater number of firms are therefore likely to be affected by the limitation on lending to a single customer.

Bank concentration ratios as opposed to product concentration, which is an outcome of oligopoly, seem to be inversely related to bank profitability offering a possible interpretation that large banks are not necessarily more profitable.

4.4.5 Summary of the impact of controls on bank risk

In summary, monetary regulation appears to impact bank risk negatively, particularly credit controls, by impacting the quality of the loan portfolio. Where adequate risk premiums are not available interest rate controls and credit controls are likely to increase bank risk. However, reserve requirements and capital are expected to impact bank risk positively.

4.5 Impact of regulatory measures on bank solvency

4.5.1 Impact of reserve requirements on bank solvency

Remedies used by authorities in Trinidad and Tobago in solving the problem of non-banks during the mid 1980s suggest a perception that reserve requirements improve bank solvency. For example, the decision to extend reserve requirements to include non-banks following the collapse of four non-banks there underscores the perceived prudential role of reserve requirements - a tool normally viewed as monetary.

Commercial bankers, however, observe that solvency in an accounting sense differs from functional solvency, noting that while the security of depositors is boosted by the holding of high levels of reserve deposits with the Central Bank, where these funds are not accessible to banks or are only accessible at prohibitive rates of interest, the traditional backing provided by the monetary authorities becomes inaccessible, so that high levels of reserve requirements begin to create problems of 'operational' solvency for commercial banks. This is the case even though on a break-up basis these banks may be classified as solvent based on high but 'frozen' reserve requirements.

4.5.2 Impact of credit controls on bank solvency

Indications are that credit limits contribute to solvency difficulties for small new banks. Smaller banks seem forced to lend to high risk customers and loan losses are therefore likely to be greater. While, in some case, solvency problems may have resulted even in the absence of credit limits, the argument is often made that the solvency of small banks is worsened by credit controls [Farrell (1989)]. Also, since reduced profitability affects net worth over time, where lower profitability is related to defaults arising from pressures to unload excess funds resulting from credit controls, bank solvency can be affected.

New banks, particularly marginal banks appear to be most affected by credit controls, while older and larger banks tend to have a greater proportion of high quality loans. To that extent, regulations, it is argued, can adversely affect the solvency of newer and smaller banks as they are pushed in to lending to marginal customers because the lower risk areas are controlled.

4.5.3 Impact of interest rate controls on bank solvency

The major impact on solvency from interest rate controls appears to be through reduced profitability.

4.5.4 Impact of prudential regulation on bank solvency

Most banks viewed the impact of capital adequacy regulations on bank solvency positively. Some noted that increasing support given by commercial banks to other financial institutions as their lender of last resort in an environment where the concern of authorities with macroeconomic stability puts pressure on the profitability and can create problems of solvency for commercial banks, and that solvency regulations must therefore be closely linked to lender of last resort facilities.

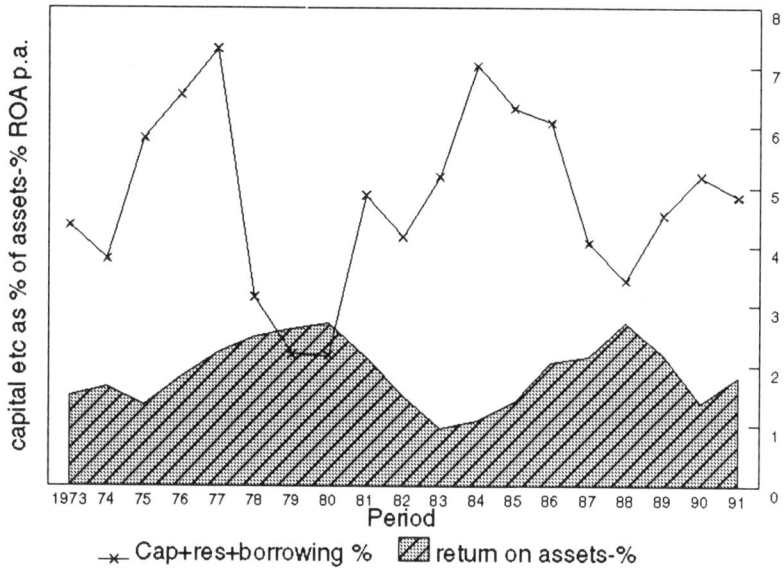

**Figure 4.7 Capital, reserves and borrowing:
comparison with profitability: Barbados**

4.5.5 Summary of impact of controls on bank solvency

The general consensus, both from responses to questionnaires and from examination of data trends, is that bank solvency is affected by regulation, particularly by credit regulations and that the solvency of smaller banks is negatively affected.

4.6 Impact of regulatory measures on bank market share

4.6.1 Impact of reserve requirements on market share

Changes in cash and reserve requirements in Barbados and the assets of non-banks show a clear positive correlation of reserve requirements with the growth of non-banks.

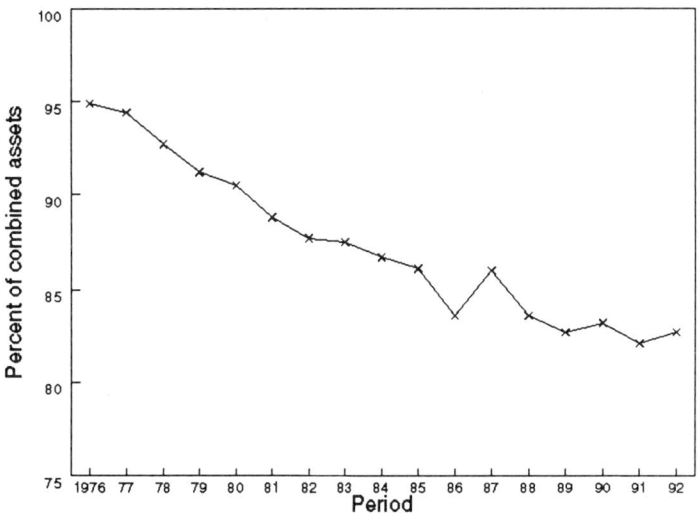

Figure 4.8 Banks' market share: Barbados

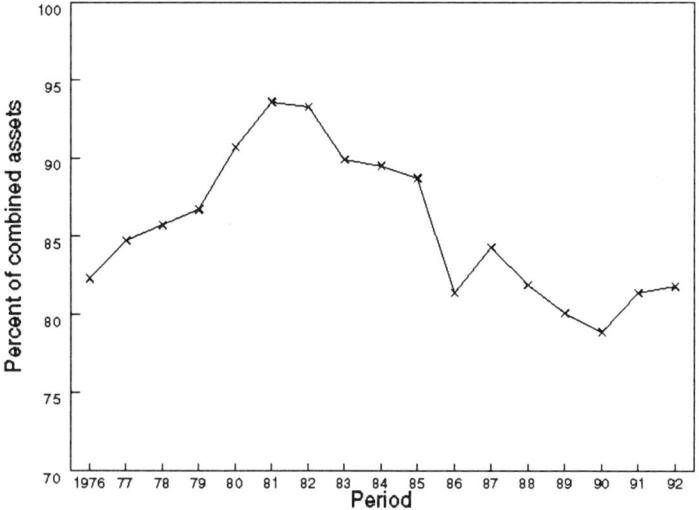

Figure 4.9 Banks' market share: Jamaica

124

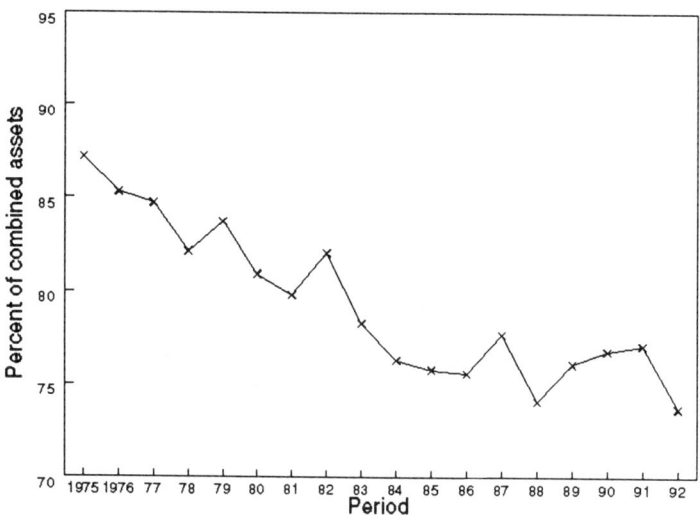

Figure 4.10 Banks' market share: Trinidad and Tobago

In some cases, the number of banks actually declined while non-banks grew. This tends to support the generally accepted view that reserve requirements reduce bank size relative to non banks and that it is related to the absence of an obligation to hold reserves or an obligation to hold only a low level of cash and securities relative to banks.[20]

4.6.2 Impact of credit controls on market share

The declining market share of banks evident in the Caribbean (see Figures 4.8, 4.9 and 4.10) occurred at different times in each country. Up to 1984 in Barbados non-banks were not subject to credit controls, and were never so subject in Trinidad and Tobago. In the Jamaica case, limits on consumer credit were extended to include non-banks, yet non-banks there grew much more rapidly than in Barbados where control was not extended until 1984. So that the answer may lie not in exclusion from credit controls but in the generally lighter regulatory burden.

Control of the ceiling on residential mortgage rates reduced the market share of banks, resulting in the virtual withdrawal of commercial banks from the mortgage market and contributing to the rise of non-banks[21] which, at first,

125

had no obligation to hold reserves either of a primary or secondary nature (Figure 4.11).

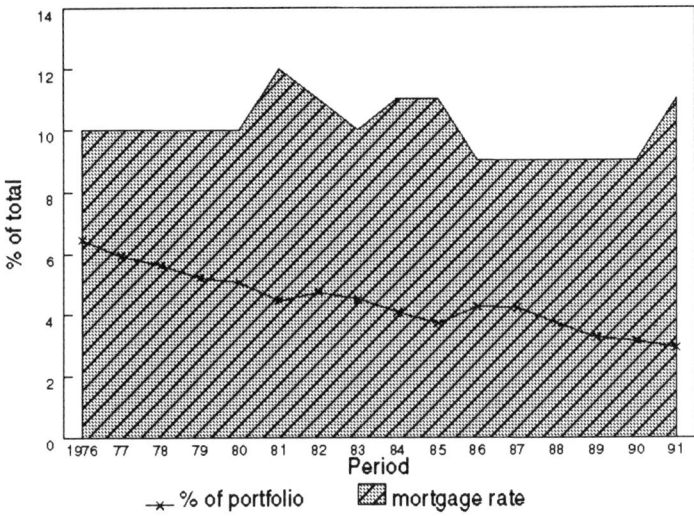

Figure 4.11 Mortgage rates and mortgage loans: Barbados

4.6.3 Impact of interest rate controls on market share

Despite the importance of interest rate spreads, actual lending rates are indicators to customers of the affordability of credit and hence influence effective demand and market share through loan volumes achieved. In periods of high interest rates, lending rates tended to bunch as ceilings on lending rates were raised[22] as non-prime customers tended to subsidise interest charged to prime customers during regimes of high interest rates. This tendency may have helped banks to retain market share of prime customers but may have been at the expense of non-prime customers. The net effect may have been loss of market share.

If interest rates were cost-axiomatic and market clearing, then interest rate controls should not have impacted as adversely on market share as would otherwise have been the case. If they were accommodative and not fully cost-axiomatic they may have had a less positive impact on bank profitability. However, neither accommodative nor cost-axiomatic pricing permits banks control over profit margins. This control over bank profits creates

126

opportunities for non-banks who have much greater flexibility in decision making.

4.6.4 Impact of prudential regulation on market share

Where capital requirements apply to banks and not to non-banks and where such unregulated institutions offer similar facilities, banks' comparative advantage in such areas will be eroded and banks' market share can be adversely affected.

4.6.5 Summary of impact of controls on market share

In summary, monetary controls are expected to impact negatively on bank market share in every case, and increases in capital are expected to impact negatively on solvency in the short run.

4.7 Summary of views and expectations

A summary of 'a priori' expectations about the impact of regulation on bank performance is set out in matrix form in Table 4.1.

Since the expected regulatory impact appears to be negative for each regulatory tool, the expectation is that a composite index of regulation will be negatively related to bank performance, principally as a result of the impact on profitability, market share and bank risk. The outcome for liquidity and solvency is mixed but seems unlikely to reverse the overall expected result of a negative impact on bank performance.

Chapters 5 and 6 develop and test a model for evaluating the impact of regulation on each of the above measures of bank performance, applying OLS regression and cointegration techniques. A composite measure of bank performance is then developed using discriminant analysis for testing the overall impact of regulation measured by a composite regulation index on the overall performance of commercial banks in Barbados, Jamaica and Trinidad and Tobago.

Table 4.1
Expectations about regulatory changes: the Caribbean experience

Effect on	Profita-bility	Liquidity	Solvency	Market Share	Risk
Monetary Selective credit controls	-	+	-	-	-
Reserve requirements (secondary)	-	-	+	-	-
Interest rate controls	-	+/-	-	-	–
Prudential Capital	-S+L	+	-S+L	-	–
Structural Setting of boundaries	-	..	-S+L	-	-

+ denotes a positive impact
- denotes a negative impact
S denotes short term
L denotes long term

Notes

1   Commercial banks in Jamaica received interest on excess liquid assets held with the Central Bank from 1979.
2   The return on government bonds and debentures is generally lower than treasury bill yields.
3   Commercial banks were allowed to exclude credit for consumer loans from the calculation of the average lending rate.

4   In the Caribbean there was generally no ceiling on deposit rates but there was a floor. This was generally the case except for the period 1973-78 in Barbados and in the early 1970s in Jamaica.

5   A comparison of spreads between the 3 month deposit rate and the prime lending rate in Barbados before and after regulation shows that on average, spreads between 3 month deposit rates and prime lending rates widened by 1% point after 1978.

6   The weighted average lending rate for compliance purposes tended to be higher than the overall weighted average on all loans (due to exemptions from the calculations.

7   This occurred in 1978 and 1979 when the required savings rate was 8% and commercial banks offered deposit rates no higher than 6.5% on non-term savings deposits despite the minimum rate set. The failure of commercial banks to comply with this directive may have been attributable to the short lead time given for compliance.

8   The disparity in interest rate spreads between banks in the Caribbean and in North America is approximately 2-3 percentage points.

9   In the case of branches of overseas banks, reserves and long term borrowing are sometimes considered substitutes for capital.

10   Leveraging constraints refer to the obligation to increase requirements in line with increased obligations and exposures, or alternatively to restrict portfolio growth.

11   Branches of foreign banks are not required to hold local capital. Five of the seven banks at the time of reporting were foreign banks.

12   Banks indicated that they borrowed overseas only as a last resort, after having launched a deposit drive and after cutting back on spending.

13   Locally owned banks, principally in Jamaica and Trinidad and Tobago, have considerably less access to overseas borrowing than do local banks.

14   In the Barbados case, the floor on the savings rate tended to keep other deposit rates down. The weighted average return on deposits differed from the minimum savings rate by on average, only approximately one percentage point.

15   The central bank discount rate is not emphasised in the study because it tends to move in tandem with other rates. In Barbados, the discount rate tended to be punitive only in periods of extreme balance of payments difficulties. In the past twenty years, this occurred twice in the Barbados case; in 1981-83 and in 1991, when rates were raised from normal levels of 8-12% to as high as 22% and 18% respectively; both being periods of Stand-by programmes with the IMF.

129

16 In some cases there is a way out through 'a material adverse change clause' which allows banks to avoid contracts if the borrowers credit worthiness declines or some other material event occurs. It is a development which has been observed in other countries in the retail banking sector, but is more common in international loan negotiations.

17 Firms which may be otherwise perfectly good credit risks based on balance sheet assets could reflect a disproportionate percentage of the bank's assets devoted to a single sector.

18 In Barbados customer concentration with respect to loans is limited to 25% of capital.

19 Branches of foreign banks who are able to base customer concentration ratios on global capital are not as seriously affected by prudential guidelines as are locally incorporated banks.

20 For a short period in 1977 and 1978 there were eight banks operating in Barbados. However, with the closure of Bank of Credit and Commerce and before the reopening of its successor in 1992 there were 6 banks operating in Barbados.

21 Banks' profits were adversely affected by in-roads into the granting of credit by commercial houses, credit unions and by the activities of companies involved in leasing.

22 The bunching of lending rates was particularly evident in Barbados in 1981 and again in 1991, both periods of particularly high interest rate regimes.

5 A model for testing the impact of regulation on Caribbean commercial bank performance

5.1 Introduction

This chapter describes the model and its assumptions, identifies the variables used, points out the constraints imposed by data deficiencies and describes the procedures used for testing. These include 1) a description of OLS regression analysis, tests for stationarity, tests establishing cointegration, the deriving of error correction models and maximum likelihood estimates, 2) the technique of multiple discriminant analysis used for developing a single composite score of bank performance and regulation and 3) Granger causality tests for testing causality between composite performance and composite regulation indices and between the main regulatory variable and the main performance measure.

Conventional methodologies employed for testing the impact of regulation on commercial banks are principally, the traditional event studies and linear regression analysis. A third possibility is comparison of the pre-regulation period with the regulated period. Traditional event studies however, require frequent data on the dependent and independent variables in order to show the response of the dependent variable to the event being studied. Therefore, data constraints do not permit the use of this methodology in the Caribbean case. In addition, since regulatory measures overlapped or were imposed simultaneously, the event studies methods is likely to have been unreliable. Informational difficulties relating to the pre-regulation period did not offer a series of acceptable length for testing of the impact on profitability of the regulated compared to the unregulated environment. The study therefore adopts the linear least squares (OLS) regression technique, an approach used in studies on bank profitability and shareholder wealth by several writers [Kane and Unal (1990), Dermine and Hillion (1992) and Bourke (1988) (1989)].

131

5.2 Assumptions

The following are some of the assumptions of the model.

1. It is assumed that costs influence choices relating to all assets and liabilities and that no liabilities are specifically earmarked for funding particular assets.
2. No special treatment is given to the impact of the mortgage rate on bank profitability. The impact of the mortgage rate is captured in the general interest rate control variable. The maximum rate on mortgages is a prescribed rate, but mortgages represent a small proportion of commercial banks' asset portfolio.
3. Earnings on government securities are exogenously determined. Earnings on credit to the private sector are subject to a ceiling on lending rates, either the average or the prime rate. The ratios in which these assets are held are partly regulated and partly endogenously determined through secondary reserve requirements and credit limits.
4. Costs are expected to influence the structure of assets and liabilities as well as deposits through size and through their influence on liquidity costs, solvency costs and the opportunity cost of equity funds, all of which influence expected profits.
5. The impact of regulation on other bank performance measures are based principally on the equation developed for evaluating the impact on profitability.
6. No single constraint on the structure of liabilities other than the capital constraint could be identified, though consideration was given to using the ratio of savings deposits to total deposits given the prescribed minimum savings rate but the need for this was not supported by interviews with commercial banks.

5.3 The model

The model employs an equation represented by the conventional profit function transformation curve:

$$\Pi = \sum_{i=1}^{m} (r_i E_i) - \sum_{j=1}^{n} (s_j D_j) \qquad (5.1)$$

Where $r_i E_i$ represents return on assets, $s_j D_j$ the cost of deposits and Π represents bank profits. This approach has been applied in efficiency studies,

132

for example by Hannan (1991) to analyze efficiency in banking firms in the U.S.

To establish the link between microeconomic analysis of costs and bank profitability and to relate this to macroeconomic impulses which give rise to regulation, the equation for the production transformation curve is combined with the representation of the balance sheet of the banking system to arrive at a modified and testable model. The model is derived from the following system of equations.

$$A = R + E = D + W \qquad (5.2)$$

Equation (5.2) represents the structural form of the consolidated balance sheet of the banking system, where total assets are represented by the symbol (A), reserves (R), earning assets (E), total liabilities, deposits (D) and equity (W). This permits macroeconomic decisions prompted by the reserve variable (R) to be combined with the production transformation function. (R) is assumed to be non income earning, changes in (W) before distribution of profits are attributable to returns on earning assets less costs of deposits in that period.

$$\Delta W = \Pi = \sum_{i=1}^{m}(r_i E_i) - \sum_{j=1}^{n}(s_j D_j) \qquad (5.3)$$

Taking account of other costs other than interest costs and restating in balance sheet form

$$\Pi = \sum_{i=1}^{m}(r_i E_i) - \sum_{j=1}^{n}(s_j D_j) - \sum_{k=1}^{p}C(D_k) - \sum_{g=1}^{h}C(E_g) \qquad (5.4)$$

Equation (5.3) represents the intertemporal profit maximising objective function of commercial banks specified in equation (5.4) where costs other than interest costs are separately identified as a function of earning assets and deposits. If we let the first expression on the right hand side in (5.4) be

$$\Pi = r_i(D + W - R) - s_j D - B - L - S - Q \qquad (5.5)$$

represented by $r_i E$, the second by $s_j D$, the third by $C(D)$ and the fourth by $C(E)$, these costs are further respecified in equation (5.5) as (Q). Substituting (5.2) and (5.5) into (5.4) and solving for Π we obtain:

$$C(D) + C(E) = B + L + S + D \qquad (5.6)$$

133

The expressions at (5.4) and (5.5) state that bank profits are determined by return on earning assets (E) less returns to depositors (rD) after adjusting for resource costs (B), liquidity costs (L), insolvency costs (S) and the opportunity cost of equity funds

$$\Pi = r_i E - s_j D - B - L - S - Q \qquad (5.7)$$

or
A modified form of the equation takes account of parameters representing asset structures and liability structures and reflects the share of the regulated portfolio in commercial banks' total portfolio. The most important asset parameter structure is identified as the share of government securities in the banks' portfolios. It also performs the function of a regulatory variable when the required portion of these assets is utilised.

The model separates commercial banks' asset into assets held in compliance with regulated primary and secondary reserve requirements and other assets, so as to facilitate testing of the effect of regulation on the chosen measures of commercial bank evaluation. The approach to the final determination of the model is an eclectic one which builds on the profit function developed above but is adjusted to more accurately reflect the perceived determinants of bank profitability in the highly regulated case of the Caribbean.

The general form of the equation is given by

$$ROA = f(TB, SF, M, RR, CON, I, LD, CAPB, dumin, dumcr, s1, s2, s3) \qquad (5.8)$$

5.4 Explanation of the independent variables used

The symbols used are:

TB = opportunity cost of equity funds
RR = asset parameter structure
M = money supply
r = loan rate net of all costs such as administration and information costs
t = nominal interest rate on deposits
I = interest rate spreads (t-r)
SF = resource costs

134

CON = bank concentration ratio
LD = loan deposit ratio proxies liquidity costs
SOLV = expected cost of insolvency and capital deficiency, proxied by the capital asset ratio and when long term borrowing is included (CAPB).

The opportunity cost of equity funds and the interest rate on Government securities are combined in the variable (TB), the treasury bill rate, in the context of the underdeveloped state of the capital markets and the dominance of Government securities. A variable representing the loan deposit ratio was also included and served as a liquidity variable.

Credit to government is represented by the holding of secondary reserve requirements and serves as a proxy for the asset parameter structure. Assets required to be statutorily held, principally Government securities are represented by the term (RR).

Deposit growth is represented by money broadly defined and is denoted by the symbol (M). This is considered the traditional measure of financial intermediation. It is expected that growth in the total market would produce the capability for banks to earn increased profits, though not necessarily at higher relative rates of return on assets.

The actual interest rate spread (t-r), the result of the regulated average lending rate (r) and the weighted average savings rate (t), is used to represent the spread on interest rates on the basis that while the minimum savings rate is the controlled rate, all other savings rates are indirectly controlled through control of the minimum savings rate. Use of the spread variable also facilitates homogeneity in tests of equations for countries such as Trinidad and Tobago where there were no controls on interest rates.

Resource and information costs are proxied by staff expenses (SF). This variable represents a large proportion of non-interest costs. These costs also serve to examine Edwards (1977) theory that excess or supernormal profits of regulated industries may be directed away from net profit into sub-optimal expenditure patterns related to management as opposed to shareholder preferences.

A concentration ratio (CON) is also employed to examine whether regulatory forbearance is greater for large banks than for small. This ratio represents the relative share of the three largest banks - the C_3 variable.[1] The concentration ratio can be determined by number of firms or by size. The size variable was chosen here. The most frequently used measure of market concentration is the 3 -bank or 4- bank ratio. This measures the proportion of the industry controlled by the 3 or 4 largest firms. Given the limited number of banks in the Caribbean countries being studied, the three-bank (C_3) ratio was used. The inability of the concentration ratio to take into account disparities of size among larger banks was not considered a handicap given the objective of the study.

Liquidity costs are seen as a function principally of primary and secondary reserves and of the bank rate, while insolvency costs are a function of capital requirements and the cost of deposit protection. The model uses capital requirements as a proxy for the cost of insolvency.[2] The opportunity cost of equity funds is a function of the market rate on the alternative use of funds and is proxied by the treasury bill yield.

The cost of insolvency is proxied by capital and reserves (SOLV) and where branch banks dominate, by a expression which includes long term borrowing as well (CAPB).

Changes in regulations are represented where possible by actual data on interest rates and reserve requirements. Where these changes could not be quantified dummy variables are used, for example the credit control variable is both quantitative and qualitative - a dummy variable was therefore employed. Both a dummy for interest rate regulation (dumcr) and a variable representing interest rate spreads (I) were included. The inclusion of both is intended to test for the possibility of cost-axiomatic or accommodative pricing. Credit was represented only by the dummy variable. These took the value 1 when restrictions were on and zero when they were off. Since the data series are quarterly, seasonal dummies were included for three of the quarters to take account of seasonality.

Private sector assets subject to control on volume are represented by credit to the distributive sector and the personal sector. Consumer credit is a subset of personal credit and is captured in the regulation of personal lending. Commercial banks are customarily granted a period of approximately three months to comply with credit control measures, therefore three months after announcement is therefore considered the effective date.[3]

The Central bank discount rate was found to be insignificant and was withdrawn from later equations.

An inflation variable, used by some researchers, e.g. Bourke (1988) in empirical tests, was not found to be significant in preliminary testing for the Barbados case and was removed from the equations.

Of the above variables those which represent regulatory control are:

(1) credit outstanding to the personal and distributive sector (dummies are also used to show when controls on this sector are on or off)
(2) primary and secondary reserve requirements

(3) interest rate spreads, and
(4) capital and reserves.

With the exception of the inflation variable, all other variables used in the model parallel variables typically used in the literature.[4] This model specifically adds four regulatory variables mentioned above to reflect the presence of financial regulation.

5.5 Profitability measures

Two different measures of profitability are employed.

These are:
(ROA) - net before tax profit as a % of total assets
(BTSETA) - net before tax profit + staff expenses as a % of total assets.

The first indicator of profitability was measured before tax to avoid a result influenced by tax payable by banks at differing time periods. This measure takes account of actual loan losses and recoveries. The second measure is included to adjust for potential net profit which is appropriated as staff expenses. Bourke(1988) notes that this provides a value added concept of net profit before tax and staff expenses. The profitability measure (profits plus staff expenses) is designed to adjust for possible inefficiencies in the use of resources. Staff expenses are the major expense item and this measure indicates the level of profits in the presence of approximately uniform efficiency levels.[5] A third measure, return on operating profits (ROPA) was included in initial tests but results did not differ materially from those obtained from using the profitability measure (BTSETA) so it was dropped from the analysis.

A measure which includes foreign long term borrowing plus capital and reserves as a dependent variable is included among the equations as a means of introducing a proxy for bank capital applicable to branches of foreign banks. Data on changes in shareholder wealth are not available for Barbados as bank shares are not listed on the stock exchange. Since the study focuses principally on Barbados and references Jamaica and Trinidad and Tobago only for comparative purposes, the impact of regulation on shareholder wealth is not dealt with except by way of reference. In addition, data series on stock prices for Jamaica and Trinidad and Tobago were only available from 1981 and 1983 respectively, half-yearly in the case of Trinidad and Tobago and annually in the case of Jamaica. These intervals were too wide and the series too short to provide dependable results on the impact of regulation on shareholder wealth.

A fourth possible measure, used by some researchers, profits plus loan loss provisions, is applied to the Barbados case in a separate run but is not used in partitioned testing because the practice of loan loss provisioning was not particularly used in Barbados during the period, partly because most of the banks were branch banks and provisioning was left largely to head office. More recently however increasing emphasis is being placed by regulatory authorities on the practice of loan provisioning. Examination of the data shows that for most of the period examined loan loss provisioning was minimal. Nevertheless, a sample OLS regression was run using this definition of profit and results are set out in Appendix 6.3.

A fifth measure of bank profitability often used in the literature is net profit as a percent of capital and reserves, but it is not deemed to be applicable to the Barbados situation because of the dominating presence of branches of large international banks which were not required to hold local capital.

There was no change in most other prudential regulatory requirements during the period. The only prudential measure included was therefore the more important measure, capital.

Negative returns on assets (ROA) in the third quarter of 1985 precluded the use of logs in initial tests. However, a log transform for the measure of bank profitability which contained only positive numbers in the series - profits plus staff expenses as a percentage of total assets (denoted BTSETA) was relied upon in most of the tests of bank profitability.

5.6 Tests using other bank performance measures: dependent variables

The impact of regulation on

1) bank profitability is treated in considerable detail since banks (see results of questionnaires in Appendix 3) place considerably more importance on this variable than on any other,
2) tests on the impact of regulation on bank solvency,
3) bank liquidity and
4) bank market share are given detailed treatment where theory and 'a priori' indications suggest this.

The general form of the equation is adjusted depending on the dependent variable being tested, but all the regulatory variables are retained.

In the equation which tests the impact on other measures of bank performance:

1) excess liquidity which is represented by the term (LIQ)
2) solvency which is represented by capital and reserves (SOLV)
3) industry market share, that is, the share of the assets of banks relative to banks and non-banks represented by the term (MKS)
4) bank risk, or profit variance, denoted by the term (RISK).

Though the study seeks to measure the impact of regulation on commercial bank performance, particularly bank profitability, and does not seek to identify the determinants of bank regulation, other variables which influence profitability but which are not regulatory are included to improve the goodness of fit. Data are standardised by division by total assets in order to minimise the impact of heteroscedasticity on the standard errors of the estimates of the regression coefficients.

5.7 Data constraints

Data differences, data unavailability, and the need to avoid near singularity in the correlation matrix required summing variables. In the case of Trinidad and Tobago and Jamaica cash and securities requirements are combined in a variable termed the liquid assets ratio and the cash reserve requirement itself is part of stipulated liquid assets. The use of a single variable also increases the degrees of freedom in those cases where only annual data were available.

Much of the data was obtained from annual, quarterly and monthly digests of statistics of the regional Central Banks. Time series data on commercial banks and data from the stock exchanges in the region provide the main monetary data base for analysis. Data from the regional central banks on the type and frequency of monetary tools used over the period establish the main tools of monetary policy in the Caribbean over the period 1972-92. Publications of chronological lists of regulatory changes were available from the three central banks and with some updating, provided the evidence on regulatory changes. Information on prudential aspects of regulation was obtained from the central banks and by an examination of the legislation of each country.

The frequency of the data series and the short length of the series in some cases posed some difficulties. Data on bank profits for Jamaica and Trinidad and Tobago were available only on an annual basis. More frequent data on commercial banks' assets and liabilities for all three countries for the past

139

twenty years were available but could not be put to maximum use as banks reported profit data much less frequently. In the Jamaica case, in order to establish a series from 1975, since data were only available from the Bank of Jamaica from 1979, data from the Jamaica Stock Exchange were used. As a result, capital ratios of privately incorporated banks are not included in data for 1975-78. Data by bank were obtainable only from Barbados and were grouped according to size and ownership structure. Individual bank data were only available for banks in Jamaica and Trinidad and Tobago whose shares were publicly quoted.

In the Barbados case, data were collected on selected assets and liabilities of all banks on a quarterly basis for the period 1972-92, but because of gaps in quarterly income expenditure data during the early period, the final equation covers the period 1977-92.

Consumer instalment credit was not included as a separate explanatory variable because it was continually in effect for the entire period and qualitative changes in the regulations such as variations in down payments and lengthening or shortening of repayment periods were not easily converted to a measurable basis.[6] Dummies for hire purchase controls were not used because hire purchase controls were continually in effect and this would have led to a near singular correlation matrix.

The first and more extensive tests were run on bank profitability as the dependent variable.

The order of testing the performance measures is:

1) bank profitability,
2) bank risk, defined here as variability of bank profits,
3) bank liquidity,
4) bank solvency,
5) and bank market share relative to non-banks.

5.8 Methods of testing

5.8.1 OLS regressions - regulation and bank performance - the profitability measure

Preliminary OLS regressions are first run to demonstrate that the inclusion of regulatory variables improve the ability of the equation to explain bank profitability.

1. The series are first tested for stationarity (see section 5.8.2).

140

2. OLS regressions are then run using ungrouped data employing first an equation which includes lagged monetary variables only and then another which includes a prudential variable, capital. The credit control dummy variable takes effect one quarter after announcement.

A constant and three seasonal dummies are included to correct for seasonality. The equations are of the form:

$$BTSETA = f(TB, SF, M, CON, RR, LD, I, dumin, dumcr, s1, s2, s3) \quad (5.9)$$

OLS regressions are also run on bank data grouped by size and according to local or foreign ownership.

3. Tests are also conducted on bank data employing other performance measures.

$$LIQ = f(RR, TB, M, CON, LD, CAPB, dumin\ dumcr, s1, s2, s3) \quad (5.10)$$

$$RISK = f(TB, M, SF, RR, CON, LD, dumin, dumcr, s1, s2, s3) \quad (5.11)$$

$$SOLV = f(TB, M, SF, RR, LD, CON, dumin, dumcr, s1, s2, s3) \quad (5.12)$$

$$MKS = f(TB, SF, M, CON, RR, LD, I, dumin, dumcr, s1, s2, s3) \quad (5.13)$$

(variables are dropped or added as indicated by the testing procedure.)

4. The regulatory variable invoking the greatest response is chosen for causality testing on bank profitability.
5. A composite index of bank performance is then developed and applied to test the impact of regulatory measures on overall performance.
6. The same composite index is then applied in causality tests to establish possible causality between bank performance and regulation.
7. Causality tests are then run on the composite indices of bank regulation and bank performance.

5.8.2 Tests for stationarity

Tests for stationarity are based on the view [Engle and Granger (1987)] that if a model includes only stationary variables then one can assume that estimates are normally distributed and confidence intervals can be calculated using the Students t-distribution. However, in the presence of non-stationarity, tests applied under such circumstances can lead to spurious results. The first requirement for stationarity is that the first and second moments are time invariant. The series is therefore said to be I(0). Where the series are not stationary, differencing replaces a global trend by a local trend and a stationary series is constructed. A series which is stationary after differencing (d) times is said to be integrated of order (d) and X $\sim$ I (d). Where two variables Y_t and X_t are non-stationary but the form of stationarity is such that their first differences are stationary, then Y_t and X_t are said to be integrated of order one, and ΔY_t and ΔX_t are I(0).

Diagnostic tests for stationarity used in the study are the Dickey Fuller(DF) and Augmented Dickey Fuller(ADF) tests. The form of the Dickey-Fuller (DF) test used in the paper is:

$$\Delta y_t = a + b y_{t-1} + u_t \qquad (5.14)$$

The term u_t is a white noise error term. When u_t serially correlated the augmented Dickey Fuller test is applied for k lagged differences. The ADF test is based on the regression

$$\Delta y_t = a + b y_{t-1} + \sum_{j=1}^{K} c_j \Delta y_{t-j} + u_t \qquad (5.15)$$

where k differenced terms on the right hand side are included to correct for autocorrelation and a trend is incorporated into (5.14) and (5.15) when testing against the alternative of trend stationarity.

5.8.3 Cointegration

The components of a vector x_t are said to be cointegrated of order d,b, denoted $x_t, \sim CI$ (d,b), if (i) all components of x_t are I(d); and (ii) if there exists a vector α ($\neq$ 0) so that

$$z_t = \alpha' x_t \text{ is } \simeq I(d-b), \ b > 0. \qquad (5.16)$$

(5.16) The vector α is called the cointegrating vector. If z_t is stationary, and d-b =0, then the cointegration equation can be consistently estimated with ordinary least squares, with any variable treated as the dependent variable.

If x_t has N components, then there may be more than one cointegrating vector α. It is clearly possible for several equilibrium relations to govern the joint behaviour of the variables of the variable. The rank of α is r, and is referred to as the cointegrating rank of x_t. The residuals from the regression will tend to be serially correlated but must be I(0). This can be tested by

142

applying unit root tests to the residuals. Residuals from the cointegrating regression are included in a second equation. First differencing is usually required for stationarity. The differenced equation is then used to confirm that the OLS residuals are I (0). This indicates cointegration. Tests used are those provided by Engle and Granger[7] (1987). This is the method applied in this study. Rejection of the null hypothesis indicates the presence of cointegration and establishes the reliability of the OLS regression results.

5.8.4 Uniqueness of vector - deriving an error correction model

Though a valid cointegrating relationship may exist, it may not be unique. Johansen's (1988) procedure is adopted as a means of testing for more than one cointegration relationship. It also permits the testing of long run relationships adjusted for shortrun changes. It is an expansion of the cointegration approach used by Granger (1983) and Engle and Granger (1987). The procedure calls for a vector autoregressive model

$$X_t = \Pi_1 X_{t-1} \ldots + \Pi_k X_{t-k} + \mu D_t + \epsilon_t \qquad (5.17)$$

where X_t and ϵ_t are of dimension (px1),$\epsilon_t \sim N(0,\Omega)$, and D_t is a vector of deterministic variables such as a constant and dummy variables to account for fixed seasonal effects, and the Πs and μ are unknown coefficients. The levels model can be reparameterised as

$$\Delta X_t = \Pi X_{t-1} \ldots \Delta X_{t-1} + \Delta X_{t-k+1} + \Gamma Z_{1t} + \epsilon_t \qquad (5.18)$$

where Δ is the difference operator, $\Pi = (\Pi_1 + \ldots + \Pi_k - I), Z_{1t}$ is the vector ΔX_{t-k+1} ,D_t, and Π and Γ are the corresponding coefficients. The Π matrix provides information about the long term relationships among the series. If the series are stationary and cointegrated, then $0 < r = \text{rank } \Pi < p$ and equation (5.18) is an error correction model. In this case, $\Pi = \alpha\beta'$ where α and β are the cointegrating relationships among the series, and β are the cointegrating vectors.

An error correction model is indicated where the short run impact of regulation on bank performance differs from the long run impact. This appears to be the case based on responses to questionnaires by banks in the Caribbean (Table 4.12). Such models allow long run components of variables to obey equilibrium constraints where short run components have a flexible dynamic specification. Equations in levels ignore all short run dynamics, while equations in first differences ignore all long run information. Engle and Granger (1987) observe that where a cointegration equation exists there exists

143

also an error correction model, and vice versa, which takes into account short run dynamics of the relationship between the variables. The error correction model is based on the assertion that a proportion of the disequilibrium from one period is corrected in the next period.

A vector time series X_t has an error correction representation if it can be expressed as

$$A(B)(1-B)X_t = \lambda Z_{t-1} + u_t \tag{5.19}$$

where u_t is a stationary multivariate disturbance, with $A(0)=I$, $A(I)$ has all elements finite, $Z_t = \alpha' x_t$ and $\gamma \neq 0$. In this representation only the disequilibrium in the previous period is an explanatory variable. However, by rearranging terms, any set of lags of Z can be written in this form. Therefore it permits any type of gradual adjustment toward a new equilibrium. Johansen and Juselius (1990) developed an approach which enabled testing of more than one cointegration relationship and delivered a clear identification of the error structure of the dynamic process. The procedure is based on the following error correction model and is applied in some of the test equations employed in the study. Using $\Delta = 1 - L$ where L is the lag operator, the error correction model may be written as

$$\Delta X_t = \Gamma_1 \Delta X_{t-1} + .. + \Gamma_{k-1} \Delta X_{t-k+1} + \Pi X_{t-k} + \mu + \Phi D_t + \epsilon_t \tag{5.20}$$

where

$$\Gamma_i = -(I - \Pi_1 - ... - \Pi_i), \qquad (i=1,.....,k-1), \tag{5.21}$$

and

$$\Pi = -(I - \Pi_1 - ... - \Pi_k). \tag{5.22}$$

Equation 5.20 is VAR model in first differences except for the presence of the lagged level ΠX_{t-k} or error correction term.

The coefficient Π contains the relevant information about the nature of the long run relationship among the variables in the vector X. The model enables 3 possible tests for the rank of Π whereby

  1) Rank Π = p, i.e the matrix is of full rank, indicating that the vector process X is stationary which suggests a levels VAR is an appropriate description of the data.

2) Rank $\Pi = 0$ i.e. the matrix Π is a null matrix and there is no long run information giving rise to a traditional differenced VAR.
3) $0 < $ Rank $\Pi = r$, where $0 < r < p$ giving rise to cointegration and implying that there are p x r matrices a and b such that $\Pi = ab'$. The cointegrating vectors b have the property that $b'X$ is stationary even though X_t itself is non-stationary and can be interpreted as an error correction model [Engle and Granger (1987)].
Thus the main hypothesis embedded in the hypothesis of r cointegrating vectors

$$H_2: \Pi = ab' \qquad (5.23)$$

where a and b are p x r matrices.

The weights with which each cointegrating vector enters each of the ΔX_t equations are captured through a. Through maximum likelihood estimation, the likelihood ratio statistics enables testing of the order of cointegration (r) and restrictions on the parameters of the Π matrix, i.e a and b.

5.8.5 Use of diagnostics

$$-T\sum_{i=r+1}^{p} \ln(1-\hat{\phi}_i) \qquad (5.24)$$

Likelihood ratio tests of the null hypothesis of no more than (r) stationary linear combinations of the series versus, respectively, the alternative of possible stationarity of all series (that is, $r \le p$) and the alternative of at most $(r+1)$ stationary combinations of the series are:

and

$$\hat{b} = \hat{V}_r = (\hat{v}_1 .... \hat{v}_r) \qquad (5.25)$$

Distributions of these test statistics depend on the number of unit roots in the model under the null hypoesis [Johansen and Juselius (1990)]. Once the cointegrating relationships among the series is determined, the cointegrating vector(s) are given by the eigenvectors corresponding to the largest eigenvalues, so for given r,

$$0 < r < p.$$

Cointegration LR tests based on the trace of the stochastic matrix are applied as a test procedure using the Johansen maximum likelihood procedure for the case of a trend in the data generation process.

This methodology was applied to test the relationship between regulatory variables and selected measures of bank performance.

5.9 Discriminant analysis: calculating composite measures of bank performance and regulation

Discriminant analysis is the technique used to develop a single composite score, in this case, a bank performance score and a bank regulation score. Multiple discriminant analysis is the appropriate statistical technique to use when the dependent variable consists of more than one group of classifications [Hotteling (1933), Levine (1977) and Hair et al (1992)]. The procedure assigns weights to each variable and adds these products together. The result is a single composite discriminant score for all individual categories within the group. A composite score derived from this procedure is of the form

$$Z = a_1 X + a_2 Y + a_3 K \qquad (5.26)$$

The usual procedure is to divide the total sample into groups or functions. A covariance or correlation matrix is then derived. These can be standardised to produce a correlation matrix of standarised variates i.e. the deviation of a variable mean divided by its standard deviation.

Eigenvectors are then derived.[8] Using the notation

$$z = \sum_{i=1}^{N} a_i z_i \qquad (5.27)$$

a linear combination of the X variables is formed, as a linear combination of the Y variables. Of the large number of possible linear combinations for each set, coefficients are chosen such that the resultant linear combination of the X set variables is maximally correlated with the linear combination of the Y set variables. If we let x^* and y^* be defined by $x^* = \sum a_i x_i$, and $y^* = \sum b_i x_i$, canonical correlation analysis selects those values for the a_is and b_is such that r^*, y^* is the maximum possible value. Thus we can say that x^* represents that combination of X set variables which have the highest correlation with any combination of the Y set variables and furthermore y^* is that combination of the Y variables normally correlated with any X combination. Of the large number of linear combinations of the two sets of variables we have found that a particular pair was most highly related to each other. The correlation coefficient between x^* and y^* is termed a canonical correlation.

The eigenvector with the eigenvalue yielding the highest variance is identified as the canonical function which contributes to the maximum amount of variation. These are the canonical discriminant functions and are identified in descending order of importance.

A structure matrix of component loadings is then developed. Each component loading factor represents the correlation coefficient between the canonical discriminant function and the set of standardised discriminating variables. Discriminant loadings referred to as structural correlations, measure the simple linear correlation between each dependent variable and the discriminant function. The solution is rotated to produce a structure which lists the variables of each function in the order of its contribution to variability.

A test of the null hypothesis that the means of all discriminant functions in all groups in the population are really equal to 0 can be based on Wilk's lambda. It provides a test of the null hypothesis that the population means are equal. When the significance level using the F test or Chi square test, is small (less than 0.05) the hypothesis that all group means are equal is rejected.[9]

The SPSS[10] package used for calculation of discriminant functions removes outliers from the list of eligible variables, but these can be reintroduced if desired, if it is the intention to show the contribution of all variables regardless of their contribution to the composite score. The pooled within - group correlation matrix is obtained by averaging the separate correlation matrices for all groups and then computing the correlation matrix.

The contribution of a variable to a discriminant function (its discriminant loading or weight) and the relative contribution of the function to the overall solution (a relative measure among the eigenvalues of the functions) can then be calculated. It is obtained by dividing the component weight of each variable by the corresponding eigenvalue.

The composite is the sum of the overall indices across all significant discriminating functions. The weights do not add to unity and may be negative. If this occurs, they can be rescaled to unity by adding 1 to each component and multiplying by 100, thus retaining the relative distance between coefficients.

Interpretation of the composite measure is useful in depicting the relative position such as the rank or order of each variable; in this case an overall bank performance measure. A similar bank performance measure called the 'Z score' or 'Zeta score' currently used by banks, investors, stock exchanges as well as regulators, has been developed by Altman (1979, 1984). Other contributions include those of Altman, Marco and Varetto (1994) Earl and

147

Marais (1979) and Taffler (1982). However, none was explicitly designed to capture the impact of regulation.

Applying this technique, a bank performance index is then calculated for Barbados Jamaica and Trinidad and Tobago, and using similar techniques, an index of regulation. On the basis of the similarities of the economies and the similarities in the monetary and prudential measures applied in the three countries, the weights calculated for Barbados are applied to Jamaica and Trinidad and Tobago, and indices of bank performance and indices of monetary and prudential regulation are calculated.

Tests for causality are conducted between the more important regulatory variable and the more important measure of performance. Similarly, causality tests are conducted between the performance index and the regulation index. The procedure for causality testing is described below.

5.10 Causality tests

To test the null hypothesis that Y does not cause X, one can apply the direct approach which is to regress X_t on $X_{t-1},..,X_{t-r}$ and $Y_{t-1},...Y_{t-s}$, and use a conventional test of exclusion restrictions to test the effect of omitting the lagged Y variables. If these exclusion restrictions are accepted, then we accept that Y does not cause X. A second method requires a regression of Y_t on past, current and future values of X. The null hypothesis is still that Y does not cause X, but the exclusion restrictions tested are that future values of X may be excluded. If these exclusions are accepted, we again accept that Y does not cause X.

The methodology used here is the Granger causality test.

$$Y_t = \delta_0 + \sum_{i=1}^{m} \alpha_i X_{t-1} + \sum_{j=1}^{m} \beta_j Y_{t-j} + \mu_t \qquad (5.28)$$

In equation (5.28), X is said to cause Y, provided some α_i is not zero and in equation (5.29) where Y causes X if some a_i is not zero. If both of these events occur there is feedback.

$$X_t = c_0 + \sum_{i=1}^{m} a_i Y_{t-i} + \sum_{j=1}^{m} b_j X_{t-j} + e_t \qquad (5.29)$$

Causality tests are conducted in a bivariate framework since only the most critical variable identified in OLS regressions and in the cointegrating

148

equation is chosen for testing. The bivariate approach is applied because we are deemed to be investigating prima facie causality [Suppes (1970) and Granger (1980)]. A (set of) variable(s) is a prima facie cause of another set of variable(s) Y if X precedes Y in time and if the conditional and unconditional probabilities of event Y are unequal, $P(Y \mid X) \neq P(Y)$. If the relationship is linear, this implies that in a regression context, $X_{t-i}(i > 0)$ and Y_t are correlated. Reliance on an extra-statistical framework in which to make causal claims have been made by Zellner (1979, 1988), Holland (1986) and Bassmann (1988). They emphasize that the necessary conditions for a variable X to be a cause of Y must include an understandable mechanism or law relating to X, and Bassman has specified that one must be able to conceive of a conceptual experiment relating X and Y in which X is controlled. This is established from the mathematical fact that returns on reserve requirements are lower than returns on private sector loans, and hence there exists the basis for expectation of a causal impact on bank performance.

Two alternatives to a complete search of the lag space are (a) to identify the appropriate lag structure for the equations based on some statistical criterion [Hsaio (1981)] or (b) to specify alternative lag structures. Hsaio's (1981) research strategy involves selection of the 'optimal' univariate lag length M*, of the autoregressive null model followed by selection of the optimal lag length, n*, conditional upon m=m*, in the full model. The structure of the optimal causal model under the alternative hypothesis of prima facie causality is given by m* and n* causal model under the alternative hypothesis. Given prior testing and prior indications of lag length, the alternative approach of using an iterative method for arriving at an optimal lag length is used in this study.

The test for causality applied is based on an F statistic that is calculated by estimating the expression below in both the constrained and unconstrained forms.
Where:

$$F_1 = \frac{SSE_r - SSE_u \ /m}{SSE_u \ /(T-2m-1)} \tag{5.30}$$

Where SSE_r, SSE_u = residual sum of squares of the restricted and unrestricted models respectively

T = number of observations

m = number of lags.

The above procedures are described in the order in which they are employed in the ensuing analysis.

Notes

1   A dummy variable for government ownership was found to be insignificant and was removed from equations.

2   Consideration was given to including the deposit insurance premium as a proxy for the cost of insolvency in the Trinidad and Tobago case but data constraints did not permit. Also, these rates seem to be heavily subsidised by government and may not have represented the true cost of insolvency.

3   A check of announcements confirm that three months is normally granted for compliance with regulations.

4   These are capital, liquidity ratios, loan deposit ratios, overhead expenses, and factors such as size, market growth and interest rates.

5   A measure of profitability which added back loan losses was considered, but differed so widely that it was removed from the measures employed. Other areas of possible inefficiencies, unrelated to labour costs, were excluded as the study identified only the major area of possible efficiencies.

6   When credit controls on volume were removed between 1987 and 1989, hire purchase controls which fixed minimum downpayments and maximum downpayment periods remained in effect.

7   Dickey-Fuller tests for unit roots assume a process with zero mean and no trend. Where there is a trend in the data generating process Augmented Dickey-Fuller tests are applied.

8   Any vector, whose direction is unchanged after transformation is said to be an eigenvector of the transformation (or of its associated matrix). The factor by which its length is increased is the eigenvalue of the vector.

9   In discriminant analysis the percentage correctly classified is analogous to regression's R^2. It reveals how well the statistical function classifies the statistical units. The F test is analogous to the Chi square test of significance in discriminant analysis.

10   SPSS is a Statistical Package for Social Sciences.

6 Regulation and bank performance: results of empirical tests

6.1 Introduction

This chapter establishes that improved results can be obtained for determining the factors which influence bank performance when such models include regulatory variables. In the tests that follow, OLS regressions are conducted using the profitability measure as the dependent variable. Cointegration tests are employed and error correction models. Maximum likelihood estimates [Johansen and Juselius (1990)] are developed where economic theory would suggest that a long run relationship exists which can be further explained by this procedure. This is likely to be the case for two of the measures of bank performance, bank profitability and market share. Tests are conducted first for Barbados, then for Jamaica and Trinidad and Tobago. Other regressions formulated as reaction functions analyse the impact of regulation on bank risk, bank liquidity and bank solvency. In each case, comparative testing is conducted for Jamaica and Trinidad and Tobago. Discriminant analysis is then employed to develop composite measures of bank performance and of regulation, and causality tests are conducted on the performance and regulation indices and on reserve requirements and bank performance.

The study focuses on the economics of the relationships between variables. Given the wide range of comparative tests to be conducted, econometric techniques are used simply as a means of establishing such relationships. More extensive testing is employed using the measure of bank profitability, before tax profit plus staff expenses (BTSETA), as it is the only measure of bank profitability without negative values and so facilitates testing in loglinear form. Tests using other measures of bank profitability are performed more sparingly and are frequently reported in the appendices. Variables are retained in the equations even though they are not significant in order to demonstrate their lack of significance.

6.2 Regulation and bank profitability: results of regressions

6.2.1 Preliminary testing

In preliminary testing using OLS regressions, the conventional variables used by Bourke (1988) and Hannan (1991) in the determination of bank performance were employed, that is, regulatory variables were excluded. Typically such variables are money or deposits, interest rates, investments (securities), staff expenses, and inflation. When regulatory variables were added and new regressions run, results establish that equations which include regulatory variables have considerably more explanatory power. All regulated monetary variables were significant (see Appendix 6.1).

6.2.2 Profitability as the dependent variable

The testing procedure then commenced with tests for stationarity. Plots of each variable were conducted to establish whether each was trend stationary or a random walk with drift. Dickey-Fuller and Augmented Dickey-Fuller tests were employed to test for stationarity. Where stationarity changed as lags were added, regression on a constant, a trend, a lagged level, and a differenced value of the dependent variable was conducted. Tests for autocorrelation were then performed to confirm whether the variable was really I(0) or I(1). Such variables carry the symbol '*' in Table 6.1. For example, in the case of the variable LBTSETA, which unit root tests showed to be I(0) for ADF1 and I(1) for ADF2, ADF3 and ADF4, tests for autocorrelation revealed that LBTSETA was an I(1) variable (having a χ^2 LM value of 8.54(0.073) for ADF(3)). ADF tests indicated that of the other variables, five were I(0), the concentration ratio (LCON) and interest rate spreads (LI), staff expenses (LSF), treasury bill yields (LTB) and the loans deposit ratio (LD). Two were I(1); money supply (LM) and reserve requirements (LRR). First differencing of these variables was therefore necessary to achieve stationarity. Below are the calculated values of the Dickey-Fuller and Augmented Dickey-Fuller tests used for comparison with critical values (see Table 6.1).

Critical Dickey-Fuller values were -2.9077 (non-trended) and -3.4812 (trended) and ADF values are -2.9084 (non trended) and -3.4824 (trended) and were computed using the formula provided by MacKinnon (1990). A long run cointegrating equation was estimated for profitability as the dependent variable in logs and was of the form

$$LBTSETA = c + x_1LTB + x_2LSF + x_3LM + x_4LCON + x_5LRR + x_6LLD +$$
$$x_7LId_1dumin + d_2dumcr + \gamma_1s1 + \gamma_2s2 + \gamma_3s3\ u_{t-j} + e_t \qquad (6.1)$$

Where (BTSETA) = return on assets plus staff expenses.
A test for unit roots was conducted on the residuals of the cointegrating vector which was derived from the equation above. The cointegrating equation represents the long run model and the coefficients are interpreted as long run elasticities (see Table 6.2). A test of the residual is of the form

$$\Delta u_t = \rho u_{t-1} + \sum_{j=1}^{n} \beta\ \Delta u_{t-j} + e_t \qquad (6.2)$$

$H_0:\ \rho = 0$
$H_1:\ \rho < 0$

Table 6.1

Dickey-Fuller (DF) and Augmented Dickey-Fuller (ADF) tests: part 1

Variable	Dickey-Fuller (DF) (logs)	Augmented Dickey-Fuller (ADF) (logs)	First differences DF	First differences ADF
LTB(NT)	-1.5890	-2.5743	-4.2815	-3.3928
LM(T)	-1.9732	-1.8836	-8.1323	-7.2444
LSF(T)	-4.7574	-3.5485	-12.351	-10.676
LRR(T)	-3.0000	-2.1857	-10.365	-6.5716
LCON(T)	-7.8548	-5.4358	-13.413	-9.3289
LI(NT)	-6.2140	-3.9740	-13.598	-7.4991
LLD(T)	-2.9001	-3.1813	-7.4217	-7.8468
LBTSETA* (T)	-4.9218	-2.1377 (ADF3)	-11.391	-10.304

(T) denotes a trend in the data series and (NT) denotes a non-trended series (The prefix (L) before the variable denotes the loglinear form.)

153

MacKinnon (1990) tables were used as a guide for computing critical values and the results of these regressions also prove useful in selecting the vector of relevance in maximum likelihood estimates later in the study. The calculated ADF1 value of the residual was -5.30, thus rejecting the null hypothesis of no cointegration. This test is based on the assumption that a system is cointegrated if a linear combination of I(0) and I(1) variables is also I(0) [Engle and Granger (1987)]. Results from the cointegrating equation are presented in Table 6.2.

The residuals from the cointegrating equation were fed into a second equation in first differences utilising the Engle-Granger two-step approach to derive an error correction model (ECM), and lags were added. The ECM combines long run effects as well as short run dynamics. The coefficient of these residuals was significant and negative and had a value of -0.715. The residual of the ECM was also white noise based on the Box Pierce Q statistic of 19.82 which was less than a χ^2 value for 20 degrees of freedom at the 95% quantile of 31.41. This suggests that the error correction model was not misspecified and that the relevant factors were included in the error term.

Diagnostic tests were conducted to confirm whether the linear regression analysis satisfied classical assumptions of homoscedasticity and serial correlation of the unobservable disturbance term. Tests for serial correlation employ Durbin-Watson tests for non-autocorrelated errors and the Lagrange multiplier tests [Breusch and Pagan (1980)]. The normality of residuals test applied is a test of skewness and kurtosis based on Bera and Jarque (1980). The test for heteroscedasticity is a simple test of the homoscedasticity assumption that the disturbances u_t have a constant variance and provides an LM test of $\gamma = 0$ in the model

$$E(u_t^2) = \theta^2{}_t = \theta^2 + \gamma (X_t' \beta)^2 \qquad (6.3)$$

Such a test is also robust with respect to non-normality of the disturbances.

A test for functional form employs Ramsey's (1969) RESET test for the case of the square of the fitted values and a test for heteroscedasticity is based on the regression of squared residuals on squared fitted values. There was no evidence of heteroscedasticity. There was however some slight serial correlation of the residuals using the χ^2 LM version so that the results of the F version were relied upon. Kiviet (1985) notes that in small samples the F version is more reliable.

Results indicate that independent variables are associated with 62% of the variation in commercial bank profitability measured by the adjusted multiple coefficient of determination in the long run.

154

6.2.3 Results of tests excluding capital (the prudential variable)

Results indicate that two monetary measures impact adversely on bank profitability both in the ECM and in the long run model (see Tables 6.2 and 6.3). The coefficients for two of the regulatory variables representing monetary regulation, i.e. credit controls and reserve requirements, were significant at the 5% level and were negatively associated with bank profitability.

In the long run model for every 10% increase in reserve requirements there was a 4% decline in bank profitability. The views of Romer (1985) and Osborne and Zaher (1992) that equity holders bear some of the costs of increases in reserve requirements tend to be supported by the results. This negative association of reserve requirements with profitability implies an adverse impact on equity holders, (since profits become the property of equity holders on declaration of dividends). The absence of a stock market precluded direct measurement of the impact on shareholder wealth and the above relationship is deduced from the association of regulatory measures with bank profitability.

The conclusion that reserve requirements constrain the size of the banking firm is also inferred from the results. To the extent that equity is needed to match increases in bank size, and since reserve requirements reduce internally generated equity financing, the views of Ramakhrisnan and Thakor (1984) and Osborne and Zaher (1992) that reserve requirements constrain the size of the banking firm are supported by the results. This conclusion remains tentative and more specific results will depend on causality tests to be conducted later in the chapter.

Similarly, results show that the imposition of credit controls was associated with a 0.79 % decline in bank profitability. Since the dummy credit control variable is retained in the ECM, the calculation of its long run effect on BTSETA was adjusted.

Generally,

$$resid_t = y_t - \hat{\alpha}_1 x_{1t} - \hat{\alpha}_2 x_{2t} - \hat{\alpha}_3 x_{3t} \ldots + \hat{a}_n x_{nt} \qquad (6.4)$$

From Table 6.2

$$resid_{t-1} = LBTSETA_{t-1} - (-1.51 + 0.226LTB_{t-1} + 0.004LS_{t-1}F + 0.179LM_{t-1} \\ - 0.409LRR_{t-1} - 0.233LLD_{t-1} + 0.275LI_{t-1} + 0.171dumin_{t-1} \\ -0.115dumcr_{t-1}) \qquad (6.5)$$

155

Table 6.2
Barbados:
results: cointegrating equation: profitability
(LBTSETA - a long run model excluding capital)

Description	Coefficient	
C	-1.51	(-3.15)
LTB	0.226	(3.95)
LSF	0.004	(0.002)
LM	0.179	(1.76)
LCON	1.790	(3.45)
LRR	-0.409	(-2.35)
LLD	-0.233	(-0.748)
LI	0.275	(2.21)
dumin	0.171	(4.21)
dumcr	-0.115	(-2.74)
R^2	0.690	-
R bar squared	0.617	-
D.W.	1.97	-
F statistic (12,51)	9.46	-
s.e.	0.110	-
Misspecification MS1 $[\chi^2 (1)]$ MS2 [F (1,50]	4.11	3.43
Normality N$[\chi^2 (2)]$	1.36	-
Heteroscedasticity LM (1) F [1.62]	0.023	0.022
Serial Correlation $\chi^2 (4)$, F [4,47]	0.439	0.081

(T-values are placed in brackets next to coefficients.)
(Results are based on quarterly data 1977q1 to 1992q4.)

Table 6.3
Barbados:
results: error correction model: profitability
(DLBTSETA - excludes capital)

Description	Coefficient	
C	-0.538	(-1.80)
LTB	1.920	(2.15)
LSF	0.593	(1.69)
DLM	1.920	(2.15)
LCON	0.145	(2.15)
$DLRR_{t-3}$	-0.690	(-2.43)
LLD	0.568	(0.787)
LI_{t-1}	-0.219	(-1.31)
$resid_{t-1}$	-0.715	(-3.13)
$dumin_{t-1}$	-0.028	(-0.403)
$dumcr_{t-1}$	-0.049	(-0.809)
R^2	0.408	-
R bar squared	0.287	-
D.W.	2.29	-
F statistic (10,49)	3.38	-
s.e.	0.157	-
Misspecification MS1 $[\chi^2$ (1)] MS2 [F (1,47]	1.26	1.03
Normality $N[\chi^2$ (2)	4.21	-
Heteroscedasticity LM (1) F[1,58]	3.93	4.06
Serial Correlation χ^2 (4) F [4,44]	11.35	2.63

(T-values are placed in brackets next to coefficients.)
(Results are based on quarterly data from 1977q1 to 1992q4.)

In general form

$$resid_{t-1} = LBTSETA_{t-1} - C - \hat{a}_1 LTB_{t-1} - \hat{a}_2\ LSF_{t-1} \ldots \hat{a}_n\ dumcr_{t-1} \qquad (6.6)$$

Solving the ECM in Table 6.3 for the long run solution we obtain:

$$0 = 0 - 0.715(LBTSETA \ldots 0.171dumin - 0.115dumcr +$$
$$0.028dumin - 0.049dumcr) \qquad (6.7)$$

The effect of the variables (dumin) and (dumcr) on BTSETA is calculated as

0.171-(0.028/-0.715)
and -0.115-(-0.049/-0.715)
=0.21 (dumin) and -0.79 (dumcr) respectively

The fact that investors are not likely to take decisions to compete for the credit market unless they think that controls are going to be temporary, complicates the interpretation of the results. (In Barbados, credit controls were in effect continuously for approximately 10 years before they were temporarily removed.) However, the sign on the credit control variable was always negative and more frequently significant than otherwise. The credit control variable was negative and significant in the cointegrating equation or long run model which excluded capital, also in the ECM (with capital) and in the model measuring profitability by return on assets (ROA).

The coefficient of the interest rate control dummy variable was more frequently positive and significant at the 1% level. This result, combined with a positive and significant coefficient for the actual interest rate spread, favours an interpretation of accommodative interest rate-setting. It suggests that while the size of interest rate spreads influences bank profitability, the level at which regulators set rates tends to accommodate banks' cost structures such that interest rate regulation does not necessarily depress bank profitability. It supports the argument of cost-axiomatic or accommodative pricing by regulators. Whether accommodative pricing by regulators was the result of bargaining determines whether this system of pricing can be considered an example of Aumann-Shapley prices [Aumann and Shapley (1974)]. Based on responses to questionnaires submitted by commercial banks, no overt bargaining was, however, evident in the setting of interest rates as is required for Aumann Shapley prices to exist; so that to the extent that prices were market clearing, they may rather be considered anonymously equitable, or cost-axiomatic. A positive association of interest rate controls with bank profitability would suggest accommodative pricing, but whether pricing as market-clearing is more difficult to confirm, so that the most definitive position on the pricing structure of interest rates indicated by the result is that at the minimum, pricing was accommodative. Accommodative pricing is a subset of cost-axiomatic pricing. However, an indication that pricing is market clearing or anonymous equitable (see Chapter 2) does not require that the interest rate spread variable be significant. Neutrality of this coefficient would appear to be sufficient.

Generally, results on bank profitability tend to support the views of banks with respect to reserve requirements and credit controls, that is, that they impact negatively on bank profitability. However, results do not support commercial banks' views that interest rate controls impact negatively on bank profitability (responses to questionnaire 4.c and Table 4.1).

6.2.4 Results of tests: including the prudential variable

A similar equation using BTSETA as the dependent profitability variable was run and included capital and reserves. Given the branch type operations which dominate the banking system in Barbados, an adjusted measure of capital, namely capital reserves and long term borrowing was substituted. This is justified on the basis that though branch banks engage in substantial long term borrowing from overseas head offices to support their operations they are not required to hold capital locally.

The cointegrating equation was put in log linear form.

$$LBTSETA = a_0 + a_1LTB + a_2LM + a_3LRR + a_4LLD + a_5LSF + a_6LCON + a_7LI + a_8LCAPB + d_1dumin + d_2dumcr + \gamma_1s1 + \gamma_2s2 + \gamma_3s3$$

$$(6.8)$$

where L denotes the log of the variable and CAPB represents capital, reserves and long term borrowing and is I(1). CAPB is a trended variable and has a calculated ADF 1 value of -5.39 compared to a critical value of -3.48 as per the Augmented Dickey Fuller test statistic.

When capital is included among the independent variables, reserve requirements are not as significant in the long run, but continue to carry a negative sign on the coefficient and is less than unity (-0.62). Credit control carried a negative sign in the ECM and was significant at the 5% level but was not significant in the long run model though the sign was negative. In the long run the variable representing capital reserves and long term borrowing was significant at the 5% level and negatively associated with bank profitability (Table 6.4) but was neither negative nor significant in the model adjusted for short run dynamics. The adjusted variable for capital and long

159

term borrowings CAPB reflects borrowing abroad by branch banks to finance their operations. Significant foreign borrowings by commercial banks in 1981 and 1990, both years in which reserve requirements were increased, would tend to support this result. However, in the long run, increased capital and borrowing appear to have been at the expense of profitability and supports the views of banks interviewed in Barbados as well as in Jamaica and Trinidad and Tobago, that capital requirements tend to reduce bank profitability (see Questionnaire result 4.c and Table 4.1).

6.2.5 Non-regulatory variables

Results tend to confirm that profitability increases with market concentration. This is inferred from the positive and significant coefficient on the concentration variable and applies both in the long run model and in the ECM, suggesting that bank profitability of the system appears to increase with the level of oligopoly as judged by concentration.

6.2.6 Other profitability measures

Subsequent testing in levels was conducted on profitability measured by (ROA) return on assets. (Negative numbers in the series did not permit use of the loglinear form.)

This equation was of the general form

$$ROA = a_0 + a_1 TB + a_2 SF + a_3 M + a_4 CON + a_5 RR_{t-3} + a_6 LD + a_7 I_{t-1}$$
$$+ d_1 dumin_{t-1} + d_2 dumcr_{t-1} + \lambda_1 s1 + \lambda_2 s2 + \lambda_3 s3$$

$$(6.9)$$

Generally, results using the profitability measure (ROA) unequivocally support the view of a negative impact of reserve requirements and credit controls on bank profitability as well as the hypothesis of cost-axiomatic pricing. Results of the error correction model (ECM) are shown in Table 6.6. Using the measure of bank profitability (ROA), where staff expenses are not added back to profits, staff expenses are revealed to vary negatively with return on assets but are not significant (Table 6.6).[1] Results do not therefore support the views of Edwards (1977) that commercial banks earning supernormal profits engage in suboptimal expenditures even in the absence of a definition of 'supernormal' profits.

160

Table 6.4
Barbados: regulation and profitability:
a cointegrating equation with capital (LBTSETA)
(a long run model)

Description	Coefficient	
C	-1.176	(-0.235)
LTB	0.092	(1.05)
LSF	- 0.062	(-0.241)
LM	0.083	(0.746)
LCON	0.198	(3.83)
LRR	-0.139	(-0.62)
LLD	-0.266	(-0.875)
LI	0.229	(1.85)
LCAPB	-0.14	(-2.06)
dumin	0.101	(1.84)
dumcr	-0.063	(-1.26)
R^2	0.710	-
R bar squared	0.634	-
D.W.	2.07	-
F statistic	9.42	-
s.e.	0.108	-
Misspecification MS1 [χ^2 (1)] MS2[F1,50]	4.31	3.84
Normality N[χ^2 (2)]	1.92	-
Heteroscedasticity LM (1) F [1,62]	0.034	0.033
Serial Correlation χ^2 (4) F [4,47]	0.695	0.126

(T-values are placed in brackets next to coefficients.)
(Results are based on quarterly data from 1977q1 to 1992q4.)

Table 6.5
Barbados:
error correction model with capital
(DLBTSETA)

Description	Coefficient	
C	-0.563	(-1.80)
LTB	0.044	(0.631)
LSF	0.520	(1.49)
DLM	1.89	(1.99)
LCON	0.155	(2.19)
$DLRR_{t-3}$	-0.639	(-2.24)
LLD	0.474	(.615)
LI_{t-1}	0.212	(-1.26)
$DLCAPB_{t-1}$	0.073	(0.458)
$RESID_{t-1}$	-0.815	(-3.33)
$dumin_{t-1}$	-0.029	(-0.411)
$dumcr_{t-1}$	-0.053	(-1.97)
R^2	0.423	-
R bar squared	0.291	-
D.W.	2.22	-
F statistic (11,48)	3.21	-
s.e.	0.157	-
Misspecification MS1 [χ^2 (1)] MS2[F (1,47]	2.91	2.39
Normality N[χ^2 (2)]	5.58	-
Hetero LM (1) F [1,47]	2.55	2.58
Ser Cor χ^2 (4) F [4,44]	11.17	2.52

(The prefix 'D' denotes first differences and the prefix 'L' denotes logs.)

Table 6.6
Barbados:
regulation and other measures of bank profitability
ROA (return on assets) - ECM in levels

Description	Coefficient	
C	-0.521	(-2.00)
TB	0.019	(2.40)
DSF	-0.165	(-.379)
DM	0.006	(1.49)
CON	0.009	(4.01)
DRR_{t-3}	-0.044	(-2.76)
LD	0.614	(0.868)
I_{t-1}	0.193	(1.56)
$RESID_{t-1}$	0.261	(1.39)
$dumin_{t-1}$	0.125	(2.23)
$dumcr_{t-1}$	-0.104	(-2.10)
R^2	0.498	-
R bar squared	0.398	-
D.W.	1.81	-
F statistic	4.98	-
s.e.	0.131	-
Misspecification MS1 [χ^2 (1)] MS2 [F (1,49]	1.19	0.978
Normality N[χ^2 (2)]	2.93	-
Heteroscedasticity LM (1) F [1,59]	0.796	0.780
Serial Correlation χ^2 (4) F [4,46]	17.65	4.680

(This regression was run in levels. T-values are placed in brackets next to coefficients. Results are based on quarterly data from 1977q1 - 1992q4.)

6.2.7 Maximum likelihood estimates: (Including capital and long term borrowing as a prudential variable - Johansen procedure)

The error correction model which included capital as a prudential variable carried a higher adjusted multiple coefficient of correlation than that which included monetary variables only, and the capital variable was significant and negative in the long run. This outcome suggests that prudential considerations need to be taken into account in the setting of monetary regulations. The Π matrix of the Johansen procedure permits further investigation of the interrelationship between these variables. Since the only other regulatory variable which is I(1) is the reserve requirement variable, the analysis will focus on the relationship between this variable and adjusted capital (CAPB). The I(1) variables are LBTSETA, LM, LRR_{t-3}, $LCAPB_{t-1}$ the I(0) variables were LCON, LI, LTB $dumin_{t-1}$, $dumcr_{t-1}$, s1, s2, s3^2.

Table 6.7 presents results of cointegration LR tests based on maximal eigenvalues of the stochastic matrix.

Table 6.7
Cointegration LR tests based on maximal eigenvalues of the stochastic matrix

Null	Alternative	Statistic	95% Critical value
$r = 0$	$r = 1$	58.27	27.07
$r <= 1$	$r = 2$	20.00	20.96
$r <= 2$	$r = 3$	31.19	14.06
$r = 3$	$r = 4$	4.54	3.76

Results based on the trace were similar. The VAR is of order 4.

Cointegration LR tests based on maximal eigenvalues of the stochastic matrix and cointegration LR tests based on the trace of the stochastic matrix both indicate that there is one vector holding the system together. However, the area of interest is the Π matrix reported by ab' (see equation 5.24). The cointegrating vector has already been identified employing the Engle-Granger two step methodology, so that this step may be omitted.

Table 6.8
Maximum likelihood procedure: cointegration LR test based on on the trace of the stochastic matrix

Null	Alternative	Statistic	95% Critical value
r = 0	r> = 1	58.27	27.06
r< = 1	r > = 2	20.00	20.96
r <= 2	r > = 3	13.19	14.07
r <= 3	r > = 4	4.54	3.76

Table 6.9
Estimated long run matrix: Johansen estimation

	LBTSETA	LM	LRR_{t-3}	$LCAPB_{t-1}$
LBTSETA	-0.26573	0.74588	1.1571	0.18897
LM	0.04736	-0.13296	0.20626	-0.03368
LRR_{t-3}	-0.01297	-0.03649	-0.05648	0.00922
$LCAPB_{t-1}$	-0.01343	-0.03769	-0.05847	0.00955

(The prefix (L) denotes the loglinear form of the variable.)

The objective is to examine the relationship between the variables more especially between the regulatory variable, reserve requirements (RR) and adjusted capital (CAPB), with a view to examining possible conflicts between prudential and monetary regulation. The results (see Table 6.9) provide a reasonable comparison with results obtained from a simple correlation coefficient of 0.04, and compare with results of the long run model from the cointegrating equation which showed a negative correlation between capital and bank profitability in the long run and suggested a possible conflict with prudential objectives.

6.2.8 Tests of partitioned data by bank grouping - bank profitability: Barbados

The data set was partitioned in order to test whether regulatory resilience was greater for large banks than for small or for foreign banks than for local. Other hypotheses relating to the relative profitability of large and small banks are also considered in the analysis. The variables were plotted to establish whether each series was trended or non-trended and Dickey-Fuller and Augmented Dickey-Fuller tests were conducted. Results of those tests can be seen in Table 6.10.

In Table 6.10 the prefix (LA) denotes large banks and the prefix (SM) denotes small banks. (LAMKS) therefore denotes the market share of large banks, and (SMMKS) denotes the market share of small banks. These are measured as that group's share in the total assets of all banks. A variable representing deposits of the group (DEP) is substituted for broad money (M) in the equation used earlier for all banks. All other symbols are the same as employed for the consolidated banking system in earlier equations with prefixes added to denote the appropriate bank group.

In the test equation for large banks four of the variables were trended and four were trend stationary (Table 6.10 shows DF and ADF values for the new variables only). Equations were run in loglinear form for large banks, small banks, and foreign banks, employing the measure of bank profitability (BTSETA). An equation in levels was employed for local banks.

A cointegrating equation was formulated and was of the general form

$$LBTSETA = a_0 + a_1 LTB + a_2 LSF + a_3 LDEP + a_4 LMKS + a_5 LRR \\ + a_6 LDD + a_7 LLI + d_1 dumin + d_2 dumcr + \gamma_1 s1 + \\ \gamma_2 s2 + \gamma_3 s3$$

$$(6.10)$$

Residuals from the three equations were all stationary, estimated by critical values in tables provided by Mackinnon 1990. Calculated values were more negative than the critical values and the series were therefore cointegrated. The calculated values were:

-6.55622 for large banks
-5.3687 for small banks
-5.3057 for foreign banks.

Table 6.10
Dickey-Fuller and Augmented Dickey-Fuller tests: part 2

Large banks	DF (logs)	ADF (logs)	First differences (DF)	First differences (ADF)
LALBTSETA(T)	-9.5034	-6.3081	-14.8700	-10.381
LALDEP (NT)	-3.8922	-2.0275	-14.2641	-6.8897
LALMKS(T)	-7.3207	-3.6831	-16.4932	-8.2347
LALLD(NT)	-6.8929	-4.7724	-12.9524	-7.7309
LALSF(T)	-4.9953	-3.5915	-12.3201	-13.726
LALI(NT)	-7.9651	-5.4375	-13.6748	-9.3323
Small banks				
SMLBTSETA(T)	-4.9049	-3.6572	-11.9512	-9.2892
SMLDEP(T)	-4.4169	-2.7848	-10.8989	-8.2434
SMLMKS(T)	-5.7457	-5.0778	-10.4160	-8.2161
SMLLD(T)	-3.7909	-2.7848	-10.0139	-6.2380
SMLI(NT)	-6.8549	-4.3029	-13.8389	-8.6462
SMLRR(T)	-4.0866	-3.1096	-10.6807	-7.3367
SMLSF(T)	-7.2453	-5.0551	-13.1956	-10.301

The residual was then included in a second equation in first differences to derive an Engle-Granger two step error correction model. For large banks that equation is of the general form

$$LLABTSETA = a_0 + a_1 LLATB + a_2 LLASF + a_3 DLLADEP + a_4 LLAMKS$$
$$+ a_5 DLLARR_{t-3} + a_6 DLLALD + a_7 DLLAI_{t-1} + RESID_{t-1}$$
$$+ d_1 dumin_{t-1} + d_2 dumcr_{t-1}$$

$$(6.11)$$

The equation for small banks (prefix SM) is given by

$$LSMBTSETA = a_0 + a_1LSMTB + a_2LSMSF + a_3DLSMDEP + a_4LSMMKS$$
$$+ a_5DLSMRR_{t-3} + a_6DLSMLD + a_7DLSMLI_{t-1} + RESID_{t-1}$$
$$+ d_1dumin_{t-1} + d_2dumcr_{t-1}$$

$$(6.12)$$

and the equation for foreign banks is given by

$$DLNLBTSETA = a_0 + a_1LNLTB + a_2LNLSF + a_3DLNLDEP$$
$$+ a_4DLNLMKS + a_5LNLRR_{t-3} + a_6DLNLLD$$
$$+ a_7DLNLLI_{t-1} + RESID\ t-1 + d_1dumin_{t-1}$$
$$+ d_2dumcr_{t-1}$$

$$(6.13)$$

The first letter denotes the first difference and the second the log and the following two the identify the group. Seasonal dummies are added to equations (6.11), (6.12) and (6.13). Coefficients of the residuals from the cointegrating equations were: for large banks -0.325 (t-value -1.94), for small banks -0.749 (t-value -4.31) and foreign banks -0.807 (t-value -4.34).

6.2.9 Profitability: large banks: Barbados

The results of the long run equation for large banks was as follows

$$LABTSETA = 0.960 - 0.006LLATB + 0.407LLASF + 0.009LLADEP$$
$$(-0.358)\quad (-1.011)\quad\quad (2.34)\quad\quad (0.019)$$

$$+ 0.04LAMKS - 0.354LLARR - 0.072\ LALD\ -0.018LAI$$
$$(0.146)\quad\quad (-3.55)\quad\quad (-0.270)\quad\quad (-0.421)$$

$$-0.032dumin - 0.47dumcr$$
$$(0.567)\quad\quad (-0.902)$$

$$(6.14)$$

The coefficients of the cointegrating equation represent long run elasticities and the coefficients of the ECM provide the short run impact. The results of the ECM are shown in Table 6.12.

Reserve requirements continued to be negatively associated with bank profitability, even of large banks. The elasticity coefficient was -0.32 in the model adjusted for short run dynamics. Interest rate controls and credit limits did not affect the profitability of large banks in the long run suggesting that for large banks regulatory resilience was rather strong. The presence of a local bank in this bank group contributed to a problem of normality in the series. Results suggest that larger banks may be able to cushion some of the impact of regulation on profitability. Also, inspection of the data indicates that large banks tend to be less profitable than small banks - a result which supports the views of Benston (1973) and Rhodes and Savage (1981) that large banks experience little in the way of economies of scale.[3] The market share variable for large banks was positive but not significant. A positive and significant sign would have been necessary to support the above view, but lack of significance of this variable did not permit its rejection for the Barbados case.

6.2.10 Profitability: small banks: Barbados

Similar equations were run for small banks (denoted by prefix SM), where the prefix (L) denotes the loglinear form. The long run cointegrating equation is given by

$$LSMBTSETA = 0.602 + 0.674LSMTB + 0.062LSMSF + 0.294LSMDEP$$
$$(0.082) \quad (4.31) \quad\quad (0.187) \quad\quad (0.372)$$

$$-1.84LSMKS -0.431LSMRR -0.125LSMLD - 0.014LSMI$$
$$(0.464) \quad\quad (-1.42) \quad\quad (-1.86) \quad\quad (-0.374)$$

$$+0.38dumin -0.32dumcr$$
$$(2.35) \quad\quad (-3.35)$$

$$(6.15)$$

Where the symbols are as before, treasury bill yields(TB), staff expenses (SF), deposits (DEP) market share (MKS) in the case of the group this refers to the market share of the group, reserve requirements (RR), loans deposit ratio (LD), interest rate spreads (I), the interest rate control variable (dumin) and the credit control variable (dumcr).
Results of the corresponding error correction model are displayed in Table 6.12.
Diagnostic results disclosed no signs of serial correlation using either the Durbin Watson tests for non autocorrelated errors or the Lagrange multiplier test [Breusch and Pagan (1980)] and no sign of heteroscedasticity based on the regression of the residuals on squared fitted values.

169

Small banks were most affected by credit controls. This variable was significant at the 5% level, its effect on BTSETA was -0.74, after adjusting to take account of its inclusion both in the cointegrating equation and in the ECM (see methodology at page 194). It was negatively associated with bank profitability. As with the entire banking system, interest rate controls were positively associated with bank profitability, again contradicting the generally held view of commercial banks that interest rate setting by authorities adversely impacts on bank profitability. There was some evidence of a problem of normality in the series and using the method of variable deletion it was attributed to the market share variable and seems related to the take-over of a small bank.

6.2.11 Profitability: foreign banks: Barbados

Similar regressions were run for foreign banks. Results of the cointegrating equation in loglinear form provided long run elasticities and were as follows.

$$LNLBSETA = -6.73 -0.433LNLTB -0.536LNLSF + 1.48LNLDEP$$
$$(-2.73) \quad (-5.26) \quad (-1.46) \quad (+2.94)$$

$$-1.84LNLMKS \quad - 0.401LNLRR + 0.711 \, LNLLD - 0.38LNLI$$
$$(-2.06) \quad (-1.82) \quad (1.70) \quad (-1.76)$$

$$0.074dumin - 0.185dumcr$$
$$(0.765) \quad (-2.22)$$

$$(6.16)$$

Where the prefix L denotes the log and the prefix NL denotes non-local or foreign. Additional tests for stationarity relevant to foreign and local banks are presented in Table 6.11.

LNLBTSETA denotes profits before tax plus staff expenses of foreign banks and LNDEP denotes deposits as a ratio of total assets of foreign banks. LNLMKS denotes market share of foreign banks. All other variables are the same except that the prefixes L and NL are added to denote log linear form (L) and with application to foreign banks (NL). The I(1) variables are LNLTBR, LNLTDPA, LNLMKS LNLRR, LNLLD, LNLI and LNLSF.

Results indicate that both in the long run and the short run, required secondary reserve requirements have punitive implications for the profitability of foreign banks. The t-value was significant and negative at the 5% level, and its elasticity was 0.40 in the long run model. Increasing size seemed to be associated with declining profitability of foreign banks in the long run model as indicated by the coefficient of the market share variable which was negative and significant. Credit controls were negatively associated with the profitability of foreign banks, but interest rate controls did not seem to influence the profitability of foreign banks, either negatively or positively.

Table 6.11
Dickey-Fuller and Augmented Dickey-Fuller tests: part 3

Variable	DF (logs)	ADF (logs)	First diff DF	First diff (ADF)
Foreign banks				
LNLBTSETA (NT)	-5.3497	-3.4064	-14.2631	-11.210
LNLMKS(T)	-2.0341	-1.9129	-9.6019	-5.1711
LNLRR(T)	-3.6892	-2.4041	-11.7522	-6.9961
LNLLD(T)	-2.9166	-2.7747	-8.9081	-7.6727
LNLI(NT)	-2.9454	-2.1829	-10.6286	-6.6162
LNLSF(T)	-3.2231	-4.4276	-14.2130	-9.4367
LNLDEP(T)	-5.8620	-2.7018	-17.0038	-7.0912
Local banks				
LBCBTSETA(NT)	-8.2739	-5.6210	-13.1585	-9.5003
LBCSF(NT)	-13.7269	-4.0404	-3.9130	-3.4875
LBCMKS(NT)	-8.3972	-2.1892	-23.1372	-8.9994
LBCRR(T)	-2.6832	-2.0476	-9.6543	-6.0871
LBCLD(T)	-2.8259	-4.5307	-13.1913	-5.2691
LBCI(NT)	-4.9579	-1.3699	-15.7772	-3.4875

'Diff' is a shortened form of difference. The prefix (BC) denotes local banks and (NL) foreign banks.

This equation tended to explain approximately one third of the fluctuations in bank profitability. However, since the objective of the exercise is not to formulate the determinants of bank profitability but rather to establish whether the selected variables influenced bank performance, the low multiple coefficient of determination simply indicated that regulatory variables do not explain all changes in bank profitability.

6.2.12 Local banks: Barbados

Modelling local banks proved very difficult, as local banks, among which is a government owned bank, did not seem to respond to the same impulses as other commercial banks. A levels model was used for the modelling of local banks because of the negative numbers in the series. Most diagnostics for local banks were acceptable but there was some abnormality in this series for the reason mentioned earlier.

In the case of local banks a cointegrating equation and an Engle-Granger two-step error correction model were employed. The result for reserve requirements was quite perverse. Most significantly, reserve requirements were positively associated with the profitability of local banks. This was the only category of bank where profitability was not negatively associated with reserve requirements. Government securities appear to have constituted a major income earning asset for local banks implying that returns on non-government held assets of local banks are relatively lower than those of foreign banks, so that higher reserve requirements would not have reduced profitability since earnings for the bank as a whole were lower. Also, the positive association of reserve requirements with bank profitability of local banks suggests that there might be a deposit-maximising aspect of reserve requirements with respect to local banks [Courakis (1984)] and that depositors may have felt safer in placing funds with local banks as reserve requirements increased (see Chapter 2).

Credit controls were, however, negatively associated with the profitability of local banks and suggest that, like small banks this category of bank depended rather heavily on credit to the personal sector, a controlled category of credit.

The interest rate coefficient, was positive but was not sufficiently significant to confirm the hypothesis of cost-axiomatic pricing. Generally, bank regulation explained the profitability of local banks to a much lesser extent than that of other banks or of the system as a whole. The negative sign of the market share variable suggests that local banks become less profitable as they increase in size and may indicate premature expansion of local banks.

While the equation was cointegrated (the ADF for the residual from the cointegrating equation was -5.556 compared with a critical value of -2.91) there was considerable abnormality in the series and results of the ECM are not therefore reported. Though results of the long run cointegrating equation are reported, results must be interpreted as only tentative (Table 6.13).

Table 6.12
Barbados: regulation and profitability: large, small and foreign banks
(ECM model - in logs)

Description	Large (LA)		Small (SM)		Foreign(NL)*	
C	0.186 (0.137)		-8.28 (1.58)		0.492 (0.801)	
LTB	-0.006 (-0.09)		0.018 (0.130)		-0.003 (-0.009)	
LSF	0.296 (1.57)		0.322 (0.885)		-0.048 (-0.678)	
LDEP	-0.086 (-1.82)*		-0.71 (-0.60)		0.404 (0.66)*	
LMKS	0.200 (0.693)		-1.33 (1.49)		-0.87 (-0.563)*	
LRR_{t-3}	-0.320 (-3.21)*		-0.27 (0.63)*		-0.879 (-2.95)	
LLD	0.086 (0.873)		-1.04 (-1.44)*		0.127 (0.23)*	
LI_{t-1}	-0.001 (-0.09)		0.03 (0.83)*		-0.246(-0.96)*	
$dumin_{t-1}$	0.089 (1.33)		-0.065 (-.467)		-0.042 (-0.551)	
$dumcr_{t-1}$	-0.091 (-1.49)		-0.080 (-2.66)		-0.021 (-2.29)	
$resid_{(t-1)}$	-0.325 (1.94)		-0.749 (-4.31)		-0.807 (-4.34)	
R^2	0.327	-	0.446	-	0.457	-
R bar squared	0.19	-	0.333	-	0.348	-
D.W	2.10	-	2.00	-	2.20	-
F statistic (10,49)	2.48	-	3.95	-	4.20	-
Misspecification MS1 [χ^2 (1)] MS2[F (4,47)]	0.042	0.034	6.99	6.36	0.28	0.227
Normality N [χ^2,(2)]	7.41	-	7.17	-	0.473	-
Hetero LM (2) F[1,59]	0.309	0.301	0.239	0.377	2.17	2.17
Ser Cor χ^2 (4) F [4,45]	7.11	1.72	1.71	0.329	5.06	1.04

(T-values are placed in brackets next to the coefficients.)
The prefix 'L' denotes logs. The symbol '*' denotes the first difference.

Table 6.13
Barbados: regulation and profitability:
cointegrating equation: local banks
(in levels)

Description	Coefficient	
C	0.185	(0.138)
TB	0.034	(-1.70)
SF	0.468	(0.591)
DEP	0.011	(-0.122)
MKS	-2.21	(-2.02)
RR	0.036	(1.72)
LD	0.379	(0.790)
I	-0.046	(-0.943)
dumin	0.122	(0.921)
dumcr	-0.219	(-2.92)
R^2	0.308	-
R bar squared	0.132	-
D.W.	7.06	-
F statistic (12,47)	1.75	-
Misspecification MS1 [$\chi^2(1)$ MS2 [F (1,51]	1.13	0.884
Normality N[χ^2 (2)]	11.33	-
Heteroscedasticity LM (1) F [1,62]	0.579	0.566
Serial Correlation χ^2 (4) F(4,48)	1.633	0.301

(T-values are placed in brackets next to coefficients.)
(Results are based on quarterly data from 1977q1 to 1992q4.)

174

6.2.13 Regulation and profitability: Jamaica

In the case of Jamaica, profitability data were available only on an annual basis and required the use of more parsimonious models. The exchange rate (ER) and the bank rate (BKR) assume much greater importance in the Jamaica case since a flexible exchange rate regime existed for most of the period. Because of the short length of the series, some of the non-regulatory variables used in earlier OLS regressions for Barbados were dropped in order to maximise on the number of degrees of freedom. All regulatory variables were however retained.

The equation employed for testing regulation and profitability in Jamaica was in log linear form and was as follows:

$$JLROA = a_0 + a_1 JLRR + a_2 JLI + a_3 JLER + a_4 JLBKR + a_5 JLINF + d_1 dumcr + d_2 dumin$$

(6.17)

where the prefix (L) denotes the log of the variable and the prefix (J) indicates that the data are for Jamaica. Tests for stationarity revealed that all variables in the six variable system (plus dummies) were I(1).

The cointegrating equation in loglinear form was as follows

$$JLROA = 0.239 - 0.299 JLRR + 0.321 JLI + 0.135 \ JLER - 0.352 JLBKR$$

$$\begin{array}{cccc} (0.151) & (-1.51) & (1.17) & (0.485) \\ (-0.991) & & & \end{array}$$

$$+ 0.245 JLINF - 0.025 Jdumcr - 0.040 Jdumin$$

$$\begin{array}{ccc} (9.841) & (-0.098) & (-0.170) \end{array}$$

(6.18)

An error correction was developed and results are presented in Table 6.14.

The exchange rate emerged as one of the most important factors influencing the profitability of commercial banks in Jamaica in the ECM equation adjusted for short run dynamics (Table 6.14). This variable was significant at the 5% level and supported the view that commercial bank profitability improved with devaluation and with a depreciating exchange rate. The equation however explained only 30% of the variation in bank profits. The interest rate control variable (dumin) and the interest rate spread variable (DI) were both positive and significantly associated with bank profitability (the latter at the 10% level).

Reserve requirements were negatively related to bank profitability at just about the 5% level. Surprisingly, controls on sectoral credit were positively associated with bank profitability. This differed from the result for Barbados

175

and tends to confirm the assertion by banks in Jamaica who responded to the questionnaires, that the controlled sector was not necessarily the sector offering the highest return, as was the case for Barbados (see Table 6.14 and Questionnaire responses 4.b).

6.2.14 Regulation and bank profitability: Trinidad and Tobago

A similar approach to testing was applied to the case of Trinidad and Tobago. Tests were run on annual data because of the data difficulties. Variables were first tested for stationarity and Dickey Fuller and Augmented Dickey Fuller tests applied. All variables were I(1).

Reserve requirements proved to be the single most important factor influencing the profitability (ROA) of banks in Trinidad and Tobago. The sign of the credit control variable was negative but not significant, reflecting the mildness of credit controls in Trinidad and Tobago.

There was no interest rate control in Trinidad and Tobago and very limited credit control. The latter was represented by a dummy variable which took the value one when controls were in place and the value zero when they were not.

Results confirm that the range of regulatory measures used in Trinidad and Tobago was much more limited than in the case of Barbados and Jamaica and that reserve requirements (or the liquid assets ratio as it was termed in Trinidad and Tobago) and to a lesser extent the bank rate were the more important regulatory variables.

6.2.15 Causality tests: reserve requirements and bank profitability

In view of the consistently negative association between reserve requirements and bank profitability, Granger causality tests were conducted to ascertain whether the relationship between reserve requirements and bank profitability was causal. Tests are based on the premise that if past values of X are better predictors of Y then it is likely that X causes Y. Tests were conducted for the case of Barbados, Jamaica and Trinidad and Tobago. Results showed no causality for Jamaica and Trinidad and Tobago, but showed causality between reserve requirements and bank profitability in the Barbados case with the direction of causality running from reserve requirements to profitability.

Table 6.14
Jamaica and Trinidad and Tobago:
regulation and bank profitability: ECM

Description	Jamaica	Trinidad and Tobago
C	-1.41 (-1.88)	-0.13 (-0.52)
DRR	-0.136(-1.99)	-2.08 (-2.88)
DI	0.56 (2.01)	-2.93 (-0.49)
DER	0.075 (2.80)	-0.21 (-0.16)
DBKR	-0.986(-2.28)	-0.03 (-1.58)
DINF	1.83 (1.40)	0.225 (0.46)
DM	-	1.05 (1.91)
DTB	-	0.781 (0.89)
dumcr	0.947(1.69)	-0.052(-0.17)
dumin	0.285 (1.76)	-
$resid_{t-1}$	-0.504(-2.11)	-0.771(-1.89)
R^2	0.628	0.665
R bar squared	0.298	0.282
D W	1.40	1.78
F statistic	1.90	1.74
Misspecification F(1,11) χ^2 (1,11)	3.61 2.00	3.63 1.76
Normality N χ^2 (2)	0.135	0.657
Hetero F (1,17) L (7,1)	3.55 3.93	0.079 0.029
Serial Correlation F (1,11),χ^2 (1)	3.61 2.00	4.44 5.38

(T-values are placed in brackets next to coefficients. The prefix 'D' denotes the first difference.)
(Results are based on annual data - 1975-92.)

Table 6.15
Granger causality tests:
(running from reserve requirements to bank profitability)

	Restricted	Unrestricted
constant	0.125 (1.76)	0.247 (2.12)
ROA(-1)	0.310 (2.42	0.325 (2.54)
ROA(-2)	0.071 (0.546)	0.098 (0.806)
ROA(-3)	0.079 (0.608)	0.002 (0.017)
ROA(-4)	0.297 (2.39)	0.320 (2.75)
RR(-1)	-	0.017(1.07)
RR(-2)	-	-0.003 (-.161)
RR(-3)	-	-0.061 (-3.21)
RR(-4)	-	-0.038 (-2.24)

(T-values are placed in brackets next to coefficients.)

The test for causality applied is based on an F statistic that is calculated by estimating the expression following in both the constrained and unconstrained forms.
Where:

$$F_1 = \frac{SSE_r - SSE_u \ / m}{SSE_u \ / (T - 2m - 1)}$$

(6.19)

Where SSE_r, SSE_u = residual sum of squares of the reduced and unrestricted models respectively
T = number of observations
m = number of lags.
Results using the F test show a critical value of 3.53 compared with a test statistic of 2.10 for 8 degrees of freedom and 53 observations; confirming causality in the Granger sense from reserve requirements to bank profitability. Reliance on extra statistical support on which to base causal claims [Zellner (1979), Holland (1986) and Bassman (1988)] seem to provide 'a priori' grounds for a case for Granger causality.

178

6.2.16 Summary of results on bank profitability

Results suggest that regulation impacted bank profitability more in the Barbados case than in Jamaica or in Trinidad and Tobago, but reserve requirements were negatively associated with bank profitability in all cases. The result tends to confirm the tentative conclusion reached earlier in support of the views of Ramakhrisnan and Thakor (1984) and Osborne and Zaher (1992) that the cost of reserve requirements are partly borne by equity holders and that reserve requirements constrain the size of the banking firm. Indications are that profitability increases with the level of concentration in the banking industry but large banks are not necessarily more profitable than small banks. Also, the impact of reserve requirements on profitability appears to be causal in the Granger sense for the Barbados case. Residuals from the cointegrating equations when included in the ECMs were negative and significant. The size of the coefficients suggest that much of the response was in the short term and that the response to regulation was not totally a long run response. This was particularly the case for Barbados and tends to support the views of Fry (1988) and Brown (1991) that in countries with fixed exchange rates monetary regulation is not a long term solution. This may have implications for the sustainability of the regulatory system and may find support in the views of Brown (1991) that high levels of monetary regulation are not sustainable over the long term.

The views of Stiglitz and Weiss (1981) that regulated ceilings on lending do not necessarily affect bank profitability (since higher rates will be accompanied by higher risks and therefore greater losses) were not borne out by the results for Barbados. Benston's (1972) observation that large banks are not necessarily more profitable than small banks is supported, based on results for Barbados.

Generally, results for the Barbados case tend to confirm the views of Bourke (1988) that regulation tends to depress profitability. For the case of Jamaica and Trinidad and Tobago this applies to reserve requirements only.

6.3 Regulation and bank risk: results of regressions

Diagnostic tests for the ECM with bank risk as the dependent variable indicate that there were no signs of heteroscedasticity but there was some serial correlation in the LM version, but not in the F version, so that the Kiviet (1985) conclusion that the F version is more relevant in small samples is relied upon. The residual was significant at the 10% level and had a value of -7.09 and was more negative than the ADF critical values as confirmed by tables provided by Mackinnon (1990). The series was therefore stationary. Risk is measured in this study by the variance of profits and is a sub-set of bank profitability. Profit variability is defined as the difference between expected profit and actual profit. Expected profit is defined as the average of the prior four years' profit.

6.3.1 Regulation and bank risk: Barbados

OLS regression results indicate that risk increases with the incidence of reserve requirements but declines with the incidence of interest rate controls. A possible inference is that interest rate controls may help to protect banks from increased risk. The overall outcome for monetary controls and bank risk therefore depends on which particular monetary measure predominates, but depending on the measure used by authorities, risk may either increase or decrease as a result of monetary measures. Risk is represented by the variable (RISK) and is I(1), having a calculated test statistic of -5.9068 compared to a critical ADF value of -2.9084. Other stationarity test results are as in Table 6.1.

The cointegrating equation includes capital as an explanatory variable. Results are as follows:

$$RISK = 1.71 - 2.77LTB - 4.96LM - 6.3LSF + 13.11RR + 0.037LI$$
$$(-0.295) \quad (-2.61) \quad (-4.51) \quad (-2.01) \quad (5.01) \quad (0.025)$$

$$-1.42LLD \quad -0.541dumcr \quad +1.39dumcr \quad -1.39LCAPB$$
$$(-0.400) \quad (-.847) \quad (2.40) \quad (-1.58)$$

$$+0.655s1 \quad +0.948s2 \quad +1.14s3$$
$$(1.44) \quad (2.07) \quad (2.24)$$

$$(6.20)$$

Both in the long run and in the ECM uncertainty of profits was influenced principally by reserve requirements. This variable was significant and positive at the 1% level. Results suggest that as reserve requirements increase banks may attempt to maintaining profitability by assuming greater risk. This tends to give support to the view that portfolio risks increase with the incidence of reserve requirements. Whether this is a result of increased lending to the more productive high risk sectors cannot be inferred from the results. The equation explained approximately 50% of the variability of profits.

Results indicate that risk increases with credit controls. The coefficient of this variable was significant at the 5% level. The sign of the capital variable

180

suggests that risk declines with increasing capital, but the coefficient, though greater than unity and therefore tending to confirm the views of bank supervisors, was not significant at the 5% level.

Lack of significance of the coefficient for the concentration ratio fails to support the Galbraith-Caves hypothesis [Galbraith, (1967)], [Caves,(1970)] that there exists a negative relationship between bank concentration and risk, and that there is risk avoidance behaviour in concentrated markets.[4] (The t-value was however, greater than unity). Similarly, lack of significance of the interest rate spread variable did not support the findings of Mingo (1978) that where banks do not rely on interest payments to attract deposit funds, there tends to be more non-price rationing which may lead to higher bank risk, though his views with regard to a positive association of reserve requirements and bank risk were supported.

6.3.2 Regulation and bank risk: Jamaica

Results of the ECM for the Jamaica case disclosed that risk was not associated with reserve requirements nor with any of the regulatory measures. The exchange rate was the principal factor explaining bank risk (see Table 6.19).

6.3.3 Regulation and bank risk: Trinidad and Tobago

The equation for bank risk in the case of Jamaica and Trinidad and Tobago was also cointegrated. In Trinidad and Tobago case, bank risk was measured by the variability of profits and was positively associated with reserve requirements. The coefficient of this variable was significant at the 5% level, even though Trinidad and Tobago is considered a mildly regulated environment. Results of the ECM are displayed in Table 6.17.

6.3.4 Conclusion

A negative sign on the credit control variable is required to support the views of Fry (1988) that credit controls discourage risk-taking. While this was so in the case of Trinidad and Tobago, the variable was not significant. The Fry (1988) view is consistent with the views of commercial banks that controls on lending did not lead to increased credit to the high-risk sectors, but the relevant variable was not significant. Reserve requirements were however positively related to bank risk in two of the three cases, supporting the Mingo (1978) view with regard to the association of reserve requirements and bank risk. A possible interpretation is that higher levels of reserve requirements force banks into taking greater risks in order to maintain profitability.

181

Table 6.16
Barbados:
regulation and bank risk: error correction model

Description	Coefficient	
C	0.079	(0.028)
LTB	-0.426	(-0.616)
DLSF	-9.21	(-3.13)
DLM	-7.57	(-0.84)
DLRR	7.52	(2.63)
DLLD	3.57	(0.52)
LCON	0.140	(0.205)
LI	0.854	(0.560)
$resid_{t-1}$	-0.904	(-5.39)
$dumin_{t-1}$	-0.410	(-0.72)
$dumcr_{t-1}$	0.482	(0.88)
R^2	0.565	-
R bar squared	0.472	-
D.W.	2.15	-
F statistic (11,51)	6.03	-
Misspecification MS1 $[\chi^2(1)]$ MS2 [F (1,47]	0.546	0.437
Normality $N[\chi^2 (2)]$	4.92	-
Heteroscedasticity LM (1) F [1,61]	0.013	0.012
Serial Correlation $\chi^2 (4)$ F(4,47)	6.19	1.28

T-values are placed in brackets next to the coefficients.
The prefix 'D' denotes the first difference.
(Results are based on quarterly data from 1977q1 to 1992q4.)

Table 6.17
Jamaica and Trinidad and Tobago:
regulation and bank risk: ECM

Description	Jamaica		T'dad & Tobago	
C	-4.62	(-0.426)	-0.246	(-0.552)
DRR	1.59	(0.604)	7.49	(2.32)
DTB	-4.24	(-0.576)	3.39	(1.91)
DI	-3.49	(-0.344)	-3.04	(-0.252)
DM	-	-	4.53	(3.48)
DER	6.48	(2.47)	2.15	(0.95)
DBKR	-5.20	(-1.02)	-	-
DINF	6.13	(0.285)	1.04	(1.35)
dumin	0.932	(0.278)	-	-
dumcr	2.93	(0.417)	-0.204	(-0.373)
$resid_{t-1}$	-1.21	(-1.86)	-1.02	(-2.73)
R^2	0.809	-	0.86	-
R bar squared	0.554	-	0.653	-
D.W.	2.38	-	1.72	-
F statistic	3.17	-	4.06	-
Misspecification MS1 $[\chi^2(1)]$ MS(2)[F(1,5]	7.66	5.21	0.945	0.289
Normality N[χ^2 (2)]	0.556	-	0.945	-
Heteroscedasticity LM (1) F [1,62]	1.13	1.06	0.963	-
Serial Correlation χ^2 (4),F [1,13]	2.57	1.03	0.007	0.005

(T-values are placed in brackets next to coefficients. The prefix 'D' denotes the first difference.) (Results are based on annual data from 1975-92.)

6.4 Regulation and liquidity: results of regressions

Excess liquidity was defined as commercial bank holdings of cash and government securities in excess of required amounts as a percentage of total assets (LIQ). A general reaction function was formulated for the liquidity equation. The equation was of the form

$$LIQ = a_0 + a_1 LTB + a_2 LM + a_3 LCON + a_4 LRR + a_5 LLD + a_6 I$$
$$+ d_1 dumin + d_2 dumcr + \lambda_1 s1 + \lambda_2 s2 + \lambda_3 s3$$

(6.21)

6.4.1 Barbados: regulation and liquidity

Equations in levels were employed because of the problem of negative values, stationarity was established and a cointegrating equation formulated. Results of the error correction model are displayed in Table 6.18.

The error correction model produced an R^2 of 0.79, and an R bar squared of 0.76. (Table 6.18.) Diagnostic tests were conducted to ascertain whether the linear regression analysis satisfied classical assumptions of homoscedasticity and serial correlation of the unobservable disturbance term. Tests for serial correlation employ Durbin-Watson tests for non auto-correlated errors and Lagrange multiplier tests [Breusch and Pagan (1980)]. The normality test is a test of skewness and kurtosis based on Bera and Jarque (1980). While there was no heteroscedasticity, and no problems of normality or misspecification, there was serial correlation of the residuals using the χ^2 LM version, though the results of the F version were acceptable. This is usually more reliable for small samples. Reserve requirements as expected were negatively associated with bank liquidity and the coefficient was significant at the 5% level. Credit controls were positively associated with liquidity and were significant at the 10% level, giving support to the views of King (1986) that credit limits increase the liquidity of banks.

Tests were also conducted employing the average lending rate and the savings rate as separate variables as opposed to simply applying the single interest spread variable. Results indicate that as interest rates rose liquidity declined but the coefficients of the variables were not significant. The interest rate control variable was not significant at the 5% level but was greater than unity and was negatively related to liquidity. The credit control variable was positive and significantly associated with liquidity and conforms to expectations since controls on credit will lead to unplaced

184

funds and to excess liquidity (see below).
The result of that equation can be written:

$$LIQ = 52.15 -0.004M2 -0.266RR +0.026CON -0.157TB$$
$$(11.39) \quad (-3.95) \quad (-2.16) \quad (1.30) \quad (-1.31)$$

$$-50.69LD -0.141SAVR -0.191LR -0.57dumin$$
$$(-9.37) \quad (-0.617) \quad (-0.731) \quad (-1.11)$$

$$+0.95dumcr +0.505s1 +0.893s2 +0.043s3$$
$$(1.99) \quad (1.29) \quad (2.22) \quad (0.104)$$

$$(6.22)$$

(The notation (SAVR) refers to the minimum savings rate and the notation (LR) to the average lending rate.)

R^2 0.914   R bar squared   0.892
DW 2.19
F statistic (12,47) 41.61
Diagnostic tests were as follows:
Misspecification χ^2 (1) 3.850   F (1), (1,44) 3.07
Normality χ^2 (2) 1.35
Heteroscedasticity (1) 1.88   F (1,57) 1.88
Serial Correlation $\chi^2(4)$ 3.52 F (4,41) 0.650

The process of testing revealed that the loan-deposit ratio and the reserve requirement variable appear to be collinear in that the coefficient on the latter increases in significance only when the loan deposit variable is excluded from the equation.

6.4.2   Impact of regulation on bank liquidity: by bank type

OLS regression equations partitioned according to small, large, foreign and local banks confirmed varying responses by each group to regulatory measures (Table 6.19, 6.20 and 6.21). Results for large banks are not reported as they did not differ particularly from results for the entire system.

In the ECM formulation, regulatory changes impacted more on the liquidity of foreign banks. Reserve requirements were negatively associated with excess liquidity of small and foreign banks. The latter result is surprising given the access of foreign branch banks to the resources of the parent.

185

Table 6.18
Barbados:
regulation and liquidity:
ECM

Description	Coefficient	
C	1.03	(0.607)
TB	-0.020	(-0.336)
DM	-0.007	(-2.06)
SF	-1.99	(-0.558)
DLD	-42.97	(-8.87)
DRR	-0.415	(-3.30)
dumin	-0.113	(-0.271)
dumcr	0.487	(1.75)
$resid_{t-1}$	-0.914	(-7.44)
R^2	0.792	-
R bar squared	0.757	-
D.W.	2.05	-
F statistic (9,53)	22.53	-
s.e.	1.01	-
Misspecification MS1 [$\chi^2(1)$] MS2 [F (1,52]	0.044	0.036
Normality N[χ^2 (2)]	0.562	-
Heteroscedasticity LM (1) F [1,61]	0.446	0.435
Serial Correlation χ^2 (4) F[4,49]	10.22	2.37

The symbol (D) denotes the first difference. T-values are placed in brackets next to coefficients.

The result tends to confirm the views of commercial banks that foreign borrowing was used only as a last resort, since evaluation in the light of their liquidity positions (see Appendix 4.b) suggests that when they do borrow abroad, deficits on required liquidity levels have already been incurred.

Credit controls seemed to influence the liquidity of small banks more so than of foreign banks. As credit controls were imposed, small banks became less liquid. This may be explained by the movement of business away from large banks (who may have exceeded their credit limits) toward smaller banks. Surprisingly, the liquidity of local banks was not strongly affected by monetary regulation. This suggests that where such liquidity difficulties exist, that the source may not be monetary regulation as is sometimes believed.

In Chapter 4 it as observed that the response of individual banks to reserve requirements depends on initial liquidity conditions. The figures at Appendix 6.4 display liquidity ratios of banks by group. Banks which are highly loaned relative to deposit levels, will experience greater liquidity difficulty in adjusting to reserve requirements than banks with lower loans deposit ratios. Appendix 6.4 suggests that small banks are more likely to experience liquidity difficulties than other banks because of initial conditions. This conforms with results of the ECM for small banks whose levels of excess liquidity declined as reserve requirements increased (Table 6.19).

6.4.3 Regulation and liquidity: Jamaica

Reserve requirements were positively associated with bank liquidity in Jamaica. Since it is unlikely that banks would voluntarily hold excess cash and securities, the logical conclusion is that monetary controls in the form of reserve requirements were imposed when liquidity was already high. Credit controls and interest rate controls were negatively associated with liquidity. Depreciation of the exchange rate was associated with declining excess liquidity, possibly because liquidity was already mopped up by increases in reserve requirements.

6.4.4 Regulation and liquidity: Trinidad and Tobago

In the case of Trinidad and Tobago, monetary regulation had only a weak association with regulation of bank liquidity. Reserve requirements were negatively associated with excess liquidity, but at the 10% level of significance. Results support the view of King (1986) that credit limits lead to a build up of liquidity by banks. Changes in the exchange rate in Trinidad and Tobago did not impact on liquidity (Table 6.23) compared with the case of Jamaica where this variable was quite significant (Table 6.22).

Table 6.19
Barbados:
regulation and liquidity: ECM: small banks
(levels)

Description	Coefficient	
C	5.37	(0.861)
SMTB	0.014	(0.091)
DSMDEP	0.197	(2.03)
DSMRR	-0.003	(-2.68)
DI	-1.51	(-1.78)
SMMKS	-0.062	(-0.455)
DSMLD	2.08	(0.325)
Dumin	-0.576	(-0.548)
Dumcr	-0.392	(-2.412)
$resid_{t-1}$	-0.907	(-7.48)
R^2	0.582	-
R bar squared	0.501	-
D.W.	1.89	-
F (10,52)	7.24	-
Ser Cor χ^2 (4) F (4,48)	1.74	0.341
Misspecification $X^2(1)$	1.12	0.929
Normality χ^2 (2)	3.41	-
Heteroscedasticity χ^2 (1) F (1,61)	3.52	3.61

T-values are placed in brackets next to the coefficients. The prefix 'D' denotes the first difference. Results are based on quarterly data from 1977q1 to 1992q4.

Table 6.20
Barbados:
regulation and liquidity: cointegrating equation and ECM:
foreign banks

Description	Foreign banks (cointegrating equation)		ECM	
C	0.614	(0.516)	0.014	(0.19)
NLTB	0.051	(5.53)	0.053	(2.11)
NLDEP	0.023	(3.77)	0.016	(1.51)
NLRR	-0.029	(-2.96)	-0.039	(-2.10)
NL1	0.256	(1.92)	0.187	(1.12)
NLMKS	-2.29	(-2.36)	-3.25	(-1.65)
NLLD	1.06	(2.06)	0.294	(.417)
dumin	0.069	(0.73)	0.031	(.457)
dumcr	-0.147	(-2.14)	-0.059	(-.918)
$resid_{t-1}$	-	-	-0.98	(-5.38)
R^2	0.662	-	0.492	-
R bar squared	0.534	-	0.394	-
D.W.	2.11	-	1.98	-
F	7.01	-	5.04	-
ser cor χ^2 (4) F (4,47)	6.06	1.23	3.22	0.647
Misspecification	0.977	0.775	5.52	4.89
Normality	13.47	-	1.457	-
Heteroscedasticity χ^2 (1) F (1,62)	3.09	-	0.405	0.394

(T-values are placed in brackets next to the coefficients.)
(Results are based on quarterly data for the period 1977q1 to 1992 q4.)

189

Table 6.21
Barbados:
regulation and liquidity:
local banks ECM

Description	Coefficient	
C	3.97	(1.37)
DBCTB	-0.227	(-0.29)
DBCSF	1.071	(0.755)
DBCDEP	-0.634	(-2.32)
DBCRR	0.642	(1.01)
DI	- 3.80	(-1.51)
dumcr	- 1.00	(-0.511)
$resid_{t-1}$	0.416	(-3.40)
R^2	0.535	-
R bar squared	0.450	-
D.W.	2.14	-
F stat	6.28	-
Normality	0.305	-
Heteroscedasticity χ^2 (1) F (1,62)	3.89	4.03
Serial Correlation χ^2 (4) F (4,45)	7.16	1.53

(T-values are placed in brackets next to coefficients.)
(Results are based on quarterly data for the period 1977q1 to 1992q4.)

Table 6.22
Jamaica:
regulation and liquidity:
cointegrating equation: long run

Description	Coefficient	
C	34.11	(10.54)
JRR	0.231	(5.66)
JER	-0.506	(-2.87)
JI	0.135	(1.28)
JLOAD	0.602	(4.69)
JDEP	-0.698	(-7.32)
dumin	-2.48	(-3.54)
dumcr	-26.07	(-8.49)
R^2	0.929	-
R bar squared	0.858	-
D W	2.54	-
F statistic	13.16	-
Misspecification F (1,11) χ^2 (1)	1.82	0.850
Normality N χ^2 (2)	7.15	-
Heteroscedasticity F (1,17) LM (1)	3.98	4.51
Serial Correlation F (1,11), χ^2 (1)	2.34	1.12

(T-values are placed in brackets next to the coefficients.)
(Results are based on annual data for the period 1975-92.)

Table 6.23
Trinidad and Tobago: regulation and liquidity: ECM

Description	Coefficient	
C	-1.28	(- 0.72)
DTRR	-1.08	(-1.77)
DTB	-2.20	(-1.86)
DTI	1.96	(2.85)
DTM	0.005	(1.97)
DTINF	0.238	(1.19)
DTBKR	0.669	(0.793)
DTER	1.76	(0.918)
dumcr	3.48	(1.85)
$resid_{t-1}$	-1.00	(-6.24)
R^2	0.908	-
R bar squared	0.790	-
D W	2.19	-
F stat	7.72	-
Misspecification LM (1) F (1,11)	2.32	0.948
Normality N χ^2 (2)	0.677	-
Heteroscedasticity LM (1) F(1,17)	0.571	0.522
Serial Correlation F (1,11) χ^2 (1)	0.647	0.237

(The prefix (D) denotes first differences.)
(T-values are placed in brackets next to coefficients.)
(Results are based on annual data for the period 1975-92.)

6.4.5 Conclusion: regulation and liquidity

Generally, banks in Trinidad and Tobago where credit controls were mild, tended to be more illiquid than banks in Jamaica and Barbados where credit controls were more binding, suggesting that credit controls may be associated with higher liquidity levels of banks (see also Table 3.20). This is borne out by cases of Barbados and Jamaica, and contrasts with that of Trinidad and Tobago.

The views of King (1986) that credit controls increase the liquidity of banks, are supported both in the case of Barbados and Trinidad and Tobago for banks as a whole, though results for individual bank groups differ. How changes in reserve requirements translated into adjustment in excess liquidity levels was shown to depend on initial conditions. Banks which were more liquid had greater tolerance for reserve requirement increases. Small banks were more adversely affected.

6.5 Regulation and bank solvency: results of regressions

6.5.1 Regulation and bank solvency: Barbados

Analysis of the role of capital has focused so far on the effects of changes in bank capital on bank performance as measured by bank profitability. We now alter the role of the capital, so that it becomes the dependent variable in a regression equation with the other variables on the right hand side. The objective of the OLS regression is now to test the impact of monetary regulation on solvency, as represented by capital.

Results of the ECM using the Engle-Granger two step with capital, reserves and borrowing as the dependent variable are shown in Table 6.24. The adjusted multiple correlation coefficient was rather low at 0.20. Results showed that capital was positively associated with reserve requirements and suggest that reserve requirements are associated with improved prudential standards.

OLS regressions run to test the impact of regulation on solvency as a performance measure show that for banks as a whole, reserve requirements were positively related to capital, suggesting that there may be no conflict between monetary and prudential objectives Table (6.24). While reserve requirements were positively association with capital in the ECM formulation at the 5% level, the interest rate control variable for all banks was negative and carried a t-value of -1.77 and was therefore significant at the 10% level. However, credit controls were not related to solvency.

193

Diagnostic tests of the ECM for all banks disclosed no sign of misspecification employing Ramsey's (1969) reset test for functional form misspecification and the normality test which applied a test of skewness and kurtosis based on Bera and Jarque (1980) was also acceptable. However, there were signs of serial correlation, but for a χ^2 (4) reading this was not serious, and the F version was acceptable. There were signs of heteroscedasticity but White's heteroscedasticity-consistent standard errors showed little change in the results (see Table 6.24).

6.5.2 Testing regulation and bank solvency by bank group

Tests using narrowly defined capital were conducted only for local banks. (They are required to hold stipulated levels of capital against local operations). In this regression it is assumed that 'actual' capital and reserves are representative of 'required' capital and reserves, since the experience is that banks tend not to hold excesses of capital over required amounts.

6.5.3 Local banks

Employing capital as a dependent variable, tests were conducted for local banks. (Local banks are required to hold stipulated levels of capital against local operations). In this regression it is assumed that 'actual' capital and reserves are representative of 'required' capital and reserves. There was some serial correlation of the residuals so that results are rather tentative. In the long run model (see below) the interest rate control and reserve requirement variables were both significant and negatively associated with capital, but in the ECM monetary regulation of local banks is consistent with prudential objectives.

The results of the long run model are

$$BCSOLV = 2.04 - 0.021BCTB - 0.714BCSF + 6.73\ BCMKS$$
$$\quad\quad (0.57)\quad (-1.12)\quad\quad (-0.93)\quad\quad\quad (3.20)$$

$$- 0.033BCRR\quad -0.255BCLD\quad -0.008\ DEP\ -0.189\ dumin$$
$$\quad (-3.21)\quad\quad\quad (-0.55)\quad\quad\quad (-0.575)\quad\quad (-1.77)$$

$$- 0.107\ dumcr\ +\ 0.053s1\ +\ 0.020s2\ +\ 0.036s3$$
$$\quad (-1.02)\quad\quad (0.573)\quad\quad (0.218)\quad (0.362)$$

$$(6.23)$$

Table 6.24
Barbados:
regulation and bank solvency (all banks)
Engle-Granger two step: ECM

Description	Values		White's adjusted s.e	
C	-0.029 (-0.04)		-0.029 (-0.04)	
TB	-0.015 (-0.94)		- 0.015 (-1.50)	
SF	0.426 (0.51)		0.427 (0.479)	
DM	-0.016 (-0.95)		-0.007 (-1.17)	
CON	0.006 (1.48)		-0.006 (2.41)	
DRR	0.057 (1.91)		0.057 (2.69)	
DLD	-3.31 (-2.94)		-3.31 (-1.57)	
$resid_{t-1}$	-0.221 (-1.92)		-0.222 (-1.72)	
dumin	-0.105 (-1.11)		-0.105 (-1.15)	
dumcr	0.067 (0.75)		-0.067 (0.991)	
R^2	0.326	-	-	-
R bar squared	0.197	-	-	-
D.W.	2.32	-	-	-
F statistic (10,52)	2.52	-	-	-
Ser. Cor χ^2 (4) F (4,48)	6.02	1.27	-	-
Misspecification χ^2 (1) F (1,51)	1.34	1.38	-	-
Normality χ^2 (2)	14.43		-	-
Heteroscedasticity χ^2 (1) F (1,61)	12.17	12.19	-	-

(T-values are placed in brackets next to coefficients. The prefix 'D' denotes the first difference. Results are based on quarterly data from 1977q1 to 1992q4.)

Table 6.25
Barbados: regulation and solvency (local banks)
ECM

Description	Coefficient
DC	0.008 (0.124)
DTB	-0.007 (-0.443)
DSF	0.053 (0.166)
DMDEP	0.014 (2.26)
DMKS	5.45 (5.18)
DRR	-0.012 (-0.855)
DLD	-1.26 (-4.08)
DI	-0.041 (-1.70)
dumin	-0.039 (-1.685)
dumcr	-0.020 (-0.495)
$resid_{t-1}$	-0.176 (-2.03)
R^2	-0.637 -
R bar squared	0.62 -
D.W.	1.62 -
F statistic	8.45 -

(T-values are placed in brackets next to coefficients.)
(Results are based on quarterly data from 1977q1 to 1992q4.)

Results suggest that in the case of local banks, in the model adjusted for short run dynamics, that reserve requirements are positively related to capital, but in the cointegrating equation the relationship of reserve requirements and solvency is negative. The signs on the credit control variable are negative but not significant. Overall, the relationship between monetary and prudential regulation remains equivocal (Table 6.25).

6.5.4 Regulation and bank solvency: Jamaica

The equation to establish the relationship of bank regulation and bank solvency was of the form

$$JSOLV = a_0 + a_1JRR + a_2JBKR + a_3JI + a_4JLOAN + a_5JDEP + a_6JNF + a_7jdumin + a_8jdumcr$$

$$(6.24)$$

The equation was cointegrated and the residual when tested for stationarity had a calculated value of -4.21 compared with a critical value for ADF1 of -3.71.

In the cointegrating model, interest rate controls were inversely associated with the solvency of banks and the removal of controls was accompanied by improved bank solvency (results not shown). In the ECM formulation which took account of short run dynamics, monetary controls were negatively signed but not significant. The results, though not conclusive, are consistent with a negative impact of controls on bank solvency and give support to views about possible conflicts between monetary controls and prudential regulations.

This OLS regression accounted for 86% of the variation in bank solvency measured by R bar squared, but suffered from a high level of heteroscedasticity. Results are not reported and any conclusions must be tentative.

6.5.5 OLS: Regulation and solvency: Trinidad and Tobago

Reserve requirements were positively associated with bank solvency in the Trinidad and Tobago case, but, credit controls were negatively associated and at the 1% level of significance (Table 6.26). The bank rate, which was quite heavily used in the post-1985 period carried a negative sign and was significant at the 10% level.

197

Table 6.26
Trinidad and Tobago: regulation and solvency
(Error correction model)

Description	Coefficient	
C	-0.916	(-0.81)
DRR	1.49	(2.98)
DTB	-0.002	(1.51)
DI	-0.353	(-0.67)
dumcr	-4.03	(-3.37)
DM	-0.002	(-1.51)
DBKR	-1.01	(-1.78)
DER	2.51	(2.06)
DINF	0.301	(2.34)
$resid_{t-1}$	-0.825	(-2.47)
R^2	0.807	-
R bar squared	0.519	-
D W	1.92	-
F stat	2.80	-
Misspecification χ^2 (1) F (1,11)	6.23	3.19
Normality χ^2 (2)	0.761	-
Heteroscedasticity LM(1) F(1,17)	0.739	0.678
Serial Correlation $\chi^2(1)$, F (1,11)	0.207	0.056

T-values are placed in brackets next to coefficients. The prefix 'D' denotes the first difference. Results are based on annual data from 1975-92.

Though regulation in Trinidad and Tobago was relatively mild, there was a surprising degree of negative association between regulation and solvency. This is consistent with the fact that of the three countries, Trinidad and Tobago experienced more solvency problems and banks there appeared more unstable. Solvency was positively associated with a depreciating exchange rate, suggesting that exchange rate liberalisation may in some circumstances (contrast the case of Chile and Argentina) be accompanied by improved solvency of banks. This compares with the case of Jamaica where solvency also improved with exchange rate depreciation.

6.5.6 Conclusion: regulation and solvency

Results of tests of the impact of regulation on bank solvency indicate mixed results. Results suggest that in Trinidad and Tobago that regulation is associated with lower solvency for the case of credit controls but is positively associated with reserve requirement, the more important monetary measure. This is a comforting result since authorities tend to increase reserve requirements when banks are experiencing solvency problems. Results for Barbados suggest that most monetary regulations were associated with prudential objectives. Interest rate controls tended to impact negatively on bank solvency, but the case of reserve requirements was unclear. Credit controls were negatively associated with solvency only for the case of Trinidad and Tobago.

6.6 Regulation and market share: results of regressions

Results of regressions run with commercial banks' market share relative to non-banks as the dependent variable confirm that market share was lost by commercial banks to non-banks as the size of the banking system increased.

6.6.1 Barbados: regulation and market share (MKS): all banks

The Engle and Granger two-step method was applied using the residual from the levels model to define a relationship which captured both long run and short run changes. Results continued to confirm that in the model adjusted for short run dynamics, the market share of commercial banks was influenced mostly by reserve requirements. Secondary reserve requirements and control of interest rate spreads were the two most significant explanatory regulatory variables. Results support the view that reserve requirements and interest rate controls contributed to reduced market share of commercial banks (Table 6.27). The long run elasticity of reserve requirements was 0.08 (not reported).

Table 6.27
Barbados:
regulation and market share:
cointegrating equation and ECM

Description	Cointegrating equation		ECM	
C	5.10	(1.74)	0.031	(2.26)
TB	-0.001	(-3.04)	0.004	(1.05)
SF	-0.032	(-0.202)	-0.008	(-0.591)*
M	-0.083	(-1.68)	-0.006	(-0.115)*
RR	0.018	(1.27)	-0.035	(-2.52)*
LD	-0.024	(- 1.27)	-0.047	(-1.51)*
I	-0.008	(-1.14)	-0.002	(-0.313)
dumin	-0.002	(-1.91)	-0.001	(-2.064)
dumcr	0.005	(2.17)	-0.007	(-0.247)
$resid_{t-1}$	-	-	-0.901	(-6.51)
R^2	0.979	-	0.528	-
R bar squared	0.974	-	0.437	-
D.W	1.86	-	2.16	-
F statistic (10,52)	203.2	-	5.83	-
Misspecification χ^2 (1), F (1,48)	0.790	0.625	0.030	0.024
Normality (2)	0.687	-	1.98	-
Heteroscedasticity χ^2 (1) F (1,51)	2.62	2.64	0.438	0.427
Serial Correlation χ^2 (4) F(4,48)	0.891	1.66	3.94	0.80

(T-values are placed in brackets next to the coefficients. The symbol * denotes those variables which are first differenced. Results are based on quarterly data from 1977q1 to 1992q4.)

200

Surprisingly, the credit control variable did not impact on market share in the short run but was associated with declining market share in the long run. This is possibly explained by the fact that the requirement that prospective borrowers place minimum down-payments was made applicable to non-banks as well, even though limits on credit outstanding to non-priority sectors did not apply to these institutions until 1984.

Interest rate spreads were not significantly associated with market share, but interest rate controls were negative and significant at the 5% level. The result gives support to the view that interest rate controls may have been cost axiomatic, but also tends to support the view that interest rate spreads may have been insufficiently wide to prevent banks from losing market share to non-banks or to prevent the exit of new small banks from the industry, so that cost-axiomatic pricing seemed insufficient to prevent the loss of market share. Loss of market share to non-banks may be associated with the exit of 4 smaller banks from the industry in Barbados. The coincidence of the exit of small banks and the entry of non-banks when matched with the results obtained here could suggest some causality, but despite the high level of correlation this cannot be inferred from the data.

It is suggested that the fact of regulation of interest rates may have adversely influenced banks' market share more so than the actual spreads that resulted from the setting of rates. It gives support to the view that the fact of interest rate-setting by authorities exerts greater influence on decisions on market entry than the actual level at which rates are set. Results would tend to support the view of [Peltzman (1986)] that in highly regulated systems entry into the banking industry is below the level which would have been achieved in the absence of regulation.

The results showed an R^2 of 0.98 and an adjusted R^2 of 0.97 in the long run model and 0.608 and 0.533 in the ECM. The ECM disclosed that the most significant regulatory measure influencing market share was reserve requirements, followed by interest rate controls.

6.6.2 Maximum likelihood estimates and market share

Maximum likelihood estimates for the tests relating to market share were derived on the basis that market share is a long run phenomenon. Cointegration LR tests based on maximal eigenvalue of the stochastic matrix revealed only one vector holding the system together: the calculated statistic was larger than the critical value at the 95% level for only one vector.

I(1) variables are MKS, M, SF, RR, and the I(0) variables are CON, LD, TB ,I, dumin, dumcr, s1, s2, s3. (Money supply (M) and loans deposit ratio (LD) have seasonal variation).

The test statistic to formally evaluate the number of cointegrating vectors holding the system together is based on the trace test which is based on the hypothesis that H_2 (r) :Π =ab', that is, there are at most (r) cointegrating vectors or Π is of reduced rank r < p versus the alternative that:

$$H_1: \Delta X(t) = \sum_{j=1}^{k-1} \Gamma_j \Delta X_{t-j} + \Pi X_{t-k} + \mu + \Phi D_t + \epsilon_t, \tag{6.25}$$

The trace test is based on the likelihood ratio test defined as

$$-2\ln Q(H_2|H_1) = -T \sum_{i=r+1}^{p} \ln(1 - \hat{\lambda}_i) \tag{6.26}$$

where r is the number of cointegrating vectors, p the number of variables and λ_i the estimated eigenvalues.
Results using the Johansen procedure are presented in Tables 6.28 to 6.30.

Table 6.28
Cointegration LR tests based on maximal eigenvalues
of the stochastic matrix

Null	Alternative	Statistic	95% critical value
r = 0	r = 1	44.21	27.07
r < = 1	r = 2	23.11	20.96
r < = 2	r = 3	8.09	14.07
r < = 3	r = 4	1.52	3.76

Table 6.29 shows results of cointegration LR tests based on the trace of the stochastic matrix and confirms the presence of one cointegrating vector.

Table 6.29
Cointegration LR tests based on the trace of the stochastic matrix

Null	Alternative	Statistic	95% critical value
r=1	r > 1	44.20	47.21
r = 2	r > 2	23.11	29.68
r = 3	r > 3	8.09	15.41
r = 4	r > 4	1.52	3.76

The cointegrated vector and its weights are shown in Table 6.30.

Table 6.30
Cointegrated vector and weights

Variable	Vector	Weights
MKS	0.2155	-1.996
	(-1.000)	(0.4303)
M	0.0011	0.880
	(-0.005)	(-0.189)
SF	4.496	-0.0023
	(-20.86)	(0.0004)
RR	0.0086	1.874
	(-0.039)	(-0.404)

The normalised eigenvectors are

$$\hat{v}=(\hat{v}_1,.....\hat{v}_5); \text{ the weights are } \hat{w}=S_{0k}* \hat{v} \qquad (6.27)$$

where S_{0k} are the product moment matrices.
The equation for the Johansen model can be written

$$MKS = 0.005M - 20.86SF - 0.04RR \qquad (6.28)$$

There is a negative association of reserve requirements with market share in the long run. Results reveal that the adjustment of reserve requirements back to equilibrium, given by the average speed of adjustment back to steady state, $a = b'$ is -0.04 (see Table 6.30). The ability of banks to raise deposits (money is defined as broad money) influences market share negatively and could suggest that banks could have some difficulty in accumulating deposits.

6.6.3. Regulation and the market share of banks: by bank group Barbados

Results for individual bank groups are not reported as the main hypothesis is not the relative share of the market by bank groups but the relative share of the market of banks compared with non-banks. However, Figures 6.1, 6.2 and 6.3 clearly indicate an increasing share of the market by small banks (SMMKSHA), and by local banks (BCMKS), while large banks (LAMKSHA) have lost market share of banks as a group and hence by implication lost share of the market of banks and non-banks combined.

As in the case of foreign banks the market share of foreign banks was negatively associated with each monetary regulation measure, including interest rate controls.

The results suggest that the market share of large banks and foreign banks was most affected by regulation and that small and local banks were not. In the case of local banks, the protection from competition offered by interest rate controls may have assisted their growth as evidence by strong positive t-values for regulatory measure, hence the declining share of banks relative to non-banks would have been spurred by the relative decline in market share of large banks and of foreign banks.

Results are not reported partly because it is not the focus of the study and partly because of unacceptably high diagnostics for normality, attributable to the purchase and sale of one bank by another.

6.6.4 Regulation and market share: Jamaica

Results for Jamaica support the view that high levels of required liquid assets restrained market share. The fact of very few new entrants market entry may be associated with high liquid assets ratios (reserve requirements). Surprisingly, interest rate controls seemed positively associated with market share in the long run but controls on credit had no impact on market share in the short run. Credit controls in Jamaica applied to both banks and non-banks almost from the inception and explain why the credit control variable would not have exerted a significant influence on the market share of banks in Jamaica (Table 6.31)

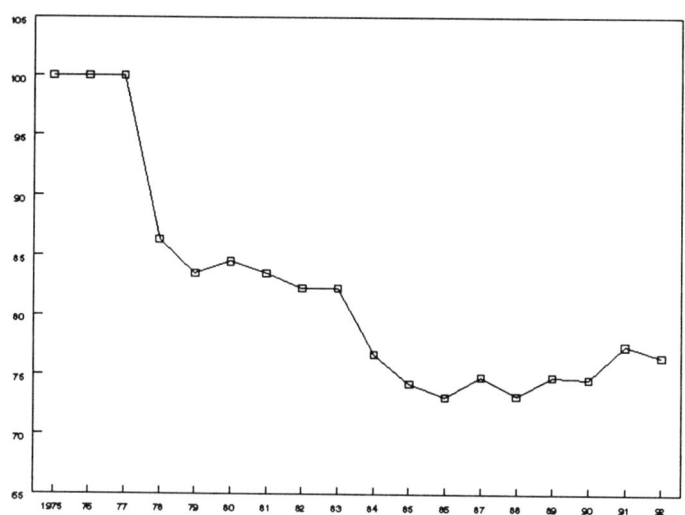

Figure 6.1 Market share: foreign banks: Barbados

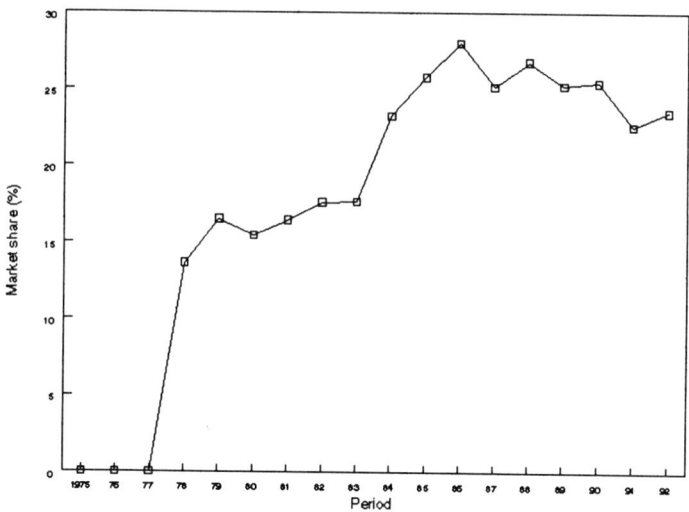

Figure 6.2 Market share: local banks: Barbados

205

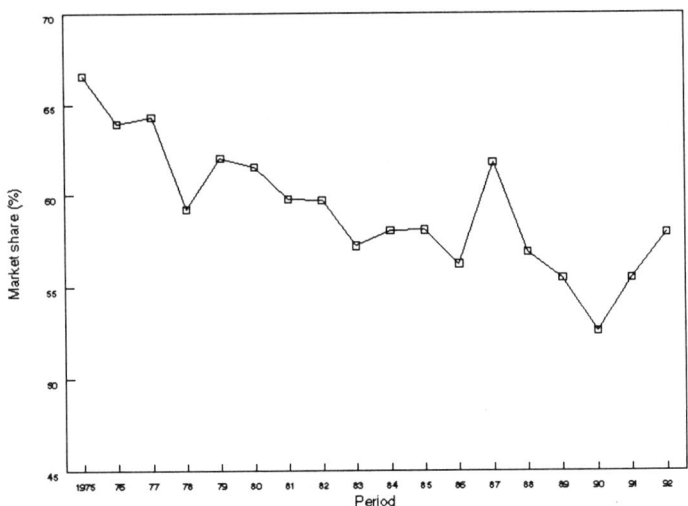

Figure 6.3 Market share: large banks: Barbados

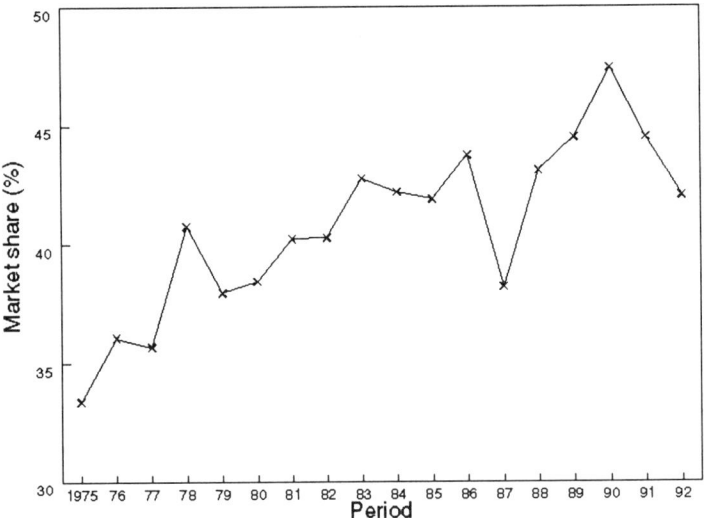

Figure 6.4 Market share: small banks: Barbados

206

Results differ for the Barbados case where credit controls were not extended to non-banks until 1984. Depreciation of the exchange rate was strongly associated with the loss of market share of banks. This tends to be confirmed by higher levels of profits which attracted non-banks to set up new business in Jamaica and tends to be confirmed by the higher level of profits which non-banks are able to make in the foreign exchange market. Interest rate spreads were negatively associated with market share, suggesting that as spreads widened and the banking system in the broad sense became more profitable and new entrants came into the market, but chose to enter the non-bank market, so eroding the market share of banks. Results of the cointegrating equation and the ECM can be seen in Table 6.31.

6.6.5 Regulation and market share: Trinidad and Tobago

In the Trinidad and Tobago case, reserve requirements and credit controls were all negatively related to market share and the coefficients were all significant at the 5 % level, supporting the view that high liquid assets ratios encouraged the entry of non-banks (Table 6.32. The sign on the exchange rate variable was negative but was not significant (1.47). These results imply that financial liberalisation of monetary controls are likely to impact positively on bank performance but that liberalisation of exchange rates seems likely to bring greater competition from non-banks.

6.6.6 Conclusion: regulation and market share

The results for market share as the dependent variable are fairly unequivocal about the negative impact of reserve requirements and to a lesser extent credit and interest rate controls on bank performance. Results support the views of Farrell (1989) that in the Caribbean context monetary and other controls prevent any meaningful level of expansion of the banking system.

Low failure rates in Barbados and Jamaica may also be associated with monetary regulation and discriminatory pricing policies, and may have resulted in the rise of non-banks and the declining share of commercial banks in the combined market share of banks and non-banks.

207

Table 6.31
Jamaica: regulation and market share:
cointegrating equation and error correction model

Description	Cointegrating equation		ECM	
C	38.63	(3.83)	-18.12	(-0.759)
JRR	0.150	(0.859)	-4.07	(-2.01)
JI	-0.255	(-0.752)	-0.374	(-2.12)
JER	-2.11	(-1.72)	-4.41	(-15.76)
JBKR	-0.231	(-1.03)	0.222	(0.930)
JINF	0.298	(5.08)	0.371	(3.50)
JDEP	-0.005	(-4.15)	-0.033	(-3.14)
JDumcr	19.81	(1.06)	5.18	(0.273)
JDumin	13.88	(4.36)	12.66	(2.62)
Resid$_{t-1}$	-	-	-0.752	(-2.47)
R^2	0.896	-	0.89	-
R bar squared	0.814	-	0.76	-
DW	2.01	-	2.64	-
F stat	10.85	-	6.38	-
Misspecification χ^2 (1) F (1,9)	0.896	0.446	4.49	1.99
Normality χ^2 (2)	0.046	-	1.69	-
Heteroscedasticity F (1,17) L(1)	4.05	-	0.012	0.011
Serial Correlation F (1,11) χ^2 (1)	0.003	0.001	4.79	2.10

T-values are placed in brackets next to the coefficients. The prefix applies
to figures in column 3.

Table 6.32
Trinidad and Tobago: regulation and market share:
Error correction model

Description	Values	
C	0.213	(0.153)
DTBKR	0.189	(0.306)
DTM	0.001	(0.594)
DTB	0.005	(0.005)
DTI	-0.468	(-0.710)
DTRR	-1.66	(-2.95)
DTINF	-0.304	(-1.87)
DTER	-2.09	(-1.47)
dumcr	-4.05	(-2.05)
$resid_{t-1}$	-0.177	(-0.823)
R^2	0.820	-
R bar squared	0.496	-
D.W.	1.94	-
F statistic	2.53	-
Misspecification MS2 [χ^2 (1)] MS1 [F (1,11]	3.70	1.31
Normality N[χ^2 (2)	0.818	-
Heteroscedasticity LM (1) F [1,17]	0.878	0.808
Serial Correlation χ^2 (4) F [1,11]	0.418	0.114

(T-values are in brackets next to coefficients. Results are based on annual data 1975-92.)

6.7 Discriminant analysis: developing a composite score

6.7.1 A composite performance index: Barbados

The analysis has so far focused on the impact of regulation on various measures of bank performance. Such an analysis gives valuable insights into the adjustment processes of commercial banks and its impact on individual performance measures, and permits authorities to predict how a particular measure will either worsen or improve in response to regulation. It is however possible to derive a composite measure of bank performance which will indicate how overall bank performance will be affected. This process involves the calculation of a composite index of performance. The process is described below.

Data are first divided into three groups or functions. Wilks' Lambda is calculated for each function using the statistical programme SPSS.[5] Eigenvalues for each function were calculated and then pooled within - group correlations between the discriminant scores and predictor variables produced. Canonical correlations were then calculated. These represented the square root of the between - group to total sums of squares. When squared they represent the total variability explained by differences between groups (Table 6.33).

Table 6.33

Canonical discriminant functions: Barbados

Fcn	Eigen value	Pct of variance	Cum pct	Canonical corr	After fcn	Wilks' lambda
					: 0	0.0001
1*	******	99.82	99.82	1.0000	: 1	0.0001
2*	178.963	0.15	99.96	0.9972	: 2	0.0224
3*	43.619	0.04	100.00	0.9887	: -	-

210

Table 6.33 cont'd
Canonical discriminant functions - Barbados

Fcn	chi-square	DF	Sig
1*	652.1116	117	0.0001
2*	283.214	116	0.0001
3*	119.642	57	0.00001

* marks the 3 canonical discriminant functions remaining in the analysis.
***** denotes very large Fcn denotes Function
cum = cumulative
Pct = percent
corr = correlation
DF = Degrees of freedom

The performance measures are the same as the earlier analysis: profitability (ROA), Liquidity (LIQ), risk (RISK), solvency (SOLV) and market share (MKS).

Table 6.34
Standardised canonical discriminant function coefficients: Barbados

	Function 1	Function 2	Function 3
ROA	0.00030	0.20662	0.97930
SOLV	-3.29606	0.00285	0.00877
LIQ	3.14287	0.98825	-0.15551

Structure matrix

The structure matrix represents pooled-within-groups correlations between discriminating variables and canonical discriminant functions. Variables are ordered by size of correlation within function.

Table 6.35
Structure matrix

	Function 1	Function 2	Function 3
LIQ	0.00030	0.97844	-0.2065
SOLV	-0.30281	0.94870	-0.0909
MKS	0.27392	-0.90361	-0.3293
RISK	0.43295	-0.85294	0.2916
ROA	0.00276	0.14688	0.9891

The eingenvalue for each function is the ratio of between group to within group sum of squares.

The entire solution is rotated with the varimax procedure to provide a simpler structure in the profiling of each function. The results are as follows:

Table 6.36
Varimax rotation transformation matrix

	Function 1	Function 2	Function 3
% Variance	95.02	2.49	2.49
Function 1	0.97566	-0.15355	-0.15658
Function 2	0.12569	0.97660	0.17452
Function 3	0.17971	-0.15059	0.97212

Table 6.37
Rotated standardised discriminant function coefficients
(Variables ordered by size of coefficient within function)

	Function 1	Function 2	Function 3
LIQ	3.21852	0.50597	0.51340
SOLV	-3.21704	0.50756	-0.50707
ROA	0.19445	0.00010	1.04335

212

Since weights which employ all variables are desired, correlations between rotated canonical discriminant functions and discriminating variables are then produced using all variables and the appropriate weights calculated as an average across each function for the Barbados case.

Table 6.38
Correlation between canonical discriminant functions and discriminating variables

	Function 1	Function 2	Function 3	Weights
ROA	-0.15661	-0.00594	0.98764	0.275
SOLV	-0.15985	0.98669	0.02970	0.285
LIQ	0.16038	0.98660	-0.02998	0.392
MKS	0.21286	-0.87494	-0.43494	0.465
RISK	0.26280	-0.94338	0.20243	0.116

The performance index can therefore be written:

$$P^* = 0.275\ ROA + 0.116\ RISK + 0.392\ LIQ + 0.285\ SOLV + 0.465\ MKS$$

$$(6.29)$$

On the basis of the above weights, performance indices were then calculated for commercial banks in Barbados (see Tables 6.41 and 6.43). A plot of these trends (Figure 6.5) demonstrates periods of improved performance, but the underlying trend is one of declining overall performance of banks in Barbados over the past 15 years. The index combines absolute and relative performances.

6.7.2 A composite performance index: Jamaica and Trinidad and Tobago

Banks as profit maximisers or market share maximisers, or both, are likely to react to regulation in predictable ways which are independent of their location. Thus having established weights for Barbados these are made applicable to Jamaica and Trinidad and Tobago and indices of performance and bank regulation can be calculated. The rationale for using the same weights is based on the similarities in the responses of banks and the

213

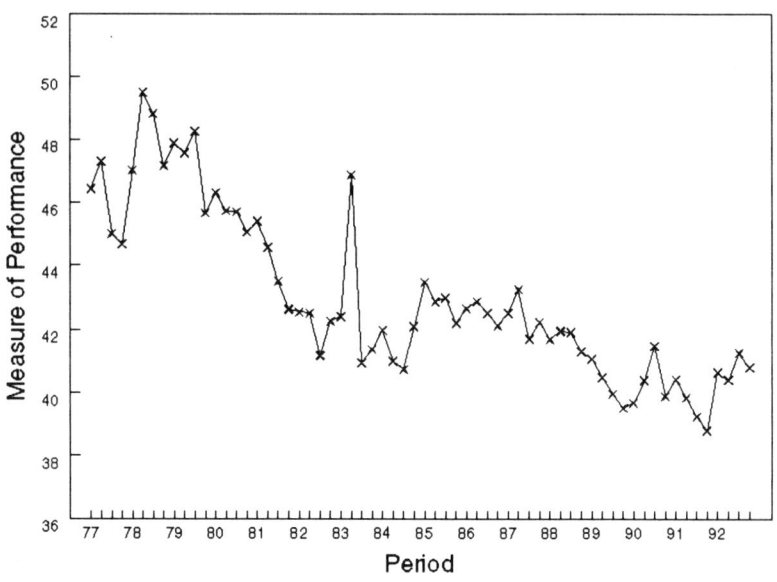

Figure 6.5 Composite index of bank performance: Barbados

assumption that companies in the same industry have the same overall objectives with regard to bank performance. This is the basis for universal application of the Altman (1984) Z score (or Zeta Score) and the basis for the general application of indices created using discriminant analysis. This is possible in the case of bank performance measures because companies are expected to use Standard Accounting Principles across countries. In the case of bank performance measures Z^* scores are therefore comparable for banks throughout the Caribbean. In the case of the regulation measure, data differences in terms of what is included in the category credit to the non-priority sectors may lead to some lack of uniformity in the indices across countries but this is not expected to be significant. Figures 6.5 and 6.6 display bank performance indices for Jamaica and Trinidad and Tobago.

6.7.3 Calculating a regulation index: Barbados, Jamaica and Trinidad and Tobago

An index of monetary and prudential regulation can be similarly created.

214

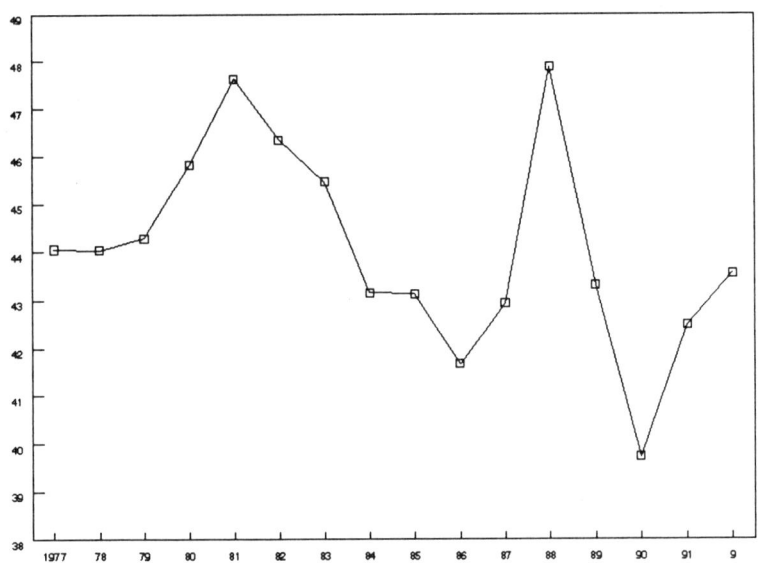

Figure 6.6 Composite index of bank performance: Jamaica

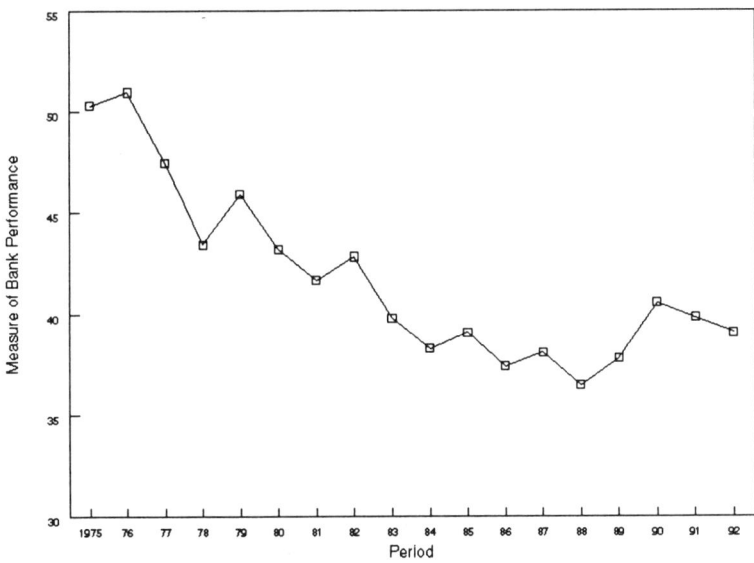

Figure 6.7 Composite index of bank performance: Trinidad and Tobago

215

Instead of dummy variables for interest rate controls and credit controls used in OLS regressions, proxies were used. Actual interest rate spreads and actual credit to the non-priority (controlled sectors) were used as proxies for controlled credit and controlled interest rates. (A preliminary run of the SPSS package for deriving discriminant scores had disclosed that the dummies were discarded by the system).

The same procedure used for calculation of the performance index was applied. A compressed form of the procedure is set out in Tables 6.39 and 6.40. Results are shown in Tables 6.42 and 6.44.

Table 6.39
Canonical discriminant functions: regulation

Fcn	Eigen value	Pct of Variance	Cum Pct	Canonical Corr	After Fcn	Wilks' Lambda
1	******	99.06	99.1	1.0000	0	0.00001
2	1102.1	0.64	99.7	0.999	1	0.00001
3	409.2	0.24	99.9	0.998	2	0.00001
4	99.2	0.06	100.0	0.995	3	0.00001

Table 6.39 cont'd
Canonical discriminant functions: regulation

Fcn	chi-square	DF	Sig
1*	919.8	236	0.00001
2*	546.5	174	0.00001
3*	329.3	114	0.00001
4*	142.8	56	0.00001

The procedure produced an index of bank regulation. Based on the procedure described earlier, a chart of the index of regulation for the Barbados case is produced below. The results display increasing levels of regulation in the period 1977-85, a decline in 1985-90 and an increase in 1991 followed by a further decline in 1992. The absolute level of regulation, however, remained high throughout the period.

216

Table 6.40
Correlation between canonical discriminant functions and discriminating variables

	Function 1	Function 2	Function 3	Function 4	Weights
RR	0.99338	0.11058	0.02620	0.0164	1.0000
CAPB	0.0058	0.91504	-0.16427	0.3684	1.121
I	-0.00013	0.29947	-0.21068	0.93055	0.2548
PERDIS	0.00067	-0.22177	0.91152	-0.34634	0.0869

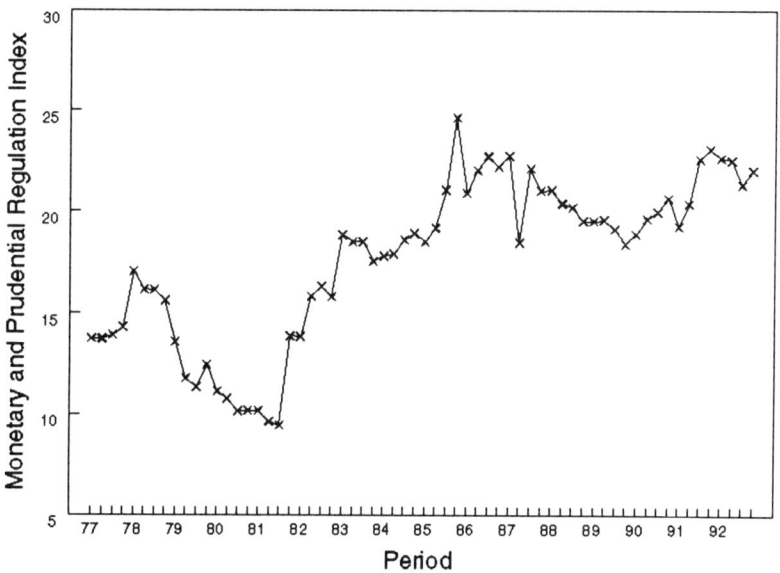

Figure 6.8 Composite bank regulation index: Barbados

The equation for the regulation index can be written

$$R^* = 1.0RR + 1.121\ CAPB + 0.255\ I + 0.086\ PERDIS \qquad (6.30)$$

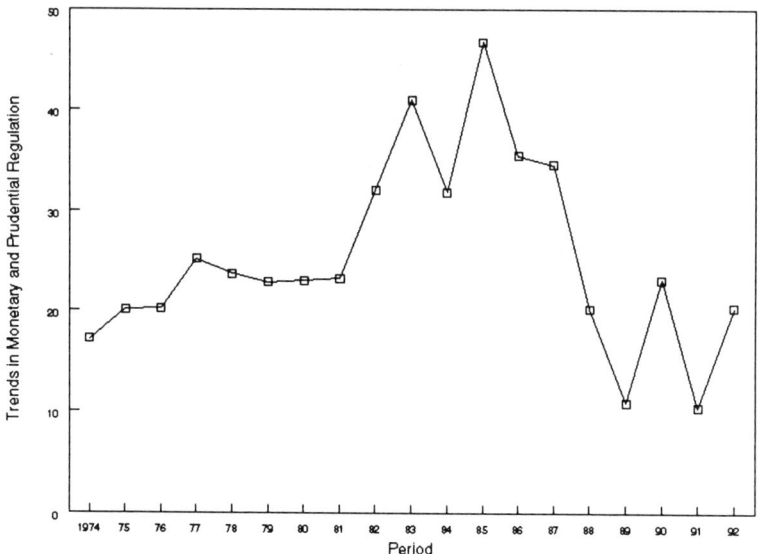

Figure 6.9 Composite bank regulation index: Jamaica

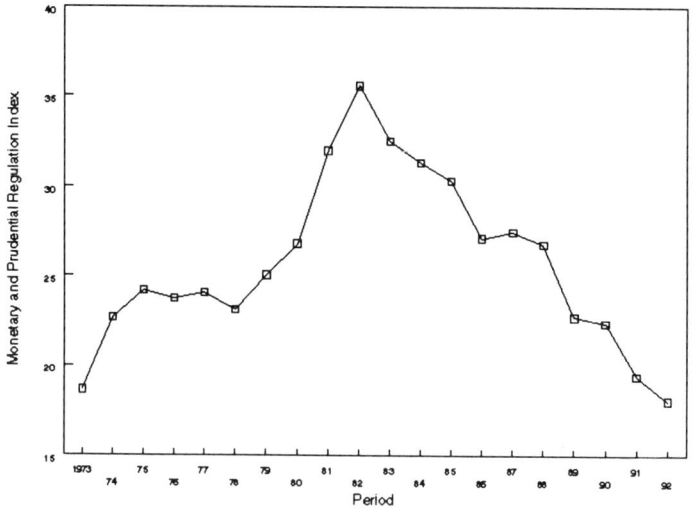

Figure 6.10 Composite bank regulation index: Trinidad and Tobago

218

Table 6.41
Index of bank performance
(normalised)
(Barbados, Jamaica and Trinidad and Tobago)

Year	Barbados	Jamaica	Trinidad and Tobago
1977	100.0	100.0	100.0
1978	105.57	99.96	91.53
1979	102.20	100.52	96.72
1980	100.84	103.99	91.04
1981	95.43	108.13	87.84
1982	94.60	105.18	90.27
1983	94.63	103.20	83.89
1984	94.23	97.96	80.71
1985	94.48	97.90	82.37
1986	94.30	94.58	78.84
1987	94.52	97.46	80.29
1988	92.46	108.69	76.85
1989	88.42	98.32	79.63
1990	89.27	90.17	85.46
1991	86.84	96.45	83.99
1992	91.32	98.87	82.35

Base year 1977 = 100

Table 6.42
Index of bank regulation
(normalised)
(Barbados, Jamaica and Trinidad and Tobago)

Year	Barbados	Jamaica	Trinidad and Tobago
1977	100.0	100.0	100.0
1978	109.16	93.91	96.18
1979	86.95	90.65	104.04
1980	70.93	91.39	111.33
1981	97.00	92.23	133.09
1982	110.38	125.58	147.99
1983	122.55	162.82	135.23
1984	132.05	126.54	130.34
1985	172.14	180.92	126.10
1986	155.29	141.15	112.10
1987	146.97	137.49	112.66
1988	136.53	80.27	114.09
1989	128.50	43.17	111.33
1990	144.46	91.67	94.45
1991	161.28	41.11	92.95
1992	153.84	80.55	80.66

Base year 1977 = 100

Table 6.43
Bank performance scores (non-normalised)

Year	Barbados	Jamaica	Trinidad and Tobago
1977	44.67	44.05	47.45
1978	47.16	44.03	43.43
1979	45.65	44.28	45.89
1980	45.05	45.81	43.19
1981	42.63	47.63	41.67
1982	42.26	46.34	42.83
1983	41.37	45.46	39.80
1984	42.09	43.15	38.29
1985	42.20	43.13	39.08
1986	42.12	41.66	37.40
1987	42.22	42.93	38.09
1988	41.30	47.88	36.46
1989	39.51	43.30	37.78
1990	39.87	39.72	40.55
1991	38.79	42.49	39.85
1992	40.79	43.55	39.07

Table 6.44
Bank regulation scores (non-normalised)

Year	Barbados	Jamaica	Trinidad and Tobago
1977	14.32	25.14	24.04
1978	15.63	23.61	23.12
1979	12.45	22.78	25.01
1980	10.15	22.97	26.76
1981	13.89	23.18	31.99
1982	15.80	32.07	35.57
1983	17.54	40.93	32.50
1984	18.90	31.81	31.33
1985	24.64	46.73	30.31
1986	22.23	35.48	27.08
1987	21.05	34.56	27.42
1988	19.54	20.18	26.76
1989	18.40	10.85	22.70
1990	20.68	23.04	22.34
1991	23.09	10.33	19.39
1992	22.02	20.25	18.05

6.7.4 Analysis of bank performance and bank regulation indices

Performance indices suggest that despite higher levels of performance in Jamaica in the early 1980s and again in 1988, bank performance in the Caribbean declined over the period measured by the calculated index of performance, but banks in Jamaica performed better than banks in Barbados and banks in Trinidad and Tobago performed poorly. Banks in all three countries appeared to recover performance levels in the period 1990-92, a period when most banking systems in the region were being liberalised in differing degrees. Improved performance appeared to be associated with the level of deregulation. This measure of bank performance differs from the bank profitability measures because of the inclusion of other measures usually omitted by banks, principally, solvency and market share.

The index of regulation shows increasing regulation in Barbados over the entire period and increasing regulation in Jamaica in the mid 1980s, but a considerable degree of liberalisation since 1985. This is consistent with the observation of Arthur Brown that the liberalisation process in Jamaica commenced at the end of 1985. For the case of Trinidad and Tobago, regulation increased in the period 1981 to 1985 and may have been associated with the tightening of prudential requirements following solvency difficulties of the early 1980s which principally involved non-banks, but which also affected banks.

Indices were calculated to a 1977 base year in order to standardise the results, though data were available for some countries for earlier periods. The indices show trends in regulation over the period but do not indicate the relative levels of regulation in the respective countries. (This can be obtained by examining the non-normalised scores (see Tables 6.43 and 6.44).) Figures 6.5 to 6.8 were based on non-normalised scores. Non-normalised scores indicate that levels of bank performance among the commercial banks in Barbados, Jamaica and Trinidad and Tobago, were relatively comparable, with the performance of banks in Jamaica on average slightly higher. The lower absolute level in the case of Barbados in the pre-1988 period seems attributable to the limited emphasis placed on capital criteria arising from the branch nature of the banking system which permits foreign branches to rely on global capital.

Using the cases of Jamaica and Trinidad and Tobago, a bold interpretation of these results would suggest that a regulation score below 20 (non-normalised scores are the appropriate scores for comparison across countries) is representative of scenarios where regulation is relatively mild (and by implication liberalisation is moderate). Similarly, bank performance scores under 40-45 represent below average performance. However, such benchmark

223

scores would need to be confirmed to have global application only after a greater number of countries have been sampled. On the basis of the three countries studied, its global application can only be tentative, but the methodology is instructive and the results, widened to offer global application should be of considerable benefit to policy makers, regulators and supervisors, particularly where off-site analysis is being relied upon.

6.8 Granger causality tests: regulation and bank performance

Despite the weight of evidence and the inference of causality in cointegrating equations, causality has not yet been unequivocally established. Granger causality tests are therefore conducted for the Barbados case employing the bank performance and regulation indices to confirm whether there is causality running from regulation to bank performance.

Table 6.45
Granger causality tests:
t - values and joint restrictions on coefficients of additional variables

	Barbados	Jamaica	Trinidad and Tobago
R*	0.792	-0.592	-2.657
R* -2	0.779	0.113	0.528
R* -3	0.773	0.005	2.041
R* -4	0.206	-1.778	2.333
Lagrange Multiplier	(5) 2.00	(4) 11.08	(4) 7.66
Likelihood Ratio	(5) 2.04	(4) 24.91	(4) 13.41
F Statistic	F (5,49) 3.45	F(4,4) 5.79	F (4,2) 1.14

In a test for unit roots the composite bank performance variable was found to be I(1) and the composite regulation score variable was I(0) at the ADF (1) level. The series was therefore differenced on the basis that if a linear combination of I(0) variables and I(1) variables is also I(0) then the relationship is cointegrated. Causality was tested in a bivariate framework for Barbados, Jamaica and Trinidad and Tobago. OLS was run on the lagged dependent variable. Up to 4 lags were included. Lags of the dependent variable were then added using variable addition. Joint tests of zero restrictions on the coefficients were applied using three diagnostic tests, the Lagrange multiplier tests, the Likelihood Ratio Statistic and the F Statistic. Tests in first differences indicated weak causality for Trinidad and Tobago applying the Lagrange multiplier and the Likelihood ratio, and stronger causality for the case of Jamaica based on two diagnostic tests. There was no causality running from regulation to performance for the case of Barbados (Table 6.44).

Economic theory would not suggest reverse causality nor would extra-statistical information discussed earlier. Tests for reverse causality were not therefore conducted.

6.9 Summary of results of empirical analysis

The four main hypotheses set out in the introduction to this thesis were, firstly, that monetary regulation impacts adversely on the performance of commercial banks, secondly that monetary regulation can conflict with the objectives of prudential regulation, thirdly, that regulators engage in cost-axiomatic pricing which mitigate some of the effects of regulation, and fourthly, that regulation depresses the market share of banks relative to non-banks. Results fully support the hypothesis on the adverse impact on bank performance and on declining market share.

Viewed as a composite group of measures (both monetary and prudential) regulation was associated with the decline in commercial bank performance. Further, causality tests confirm weak causality running from regulation to performance in the cases of Jamaica and Trinidad and Tobago. Results indicate that, except for a few years when increases were recorded, composite bank performance declined over the past 15 years in Barbados. This was especially so in the peak years of bank regulation. In the Jamaica case, peak years of regulation, coincided with low periods of bank performance. A distinct pattern of declining bank regulation is observed in Jamaica and Trinidad and Tobago since 1985 and seems associated with the monetary liberalisation of these economies and with the freeing of the exchange rate. In the Barbados case, despite the partial freeing of interest rates and the removal of credit controls, reserve requirements remain high, and explain the continuing high regulation index for Barbados compared with declining indices for Jamaica and Trinidad and Tobago.

Bank performance is more influenced by reserve requirements than by any other regulatory measure and is associated with adverse performance of several individual performance measures. The profitability of local banks

225

improved however, with increasing reserve requirements, prompting examination of the theory of growth-maximising reserve requirements for the case of local banks where reserve requirements may have offered some form of comfort to customers. In the long run, the banking system was negatively affected by credit controls in Barbados and mildly so in Trinidad and Tobago, but the profitability of foreign branch banks and small banks was more influenced by credit restrictions than was that of local banks. Regulatory resilience seemed very much determined by size and small banks had difficulty in adjusting to credit limits. However credit limits did not seem to affect local banks in the Barbados case.

Results of tests on the potential for conflict between monetary and prudential regulation are mixed. Reserve requirements are negatively associated with bank solvency in Trinidad and Tobago, suggesting a potential conflict, but the association is positive in the Jamaica case. In the Barbados case, reserve requirements are differently associated with solvency in the short run from in the long run and for the case of local banks, the correlation of capital and regulatory variables is not negative in all cases.

The hypothesis of cost-axiomatic pricing is supported by the results for the banking system in Barbados. Results suggest accommodation by regulators in their approach to the setting of interest rate ceilings and floors and contradict the conventional literature which posits that interest rate regulation impacts adversely on bank profitability - and in the case of Jamaica the theory of cost-axiomatic pricing is not rejected.

The fourth hypothesis that regulation contributes to the loss of market share of commercial banks is strongly supported by empirical analysis. Loss of market share to non-banks is principally attributable to reserve requirements. In the Barbados case, results revealed that as local banks became larger, profitability declined.

Some of the other issues cited were supported by the empirical analysis and others were rejected. Results suggest that equity holders bear some of the cost of increases in reserve requirements through the relationship of dividends to bank profitability and hence to equity. This was indicated for all three countries. The views Stiglitz and Weiss (1981) that regulated credit ceilings do not affect bank profitability are not supported by results for the Barbados case but results for the Trinidad and Tobago case are neutral. However, weak support, is found for this view in the case of Jamaica and this is attributable to the fact that in the Jamaica case there was no ceiling on lending rates so that banks could price in relation to their perceptions of bank risk and unrestrictedly trade-off risk against return. The view of Mingo (1978) that reserve requirements are associated with increased bank risk also found support in the case of Barbados and Trinidad and Tobago. However, the views of commercial banks that reserve requirements and interest rate controls are the most important factors influencing the performance of banks is supported for the case of reserve requirements and rejected for the case of interest rate controls.

A model with profitability as the dependent variable confirms that regulatory variables are important in establishing the determinants of bank profitability in the Caribbean compared with models which exclude them and the resulting model could be viewed as a model of the determination of commercial bank performance in developing countries where monetary controls are still in effect.

Results tend to support the observation of Revell (1980) that banks in countries without foreign banks tend to have higher gross margins than countries with foreign banks. However, data did not support the view that large banks are more profitable than small. Indeed, results failed to reject the views of Rhodes and Savage (1981) and Hannan (1991) that there may not be the economies of scale in banking that are frequently assumed.

Liquidity was negatively associated with interest rate spreads and declined as lending rates were raised, suggesting relatively significant price elasticity of demand for credit but the relationship between interest controls and liquidity of foreign branch banks was less significant than that of local banks and may have been influenced by the fact that foreign branches can resort to head offices abroad to ease liquidity difficulties. As expected, liquidity increased with credit controls, the exception being the case of local banks, where controls on credit seemed to lead to reduced bank liquidity.

The failure of the manufacturing sector to grow could not be attributed to interest rate controls. The examples of Trinidad and Tobago where credit controls were imposed but were not accompanied by interest rate controls, and the case of Jamaica between 1985-90 when credit controls were in place but no interest rate controls were in effect, (and where credit to the manufacturing sector grew steadily), suggest that credit to the high-risk sectors will increase more rapidly in the presence of credit controls if interest rate controls are not simultaneously in effect.

Measured by the indices calculated, except for Jamaica, the performance of commercial banks in the Caribbean was generally less than robust and declined in at least one case; simultaneously, levels of bank regulation rose up to the mid 1980s (1983-85) and declined thereafter, but remained high in Barbados up to the end of 1992.

Notes

1   The significance of this variable would have been offset by the process of adding back.

2   Regressions on a constant, a trend and a lagged level of BTSETA indicate that this variable is I(1). It also becomes I(1) for tests of ADF3 and ADF4.

3   The outturn for this group may have been influenced by the presence of a government owned bank in this category which was not subject to the same capital criteria as were other banks.

4   This is consistent with the literature on empirical work on bank profitability.

5   SPSS is a Statistical Package for Social Sciences.

7 Conclusion and implications for the future

Generally, the study demonstrates that bank performance is negatively influenced by monetary regulation. In summary, primary and secondary reserve requirements impacted adversely on profitability in all three countries but not for all bank groups, and caused profitability to decline in the Barbados case. Credit controls impacted adversely on profitability in varying degrees; more strongly in Barbados, less so in Jamaica, and hardly at all in Trinidad and Tobago. Cost-axiomatic pricing appeared to be practised in some countries but could not offset the overall impact of regulation. Regulation affected market share negatively in all three countries. Other observations include the almost total absence of entry by banks into the industry, even in the presence of wide interest rate spreads and even in times of improved bank profitability. This seems associated with the fact of regulation and not necessarily with the profitability of the banking industry. Liberalisation was associated with improved bank solvency in Trinidad and Tobago, but did not result in any increase in the number of banks over the past 20 years. The rise of non-banks in Jamaica and Trinidad and Tobago seemed associated not only with the regulation of banks but with the advantage created for non-banks particularly as a result of structural regulation which set boundaries for banks and non-banks but which were less restrictive of non-banking activity.

Though results were mixed on the question of a potential conflict between monetary controls and prudential criteria, the inference still remains that measures to protect the balance of payments via financial regulation compromise the development of commercial banks and that central banks in endeavouring to control money and credit, run the risk of restraining the development of the banking system. Capital adequacy and other prudential criteria must be consistent with monetary targeting as changes in capital requirements impact the level of economic activity particularly where the banking sector is significant relative to other sectors. Timing of prudential regulations and the length of the adjustment period needed for compliance with capitalization criteria[1] are particularly important for developing countries whose financial systems are not liberalised and where the banking system is used for achieving macroeconomic objectives. Discrete changes in regulation must therefore be based not only on considerations of safety of financial institutions but must take the adjustment process into account as well as the macroeconomic context in which the adjustment is taking place.

The study has highlighted that despite the effectiveness of monetary controls in the past, with the erosion of the monopoly of commercial banks over the financial system, monetary regulation through commercial banks can no longer be relied upon to achieve balance of payments equilibrium in an increasingly liberalised environment, so that structuralist views will require some modification. In order for the banking system to benefit from greater vibrancy and for the entire financial system to become more dynamic, monetary controls may need to be loosened. However, given the balance of payment constraints which gave rise to such controls, this will require that some means for control of the balance of payments other than direct monetary controls over the banking system be found.

Technological advances, telecommunications, information technology, advances in financial theory and globalisation of the market place will help to foster deregulation. In addition, worldwide competition will put pressure on existing structures and dramatically expand the breadth of product markets. Globally the movement toward universal banking is inexorable, and despite the risks pointed out by Gill (1983) that weaker contractual savings could result, the advantage of greater financial deepening is an alternative offered by liberalisation for developing countries with thin financial markets and underdeveloped financial instruments, which needs to be grasped.[2]

Advocates of the conservative position who argue that effective monetary policy requires narrowly defined banks are gradually giving way to advocates of the functional position who argue for an integrated system. The drawback of this holistic approach is the risk of systemic failure and 'infection'.[3] Yet limits on the permissible range of activities of different types of institutions undermine efficiency and to a lesser extent stability. The option is for regulation to be as close to neutral as possible between different financial intermediaries and markets. Such functional regulation would permit the free affiliation of various parts of the financial sector and would allow institutions to enter whatever market they choose. This would effectively avoid asset or product restrictions, which though constraining, are at the same time a central feature of current regulation.

Essentially, the study demonstrates that where banking activities are restricted, the scope for profit maximising behaviour is reduced and the banks' opportunity set is curtailed. Monetary regulation tends to inhibit competition and liberalisation increases it. In the process of determining the effects of regulation on bank performance, the study has identified a model of determination of commercial bank performance appropriate to developing countries where controls are still in place. However, the changing market will, however, alter the prescription for appropriate profit maximising behaviour and new theories of the banking firm appropriate to the new scenario are likely to evolve. Effective monetary policy as a control tool in the new structure of the financial system will probably require different transmission mechanisms. Also, monetary and prudential controls must allow for global maximisation of economic welfare and require a general equilibrium approach in both the setting of monetary policy and in the setting of structural and prudential regulations, since these are interdependent areas of control.

In the Caribbean, the experiences of the 1980s have forced policy makers to accept the deficiencies of the structuralist approach of which monetary control was a part. Indeed it is ironic that those Caribbean countries which were most wedded to the structuralist approaches have abandoned these views and now adhere to more monetarist IFI prescriptions. Countries which were more moderate in the application of these theories have managed to accept the monetarist approach of the international financial institutions while retaining some of the features in their economic structure which reflect the structuralist point of view. Examples in the Caribbean are Barbados and Trinidad and Tobago. In Jamaica and Trinidad and Tobago, for example, credit controls formed part of IMF programmes, and in the case of Trinidad and Tobago were used more during the programme period than before.

The observation of the structuralists that elasticities are lower and weaker in developing countries than in industrialised countries still apply in the Caribbean context, so that even if it might be appropriate to reject the extreme structuralist approach, there are still some elements of the structuralist views which remain relevant to the Caribbean and in some ways have not yet been completely removed from the policy prescriptions of some Caribbean countries. Also, recent research points to the view that liberalisation will not necessarily lead to higher economic growth as propounded by the liberalisation theorists led by McKinnon (1973) and Shaw (1973) and can rather lead to financial instability as has been experienced in the southern cone of Latin America.

In the Caribbean, the example of Jamaica demonstrates that when markets are fully liberalised the exchange rate can come under further pressure and inflation rates soar as countries try to seek this new competitiveness while

231

giving full rein to market forces. The complete freeing up of markets in the Jamaican economy which was announced at the start of 1991 has been accompanied by further devaluation of the dollar and by growing rates of inflation. It is worth considering whether devaluation should be sudden or whether the shift to full dependence on market forces should be a gradual process, particularly in small economies where sudden policy shifts can cause high levels of economic instability.

There remains the underlying monetarist assumption that free markets work more efficiently than imperfect markets and that state intervention should be abandoned and free markets put in their place. The study has certainly shown that bank performance declines with increases in regulation, implying that development of the banking system requires monetary liberalisation. Most Caribbean countries in structural adjustment programmes are beginning to embrace these prescriptions. However, despite the need for greater liberalisation, greater attention may need to be paid to some of the concerns of the structuralist - for example their views about institutional restraints and observations about some of the negative effects of market forces on developing economies.

Where capital markets are underdeveloped and the economies of scale do not exist, liberalisation does not ensure the same results as in large economies. The view which prevails in the banking and capital market, that markets must be of a certain minimum size to work efficiently and that markets without depth cannot function as effectively, must be transferred to policy approaches of economic management. Despite the acceptance of this view in financial circles there is only the occasional concession to the special situation of small countries and International Financial Institutions are still generally reluctant to make concessions to the constraints of size.

It is suggested that small Caribbean countries do not neatly fit into either the structuralist, the dependency or the monetarist mode, but that aspects of all three are relevant, so that a more pragmatic approach to policy prescriptions which takes into account market rigidities and special circumstances of the Caribbean is desirable. There is no doubt that liberalisation approaches to development in the Caribbean must be embraced by Caribbean countries if they are not to be left out of the global search for competitiveness. Globalisation will make it more difficult for credit controls and interest rate controls to work, and the scope for reserve requirements will be reduced. In this scenario the sequencing of the liberalisation process and the way in which structuralists' concerns are accommodated will become important. The study points to the need for further research on how monetary objectives of macroeconomic stabilisation can be achieved in a liberalised environment where banks are no longer the vehicle for giving effect to monetary controls, for in the final analysis the failure to achieve macroeconomic stability will undermine the process of financial development.

Finally, the study shows that global regulation scores and by implication (liberalisation scores) can be derived which can indicate to policy makers what are acceptable levels of regulation/liberalisation, relative to the past and to other countries. Similarly, the study develops bank performance scores for the Caribbean and lays the foundation for development of performance scores with global application. Inspection of the calculated scores would suggest that there is some level of regulation which is consistent with some level of bank performance and that if similar studies are conducted of other countries it is possible to arrive at a global benchmark measure of bank performance below which the concern of bank supervisors worldwide (and of banks themselves) is triggered, and similarly, benchmark measures of regulation above which the attention of policy makers is triggered. To derive such benchmarks with application beyond the Caribbean, would however require a sample which includes several other countries so as to give such benchmarks global application and therefore suggests an area for further research. Such indicators have the potential for facilitating improved monitoring of both the process of liberalisation and the stability of the banking system.

Notes

1   It has been suggested [Bank of England (1990)] that the agreement by Central Banks who were part of the Basle Committee, to increase capital requirements came at a time when the world economy was weak and the balance sheets of many banks found the accommodation difficult.

2   The 1933 Banking Act in the U.S., commonly referred to as the Glass-Steagall Act, was designed to separate the activities of banking and investment, ostensibly to prevent conflicts of interests. It prohibited a) underwriting of securities by the member banks, b) affiliation between banks and securities houses, c) deposit-taking by securities firms and d) management interlocks between banks and securities firms.

3   The term 'infection' refers to situations where problems of one institution create difficulties of loss of confidence in other institutions which are other wise sound.

233

Appendices

Solution via the method of Lagrange multipliers

The problem is to maximise

$$\pi = p\ (a,A)A + rA' - g(K)K - h(D)D \qquad \text{2.A1}$$

Subject to the soundness constraint

$$\tau = aA + a'A' + cC + kK + cD \qquad \text{2.A2}$$

and the balance sheet constraint

$$A' + A + C - K - D = 0 \qquad \text{2.A3}$$

The Lagrangean expression is formed from (2A.1) (2A.2) and (2A.3) eliminating C via C = (1-v)D.

$$L = pA + rA' + gK - hD + \lambda_1 (\tau - aA - a'A' - kK + cvD) + \lambda_2(A' + A - K - vD) \qquad \text{2.A4}$$

The first order conditions are

$$\frac{\delta L}{\delta A} = p_A A + p - \lambda_1 a + \lambda_2 = 0$$

$$\text{2.A5}$$

234

$$\frac{\delta L}{\delta A'} = r - \lambda_1 a' + \lambda_2 = 0$$

2.A6

$$\frac{\delta L}{\delta k} = -g_k K - g - \lambda_1 k_1 - \lambda_2 = 0$$

2.A7

$$\frac{\delta L}{\delta D} = -h_D D - h + \lambda_1 cv - \lambda_2 v = 0$$

2.A8

$$\frac{\delta L}{\delta a} = p_a A - \lambda_1 A = 0$$

2.A9

$$\frac{\delta L}{\delta \lambda_1} = \tau - aA - a'A' - kK + cvD = 0$$

2.A10

$$\frac{\delta L}{\delta \lambda_2} = A' - A - K - vD = 0$$

2.A11

The solutions to the Lagrangean multipliers are

$$\lambda_1 = 1 = p_a$$

$$\lambda_2 = -r + p_a a'$$

235

Then eliminating A' by rewriting (2.A10) as

$$\tau - aA + a'A - (a' + k) K - (a'-c)vD = 0 \qquad 2.A12$$

We are left with four equations (2.A5), (2.A7), (2.A8) and (2.A12) in four unknowns (A a,D, K).

To solve for changes is in the endogenous variable with respect to a change in soundness, total derivatives of equation (2.A5) (2.A7) (2.A8) and (2.A12) are taken, yielding

$$Ap_{AA} \frac{dA}{d\tau} + 2p_A \frac{dA}{d\tau} + (a'-a) \; p_{aa} \frac{da}{d\tau} = 0 \qquad 2.A13$$

$$- Kg_{kk} \frac{dK}{d\tau} - 2g_k \frac{dK}{d\tau} - (a' + k) p_{aa} \frac{da}{d\tau} = 0 \qquad 2A.14$$

$$-Dh_{DD} \frac{dD}{d\tau} - 2h_D \frac{dD}{d\tau} - (a - c) \; vp_{aa} \frac{da}{d\tau} = 0 \qquad 2.A15$$

$$1 -a \frac{dA}{d\tau} - A \frac{da}{d\tau} + a' \frac{dA}{d\tau} - (a'+k) \frac{dk}{d\tau} - (a'-c)v \frac{dD}{d\tau} = 0 \qquad 2.A16$$

236

Appendices to Chapter 3

Appendix 3.1

Barbados:

monetary and prudential regulatory changes: 1972-92

Effective dates		Cash reserve require -ments	Secondary reserve requirements	Credit controls + tighter -easier M = modified	Interest spreads (av lending- min savings)	Dis- count rate
1973						
q1						
q2						
q3						
q4	Dec 3	+2%	+1%			
1974						
q1	Jan 31		+1%			
	Feb 28		+1%			
q2						
q3	Sept 5	+2%	+1%			
q4	Oct 31		+1%			
	Nov 30		+1%			
1975						
q1	Mar 1					-1%
	Mar 24		+2%			
q2						
	June 1					-1%
	July 31		+1%			
	Aug 1					
q3		+2%				
q4	Oct 1					-1%

Source: Central Bank of Barbados

Appendix 3.1 cont'd
Barbados

Effective dates	Cash reserve require-ments	Secondary reserve requirements	Credit controls +tighter -easier M=modified	Interest spreads (av. lending- min savings)	Discount rate
1976					
q1					
q2 May 1					-0.5%
q3					
q4 Dec 1		+3%			
Dec 31					-1.0%
1977					
q1			+		
q2					
q3 Aug 3			+		
Aug 18	+2%				
Sept 27			-		
q4					
1978					
q1					
q2					
q3 Aug 1				-2%	
Q4 Nov 1			-	(incr)	
1979					
q1 Feb 14			-		
q2					
q3					
q4					
1980					
q1					
q2 Apr 15			- (M)	+1%	
June 1			+(M)	(decr)	
q3 Sept 22			-		
q4					

Source: Central Bank of Barbados

Barbados

Effective dates	Cash reserve require -ments	Secondary reserve requirements	Credit controls +tighter -easier M=modified	Interest spreads (av. lending - min savings)	Discount rate
1981					
q1 Jan 1				+0.5%	+3%
q2				(decr)	
q3					+8%
q4 Oct 1			+	-1%	+4%
Oct 26				(incr)	
Oct 27				-0.5%	
Nov 4		+5%		(incr)	
1982					
q1 Mar 3		+2%			
q2					
q3					-2%
q4 Oct 1					
1983					
q1					
q2 Apr 1			- (M)	-1%	
Apr 30				(incr)	-4%
Jun 30				+1%	
q3				(decr)	
q4				+0.5%	
				(decr)	
1984					
q1 Mar 9			-		
q2 Apr 19					
May20					
Jun 19			+ (M)	-0.5%	
q3 Jul 1				(incr)	
q4					

Source: Central Bank of Barbados

239

Barbados

Effective dates	Cash reserve require -ments	Secondary reserve require -ments	Credit controls +tighter -easier M = modified	Interest spreads (av lending - minimum savings)	Dis- count rate
1985					
q1 Feb 1				+1%	
q2 Apr 1				(decr)	-3%
May 15			- (M)		
May 20					
q3					
q4					
1986					
q1					
q2 Apr 1				+0.5%	-2%
Apr 3				(decr)	
q2				-1%	
q3 Sept 17		+3%		(incr)	-3%
q4					
1987					
q1					
q2 Jun 5			-		
q3			(controls		
q4			removed)		
1988					
q1					
q2					
q3					
q4					

Source: Central Bank of Barbados

240

Barbados

Effective dates	Cash reserve require- ments	Secondary reserve requirements	Credit controls +tighter -easier M=modified	Interest spreads (av lending- min savings)	Discount rate
1989					
q1					
q2					
q3 Sept 20			+ controls		+3.5%
q4 Oct 16			reinstated		
Dec 4					+2%
1990					
q1					
q2 Jun 1			-(M)	+0.5%	
q3				(decr)	
q4					
1991					
q1				(0.9%)	
q2				(incr)	
q3 Aug 1	+2%				
Aug 15	+1%		-	Determined	
q4 Oct 16				by banks	+2.5%
Nov 1				after Aug 1	
Dec 31				(-1.1%incr)	
				by bks	
					+2%
1992				(-1.4%	
q1			-	increase	
q2			(controls	by banks)	
q3 July 1			removed	(-0.4%	-3%
Aug 1	-2%		May 1 '93)	increase	
Sept 15				by banks)	-3%
Sept 28					
q4					

Source: Central Bank of Barbados

Appendix 3.2
Jamaica:
monetary and prudential regulatory changes: 1973-92*

Effective dates	Cash reserve requirement	Liquid assets ratio (includes cash)	Credit controls +tighter -easier M = modified	Minimum interest rate on savings deposits	Discount rate (bank rate)
1973					+1
q1				+1/2%	(Jan 1)
q2				to 4%	
q3		+2.5%		(Feb)	
q4		Dec			
1974					+2%
q1				+2%	Jan 24
q2		+1.5%		to 6%	
q3		May	+(M)	(Feb)	
q4			Nov		
1975					-1%
q1					Feb 19
q2					
q3	+1%				
q4	Dec 12				
1976					
q1					
q2					
q3					
q4					
1977					
q1		+2%			
q2		Mar 21			
q3					
q4					
1978					
q1					
q2					
q3	Aug 1				
q4					

* Selective credit controls were first introduced in November 1969, and control of the prime rate in May 1969 and control of both the savings and prime lending rates in July 1972. The Bank of Jamaica commenced payment on cash reserve (clearing account balances) in October 1984. Source: Central Bank of Jamaica.

Effective dates	Cash reserve require -ments	Liquid assets ratio	Credit controls +tighter -easier M = modified	Interest spreads (prime -min savings)	Dis- count rate
1979		40%		-(M)	
q1		voluntary		Feb 15	
q1					
q3					
q4					
1980				(Credit	
q1				ceilings	
q2				established	
q3				(personal and	
q4				distribution))	
1981					
q1					
q2					
q3					
q4					
1982					
q1					
q2					
q3					
q4					
1983					
q1		+6%			
q2		voluntary			
q3		ratio of 40%			
q4		terminated			

Source: Central Bank of Jamaica

Jamaica

Effective dates	Cash reserve requirements	Liquid assets ratio (excludes cash)	Credit controls +tighter -easier M = modified	Minimum savings deposit rate	Discount rate
1984 q1 q2 q3 q4	+2% Jan 25 +2% Mar 12 +1% May 11 +2% Sept 30 +2% Oct 22	+4% Feb 9 Voluntary liquid assets ratio reintroduced at 44% permitting up to 50% Formalised 01.11.84	Credit ceilings on private sector 12% Jan 24	to 12% (Feb) +1% to 16% (Sept) +1% to 13 % (Nov)	+1% to 13% Jan 25 +1% to 14% Aug 8 +2% to 16% Oct 16
1985 q1 q2 q3 q4	+1% to 15% Apr 4 +2 to 17% June 6 +2% to 19% June 21 +1 to 20% July 8	+4% to 48% *certificates of deposits introduced Nov 18	+ global ceilings Aug 3 + tightening of global credit June 11 Credit ceiling removed except consumer credit Oct 10	+2% to 15%, Feb +3% to 18% Apr +3% to 20% May	+1 to 17% Feb +4 to 21% Apr 1
1986 q1 q2 q3 q4		Feb 1 48% to 44% May 1 44% to 38%	+ August consumer credit tightened controls on personal and distribution reinstated	-4% to 16% May -1% to 15% Aug	

Source: Central Bank of Jamaica

244

Jamaica

Effective dates	Cash reserve requirements	Liquid assets ratio (excludes cash)	Credit controls +tighter -easier M=modified	Minimum savings deposit rate	Discount rate (bank rate)
1987 q1 q2 q3 q4		March 26 +3% to 35%			
1988 q1 q2 q3 q4	March 30 - Interest on payment of cash reserve increased from 15% to 30%	-5% to 30% Jan 27 -5% to 25% Feb 24 -5% to 20% Mar 20			2% to 13% Sept
1989 q1 q2 q3 q4	20% to 19% July 1 termination of interest paid on cash portion of cash reserves		+ Credit ceilings reimposed Dec 31	+5% to 18% Nov	
1990 q1 q2 q3 q4	+.5% to 19.5% +.5% to 20% May 1	+5% to 25% Apr 1 +2.5% to 27.5% May +5% to 32.5% Nov 1		Savings rate deregulated (Oct)	

Source: Central Bank of Jamaica

245

Jamaica

Effective dates	Cash reserve requirements	Liquid assets ratio (excludes cash)	Credit controls +tighter -easier M=modified	Minimum savings deposit rate	Discount rate (bank rate)
1991					
q1		+1% to	credit		
q2		33.5%	ceilings		
q3	-1% from	Jan 10	removed		
q4	20% to 19%		Jan 1		
	Oct 1	-13.5% to			
		20% Apr 1			
		Schedules			
		provided			
		for			
		liquid			
		assets			
		ratio.			
1992	+2% to 21%	liquid			
q1	May 1	assets			
q2	+2% to 23%	ratio			
q3	June 1	increased			
q4	+2% to 25%	to 50%			
	July 1	July 1			

Source: Bank of Jamaica

Trinidad and Tobago:
monetary and prudential regulatory changes: 1972-92

Effective dates	Cash reserve require- ments	Liquid assets ratio (includes cash)	Credit controls +tighter -easier M=modified	Minimum savings deposit rate (not applicable)	Discount rate (bank rate)
1973					
q1					
q2		+2% to 7%			+1% to
q3		July 2			6% July
q4					
1974		+2% to 9%			
q1		Nov 27			
q2					
q3					
q4					
1975					
q1					
q2					
q3					
q4					

Source: Central Bank of Trinidad and Tobago

247

Appendix 3.3 cont'd

Trinidad and Tobago

Effective dates	Cash reserve require- ments	Liquid assets ratio (includes cash)	Credit controls +tighter -easier M=modified	Minimum savings deposit rate (not applicable)	Discount rate
1976 q1 q2 q3 q4			Minimum down payments and maximum repayment periods for consumer credit revised.		
1977 q1 q2 q3 q4					
1978 q1 q2 q3 q4	Aug 1				
1979 q1 q2 q3 q4			Selective credit control. Non-business loans restricted to 25% of incremental credit. Nov.		

Source: Central Bank of Trinidad and Tobago

248

Trinidad and Tobago

Effective dates	Cash reserve requirements	Liquid assets ratio	Credit controls +tighter - easier M=modified	Minimum savings deposit rate (not applicable)	Discount rate
1980 q1 q2 q3 q4	9% marginal reserve require- ment of 15%, Feb 2				
1981 q1 q2 q3 q4					
1982 q1 q2 q3 q4					
1983 q1 q2 q3 q4					+1.5% to 7.5% Nov 9

Source: Central Bank of Trinidad and Tobago

Trinidad and Tobago

Effective dates	Cash reserve require -ments	Liquid assets ratio (excludes cash)	Credit controls +tighter -easier M=modified	Minimum savings deposit rate (not applicable)	Discount rate
1984					+1% to 13%
q1		+2% to			Feb 9
q2		17%			+1% to 14%
q3		Nov 7			Aug 8
q4					+2% to 16%
					Oct 16
					bank rate
					7.5%
1985					
q1					
q2					
q3					
q4					
1986			Selective credit control		
q1		-2% to	formula		
		15%　July	changed from		
q2		2	an incremental		
			basis on		
q3			consumer		
			loans. Not to		
q4			exceed 30%		
			of average		
			loans. On Sept		
			30		
			Minimum		
			downpayment		
			removed and		
			maximum		
			repayment		
			periods		
			extended		

Source: Central Bank of Trinidad and Tobago

Trinidad and Tobago

Effective dates	Cash reserve require- ments	Liquid assets ratio (excludes cash)	Credit controls +tighter -easier M = modified	Interest spreads (not applicable)	Dis- count rate (bank rate)
1987 q1 q2 q3 q4	Cash and secondary reserve split. Cash require- ment 9% Dec 16	Secondary 11% Dec 16			
1988 q1 q2 q3 q4					+2% to 9.5%
1989 q1 q2 q3 q4	Statutory cash require- ment increased by 3% to 12% July 26	Reduced to 9% Jan 25 - 2% to 7% May 3 -2% to 5% July 26			
1990 q1 q2 q3 q4					

Source: Central Bank of Trinidad and Tobago

251

Trinidad and Tobago

Effective dates	Cash reserve require-ments	Liquid assets ratio (excludes cash)	Credit controls +tighter -easier M = modified	Interest spreads (not applicable)	Discount rate Bank rate)
1991 q1 q2 q3 q4			Jan 1991 new instalment credit guidelines		+1% to 10% Oct +1% to 11.5% Dec
1992 q1 q2 q3 q4					+1.5% to 13% Jan

Source: Central Bank of Trinidad and Tobago

252

Appendix 3.4
Foreign exchange reserves in Barbados, Jamaica and Trinidad and Tobago

	Barbados BDS$million	Jamaica J$million	Trinidad & Tobago TT$million
1972	46.4	77.6	97.4
1973	35.7	55.2	78.1
1974	46.4	92.8	776.7
1975	82.2	3.1	1722.9
1976	53.5	-222.7	2397.7
1977	74.3	-221.7	3192.5
1978	126.1	-484.2	4058.7
1979	143.8	-793.9	4996.0
1980	167.2	-852.3	6491.3
1981	125.5	-1380.2	7677.2
1982	184.6	-1676.0	7034.8
1983	227.2	-3587.0	4950.9
1984	238.5	-4799.6	3579.9
1985	321.7	-6456.1	1528.4
1986	296.3	-6442.2	314.6
1987	289.6	-5301.0	284.9
1988	328.8	-4678.5	-23.8
1989	255.9	-4993.6	534.3
1990	165.1	-5068.5	796.8
1991	70.0	-8640.0	105.9
1992	235.0	-785.0	-36.7

Source: Monthly Digests of Statistics, Central Banks of Barbados, Jamaica and Trinidad and Tobago.

Appendix 3.5
Total assets of commercial banks:
Barbados, Jamaica and Trinidad and Tobago
$million

	Barbados BDS$	Jamaica J$	T'dad & Tobago TT$
1972	331.6	632.3	759.0
1975	450.9	1010.9	1555.8
1976	486.6	1066.1	1857.8
1977	538.2	1183.9	2406.4
1978	646.4	1538.6	3112.6
1979	795.4	1643.8	3942.2
1980	883.8	2100.4	4694.7
1981	1011.0	2634.2	5752.6
1982	1109.6	3150.4	8553.0
1983	1211.3	4319.6	9607.6
1984	1310.9	5426.0	10059.8
1985	1416.2	6623.3	10165.1
1986	1511.3	8240.2	9913.2
1987	1781.3	9600.0	10744.4
1988	1844.7	12812.0	10765.6
1989	1923.1	15320.0	11107.3
1990	2186.4	17327.0	12187.2
1991	2160.1	27691.0	13254.2
1992	2266.2	47865.0	13100.5

Source: Monthly Digests of Statistics, Central Banks of
Barbados, Jamaica and Trinidad and Tobago.

Appendix 3.6
Share of banks in total assets of banks and non-banks
$million

Year	Barbados (%)	Jamaica (%)	T'dad & Tobago (%)
1976	-	82.3	85.3
1977	94.4	84.7	84.7
1978	92.7	85.7	82.1
1979	91.2	86.6	83.7
1980	90.5	90.7	80.9
1981	88.8	93.6	78.0
1982	87.9	93.3	80.2
1983	87.4	89.8	78.2
1984	86.7	89.5	77.9
1985	87.5	88.6	76.7
1986	86.1	81.4	80.7
1987	86.0	84.3	82.3
1988	83.6	81.9	81.2
1989	82.7	80.1	81.8
1990	83.2	78.9	81.3
1991	82.1	81.8	81.5
1992	82.7	81.2	78.8

Source: Central Banks of Barbados, Jamaica and Trindad and Tobago.

Appendix 3.7
Comparative bank rates:
Barbados, Jamaica and Trinidad and Tobago
(%)

Year	Barbados	Jamaica	T'dad & Tobago
1972	-	6.0	5.0
1973	-	7.0	6.0
1974	10.5	9.0	6.0
1975	7.5	8.0	6.0
1976	6.0	9.0	6.0
1977	6.0	9.0	6.0
1978	6.0	9.0	6.0
1979	6.0	9.0	6.0
1980	7.0	11.0	6.0
1981	22.0	11.0	6.0
1982	20.0	11.0	6.0
1983	16.0	11.0	7.5
1984	16.0	16.0	7.5
1985	13.0	21.0	7.5
1986	8.0	21.0	5.97
1987	8.0	20.6	7.5
1988	8.0	17.35	9.5
1989	13.5	25.10	9.5
1990	13.5	30.73	9.5
1991	18.0	46.94	11.5
1992	12.0	25.49	13.0

Source: Central Banks of Barbados, Jamaica and Trinidad and Tobago.

Appendix 6.1
Results: excluding and including regulatory variables

Description	ROA - Excluding regulatory variables		ROA - Including regulatory variables	
C	1.14 (1.71)		0.504 (1.17)	
TB	0.016 (1.91)		0.026 (3.64)	
SF	-0.82 (-1.36)		-1.15 (-2.50)	
M	-0.002 (-.314		0.147 (2.00)	
CON	0.007 (.113)		0.007 (3.03)	
RR			-0.024 (-2.14)	
LD	-0.639 (-1.27)		-0.226 (-.57)	
I	0.114 (1.67)		0.202 (1.91)	
Inf	0.007 (.659			
dumin	-		0.211 (5.40)	
dumcr	-		-0.083 (2.00)	
R^2	0.405		0.700	
R bar squared	0.292		0.630	
D.W.	1.09		1.86	
F statistic	3.61	9.92	9.92	
s.e.	0.146		0.105	
Misspecification MS1 [F (1,50] MS2 [χ^2 (1)]	8.76	9.22	0.039	0.049
Normality N[χ^2 (2)	0.397		0.108	
Hetero F [1.62] LM (1)	1.18	1.19	3.20	3.14
Ser Cor F [4,47] χ^2 (4)	8.31	25.86	0.485	2.54

ROA denotes return on assets.

Appendix 6.2

Results of regression using the narrow definition of capital as an explanatory variable

R^2 0.785
R bar squared   0.726
RSS   0.367
DW   2.00
F stat   13.24
s.e.   0.088

The equation is expressed as:

$$ROA = 0.642 + 0.012 \ TB -1.22 \ SF+ 0.003 \ M + 0.006 \ CON$$
$$(1.71) \quad (1.88) \quad (-3.00) \quad (4.84) \quad (4.95)$$

$$-.050RR -0.071LD + 0.167I- 0.041CAP +0.206dumin -0.065dumcr$$
$$(-5.11) \quad (-0.181) \quad (1.99) \quad (-1.13) \quad (4.89) \quad (-2.24)$$

$$-0.052s1 - 0.159s2 -0.034s3$$
$$(1.54) \quad (-4.67) \quad (-0.99)$$

Results showed that the coefficient for capital, though having a t-value greater than unity, was not significant, indicating that capital defined to include paid-up capital and reserves may have no impact on bank profitability. Lags used in that regression equation are the same as those included in the earlier equation. The explanatory power of the equation improved only marginally as measured by the multiple correlation coefficient but the F- statistic slipped slightly indicating that the results as a whole were less robust when lags were added. Diagnostic tests for this equation indicate no sign of serial correlation or heteroscedasticity.

Results of diagnostic tests:

Misspecification F, 0.608 (1,46) X^2 0.796 (1)
Normality 0.243 (2)
Heteroscedasticity F, 1,422 (1,59) X^2 1.436 (1)
Serial correlation F, 0.295 (4,43) X^2 1.63 (4)

Appendix 6.3
Regression results with loan loss provisions (and staff expenses)
(included in return on assets (btfxla): Barbados)

btfxla = 0.67 + 0.005TB +0.207M +0.86SF -0.04RR +0.007CON
$\quad$ (1.9) $\quad$ (0.096) $\quad$ (2.72) $\quad$ (1.90) $\quad$ (-4.02) $\quad$ (4.30)

$\quad$ -0.37LD + 0.09I +0.11dumin -0.09 dumcr -0.04s1 -0.05s2 -0.003s3
$\quad$ (-0.876) $\quad$ (1.02) $\quad$ (2.47) $\quad$ (-2.83) $\quad$ (-1.22) (-1.57) (-1.00)

R^2 = 0.636
R bar squared = 0.541
DW = 1.66
F stat (12,46) 6.70
Max log likelihood 68.99

Diagnostic tests
ser. cor. LM (4) 5.46 F (4,42) (1.07)
Functional form LM (1) (0.036) F (1.45) (0.028)
Normality LM (2) (.537)
Hetero LM (1) (1.15) F (1.14)

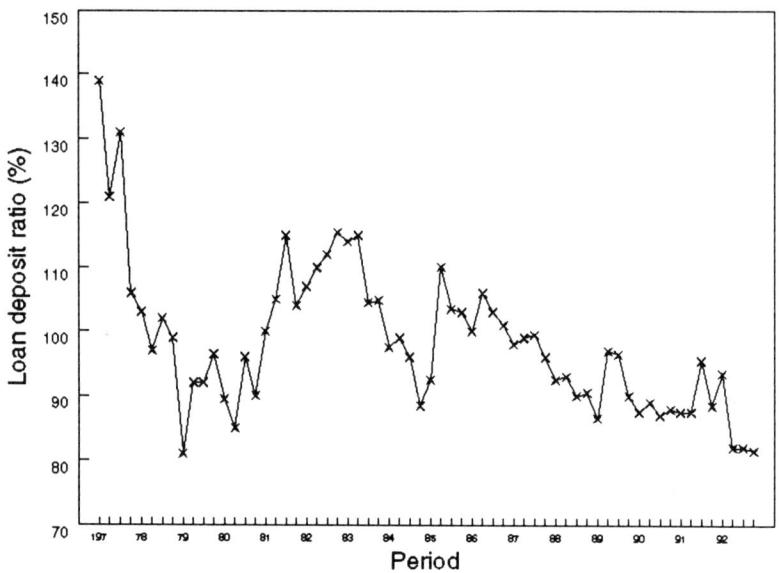

Appendix 6.4 Loan deposit ratio: small banks: 1977-92

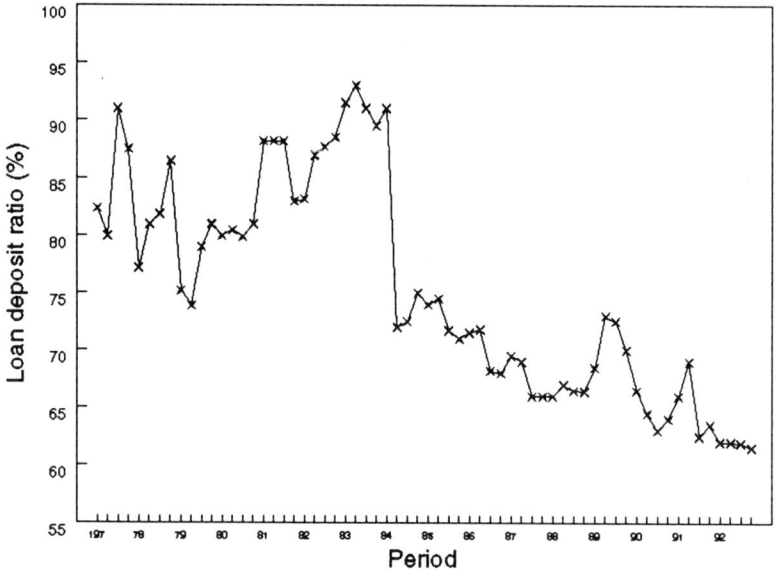

Appendix 6.5 Loan deposit ratio: large banks: 1977-92

260

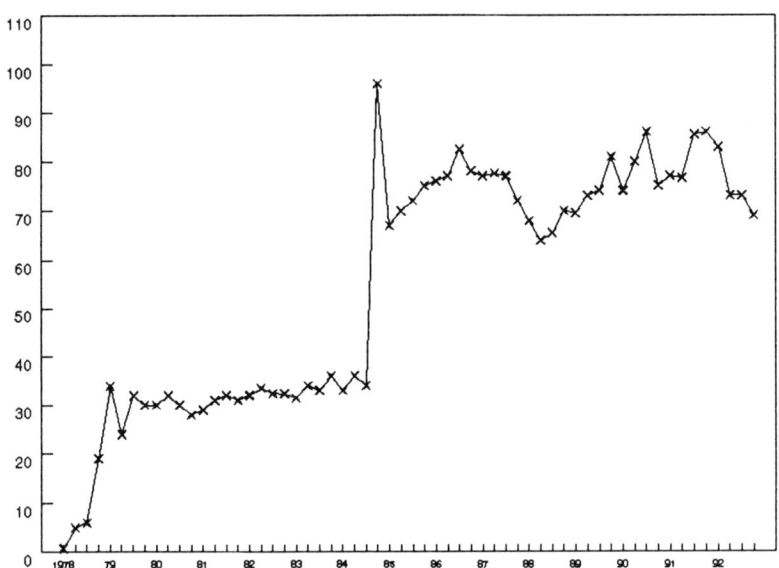

Appendix 6.6 Loan deposit ratio: local banks: 1977-92

Questionnaire

(a) Reserve requirements

1. What are the steps which your bank would take in order to meet increases in reserve requirements?

2. How long would it ordinarily take your bank to satisfy a 1% increase in reserve requirements?

3. What is the impact on your loan commitment profile of an increase in reserve requirements?

4. What areas of your bank's lending would you first restrict in order to assist in satisfying reserve requirements?

5. Do you intensify your marketing for deposits when cash reserve requirements are increased?

6. Does the adjustment required to the announcement of increases in reserve requirements often entail an increase in interest rates offered on deposits?

7. a) Does your bank ordinarily keep sufficient cash or liquid assets on hand and in your portfolio in anticipation of a cash reserve requirement increase?
   b) If the answer to 7a) above is yes, what size excess cash and liquid assets would your bank normally aim to keep in excess of your working capital needs?

8. Does the adjustment response of your bank differ when there is an increase in secondary reserves; e.g. treasury bills or debentures? Please state how.

9. Other than the fact that secondary reserves are interest bearing assets, is it otherwise easier to satisfy that requirement?

10. Does your bank as a matter of policy keep a sufficient stock of securities to satisfy an increase in secondary reserves?
    a) as much as 1% of deposits?
    b) 2% of deposits?
    c) 3% of deposits?
    d) other (please specify)

11. Does your bank borrow from its head office (in the case of branches) in order to satisfy primary or secondary reserve increases?
    Yes____   No____

12. Would the rate of interest obtaining abroad influence your decision at 11 above?
    Yes____   No____

13. In the case of branches would borrowing from head office, if undertaken, be undertaken before:
    a) launching a deposit drive?
    b) cutting back on private sector lending?
    (please tick)

14. If your bank had to restrain its lending in order to satisfy reserve requirements, what sector would likely be the most affected? Rank in order of 1 to 4
    --- personal lending
    --- distribution
    --- manufacturing
    --- services
    --- other (please specify)

(b) Credit controls

1. Do you think there are ways for banks to circumvent credit controls? (please tick)

    1) only slightly
    2) partly so

3) almost fully
4) not at all

2. Do the limits on credit to selected sectors lead to increases in credit to other sectors in the private sector?   Yes_____   No_____
   If 'yes', please specify and rank the sectors which benefit.

3. Do credit controls affect the profitability of your bank?
   Yes _____   No_____
   If 'yes', please specify.

4. Are there more applications from the protected sectors when controls are in place?
   Yes_____   No_____

5. Are the potential returns from the controlled sectors greater than the potential returns from the eligible sectors?

6. If 'yes', are the eligible sectors likely to bear a higher rate of interest?
   Yes_____   No_____

7. Is there a pent up demand for credit from the controlled sectors?
   Yes_____   No_____

8. If and when global credit limits are in place, to what sectors would credit first be cut? Please rank.
   1.
   2.
   3.
   4.

9. In the case of branches, does your head office give your branch quantitative guidelines for lending to specific sectors?
   Yes_____   No_____
   If 'yes', which sectors are given priority?
   1.
   2.
   3.

10. Is the size of your bank a constraint in meeting official guidelines relating to credit or reserve and securities requirements?

(c) Interest rates

1. What are the major difficulties for banks when ceilings are placed on:
    a) the average lending rate?
    b) the prime lending rate?

2. What areas of banking activity are first affected when the ceiling on the average lending rate (or prime rate if applicable) is lowered?   Please state.

3. Do banks immediately attempt to lower deposit rates when lending rates are lowered?
    Yes_____   No____

4. What scope is there for cutting other costs when lending rates are lowered?

5. Would increased bank charges tend to be the first or last recourse before lowering deposit rates where possible?
    a) first____
    b) last____
    c) other (please specify)

6. Is it a disadvantage to banks in having a minimum savings rate (where applicable)? Please tick.
    a) slight advantage
    b) great advantage
    c) advantage

    Please give reasons for your response.

7. To what extent do you think that a higher minimum savings rate raises the level of savings deposits when these rates are similar for all banks?
    a) helps a little
    b) helps a lot
    c) other (please specify)

8. Is the competition for deposits greater when:
    a) interest rates are high
    b) when banks are illiquid

265

9. Has liquidity of your bank ever been a serious problem?
   Yes_____   No___

   Please comment on the circumstances.

10. Do interest rate controls influence the liquidity of your bank?
   Yes_____   No___

   Please state how.

(d) Prudential regulation

1. (In the case of local banks.) Do you find the minimum capital requirements:
   a) adequate
   b) too low
   c) too high

2. Do you think prudential regulations which require banks to capitalise in line with the riskiness of their portfolios are:
   a) reasonable
   b) too strict
   c) unreasonable

3. Are prudential regulations likely to affect the profitability of banks?
   Yes___   No___

4. Does the limit on lending to a single customer adversely affect your bank?
   Yes___   No___
   If 'yes' please state how.

5. Does the restriction on the holding of equity by banks in commercial operations affect the profitability of banks?
   Yes___   No___
   If 'yes' please state how.

6. a) Do capital adequacy provisions affect the liquidity of your bank?
   Favourably_____   Unfavourably___
   Please state how.

266

b) Do capital adequacy provisions affect the solvency of banks?
Favourably___   Unfavourably___

Please state how.

c) Do capital adequacy provisions affect the profitability of banks?
Favourably___   Unfavourably___

Please state how.

Responses to questionnaire

Responses to the questionnaire sent to commercial banks in Barbados, Jamaica and Trinidad and Tobago.

The questionnaire received an 83% response from commercial banks in Barbados, a 50% response from banks in Trinidad and Tobago and a 25% response from banks in Jamaica. Most banks felt that profitability was adversely affected by increases in primary and secondary reserve requirements. They viewed the savings rate as restricting pricing flexibility and considered ceilings on lending, whether average lending or prime lending, as disadvantageous to high risk borrowers but felt that the impact of interest rate controls on profitability depended on spreads rather than on the absolute level at which rates were set. All banks responding observed that credit controls adversely affected profitability and felt that scope for circumvention was slight. Most banks viewed prudential controls as adequate and many thought concentration guidelines adversely affected profitability. Most felt that initial capital requirements were adequate but were non-committal about the use of risk-based capital guidelines.

The results of the questionnaire are summarized below.
Abbreviations
Bds = Barbados
Jca = Jamaica
T&T = Trinidad and Tobago

Responses marked 4.a refer to reserve requirements
4.b to credit controls,
4.c to interest rate controls,
4.d to prudential regulations.

4.a Responses on reserve requirements

Table 4.a.1
Ccmmercial banks' reaction to increases in reserve requirements
(primary and secondary)

Response	% of times mentioned		
Country	Bds	Jca	T&T
Increase deposits	100%	100%	33%
Restrict lending generally	83%	50%	100%
Reduce credit Lines	33%	-	-
Offer higher interest rates	50%	50%	33%
Cancel loan commitments	17%	-	-
Sell excess treasury bills	17%	33%	-

Table 4.a.2
Length of time taken to satisfy a 1% increase in reserve requirements
(liquid assets ratio)

Length of time taken	Percent of responses		
Country	Bds	Jca	T&T
Virtually no time	17%	100%	33%
Up to 2 weeks	17%	-	33%
Up to 2 months	33%	-	-
Over 2 months	33%	-	-
Various times	-	-	33%

4.a.3

Most banks indicated that the impact of increased primary and secondary reserve requirements on loan commitments would depend on liquidity at the time. Generally, however the response would be as follows.

Table 4.a.3
Banks' response to loan commitments following an increase
in reserve requirements

Response	% of respondents		
Country	Bds	Jca	T&T
Lower commitments	20%	100%	33%
Honour on a first come first served basis	20%	-	-
Restrict drawdown	40%	-	-
Indicate inability to meet commitments	20%	-	-
No effect			33%
		100%	

Most banks indicated that they would not use any one approach but the response represented the most generally used approach by them.

4.a.4

The following table summarizes those areas of lending first restricted in order to meet increases in official reserve requirements.

Table 4.a.4
Sectors which suffer credit cutbacks following credit controls

Sectors of credit cutbacks	% of responses
Personal lending	40%
Commercial lending	20%
Excess overdraft	20%
Across the board	20%

4.a.5

Banks indicated that they intensified marketing of deposits when reserve requirement were increased, especially banks in Jamaica and Trinidad and Tobago.

4.a.6

Banks confirmed that increases in reserve requirements very often required increased interest rates.

4.a.7 a) and b)

The evidence is that most banks tend to hold reserves and securities in excess of the stipulations, but almost all banks indicated that this was not done in anticipation of, or as a contingency against, increases in reserve requirements. Banks in Jamaica or Trinidad and Tobago which responded to the questionnaire indicated that they did not deliberately hold excess reserves in anticipation of increased cash reserve requirements. In Barbados a very small percentage indicated that they held excesses with official requirements in mind.

The responses to this question are summarized below.

Table 4.a.7
Holding of excess reserves as a contingency against future increases

Holding of excess reserves	Percent	Quantity
Country	*Barbados only*	*Barbados only*
As a contingency against increased requirements	17%	$5.0 million approximately
Excess not held as a contingency against increases	83%	n.a.

4.a.8

Most banks observed that action taken to satisfy reserve requirements was little different from action taken to satisfy secondary reserve requirements

271

except where they were in a position to sell treasury bills in satisfaction of cash reserve requirements. In such cases it was easier to satisfy cash reserve requirements. The cost was of course lower in the case of secondary reserve requirements, but the difference in adjustment was largely one of degree.

Table 4.a.8

Difference in banks' responses to cash reserve requirement increases compared with increases in secondary reserve requirements

Response to increased cash reserve requirements vs secondary reserve increases	Percent of responses		
Country	Bds	Jca	T&T
The same	83%	50%	66%
Different	17%	50%	33%
Easier	83%	-	33%
More difficult	easier	50%	-

4.a.9

Other than the fact that secondary reserves were interest bearing, banks felt that it was not otherwise easier to satisfy secondary reserve requirements in circumstances where they held no excess securities.

4.a.10

Most banks had no policy on holding of excess reserves but seemed to allow demand and supply conditions to dictate their holding of excess primary and secondary reserves. Banks in Jamaica had a policy not to hold excess reserves.

Banks in Barbados indicated that they borrowed abroad to satisfy primary or secondary reserve requirements. In such cases the interest rate obtaining abroad was not a major consideration; this either indicates that interest rates abroad were generally lower than local rates or that banks placed a high priority on compliance. Commercial banks in Jamaica and Trinidad and Tobago, where most banks are locally owned and controlled, did not borrow abroad to satisfy reserve requirements.

272

Table 4.a.10
Is there a policy on excess reserves?

Indications	% of responses		
Country	Bds	Jca	T&T
Policy	0%	-	-
No Policy	83%	-	100%
Policy to hold excess	0%	-	-
Policy not to hold excess	0%	100%	-
Policy to hold excess if possible	17%	-	-

4.a.11 and a.12

Table 4.a.12
Borrowing abroad to satisfy reserve requirements

Borrowing abroad	% of responses	Influenced by interest rate
Country	Barbados only	
Yes	25%	no
No	75%	..

4.a.13

Those banks in Barbados which indicated that they would borrow abroad also indicated that they would first launch a deposit drive or cut back on private sector lending. It was interesting that this response was only obtained when the question was specifically asked but was not mentioned voluntarily among the earlier responses to increased reserve requirements, indicating perhaps that it is usually a last resort.

4.a.14

In identifying which sectors were more likely to be affected by cutbacks in lending as banks sought to satisfy reserve requirements, the sector most frequently mentioned was services in Barbados, and personal lending in Jamaica and Trinidad and Tobago.

Table 4.a.14
Sectors likely to suffer cutbacks in lending
(ranked by frequency mentioned)

Sector	*Rank*		
Country	*Bds*	*Jca*	*T&T*
Services	1	4	3
Distribution	2	3	2
Manufacturing	3	2	4
Personal lending	4	1	1

4.b Responses on credit controls

Most commercial banks thought circumvention of credit controls was possible but that the possibilities were few.

4.b.1

Table 4.b.1
Can credit controls be circumvented?

Likelihood of possible circumvention	*% of respondents*		
Country	*Bds*	*Jca*	*T&T*
Only slightly	40%	-	-
Partly so	40%	66%	50%
Almost fully	0%	33%	-
Not at all	20%	-	50%

4.b.2

Banks were unanimous in the view that credit controls on the consuming sectors did not lead to increases in credit to the productive or officially preferred sectors.

Table 4.b.2
Do credit controls lead to increases in credit to the productive sectors?

Credit controls: leads to increase in credit to productive sectors?	% of respondents		
Country	Bds	Jca	T&T
Yes	0%	0%	0%
No	100%	100%	100%

4.b.3

Most banks thought that credit controls affected profitability adversely.

Table 4.b.3
Effect of credit controls on profitability

Effect of credit control on profitability	% of respondents		
Country	Bds	Jca	T&T
Adverse	100%	66%	100%
Positive	0%	33%	–
None	0%	-	–

4.b.4

Most banks observed that there was no increase in applications from the productive sectors when credit controls were in place.

4.b.5 and b.6

Most banks in Barbados felt that returns from lending to the controlled sectors were greater than returns from the protected sectors suggesting that interest rates charged were higher, but not all banks in Jamaica were of that view, nor were one-third of the respondents from Trinidad and Tobago.

Table 4.b.6
Relative returns from credit to the protected sectors

Response	Returns from credit to the protected sectors		
Country	Bds	Jca	T&T
Greater	25%	-	33%
Lesser	75%	50%	66%
The same	0%	-	-
Not	25%	50%	-

necessarily
greater

4.b.7

Commercial banks in Barbados observed that there was no pent up demand for credit from the controlled sector. This differed from responses from commercial banks in Jamaica who observed that there was considerable pent up demand from the controlled sectors when controls were in place.

4.b.8

In response to the question concerning which sectors were affected by global credit limits, the personal sector was mentioned more frequently by respondents. The following is a summary of those responses.

Table 4.b.8
Sectors affected by global credit limits
(ranked by the frequency and the order in which mentioned)

Sector	No of times sector mentioned		
Country	Bds	Jca	T&T
Personal	1	1	1
Distribution	2	1	1
Services	3	1	-

Table 4.b.8 (cont'd)
Sectors affected by global credit limits
(ranked by the frequency and the order in which mentioned)

Sector	No of times mentioned		
Country	Bds	Jca	T&T
Manufacturing	4	-	-
Construction	4	2	2
Agriculture	5	3	-
Tourism	-	-	-
Across the board (least profitable)	4	1	2

4.b.9

Only a few banks in Barbados indicated the existence of head office guidelines for sectoral lending. There were no such guidelines in Jamaica or Trinidad and Tobago where most banks were locally owned.

Table 4.b.9
Head office guidelines on sectoral credit

Are there head office guidelines on sectoral credit?	% of respondents		
Country	Bds	Jca	T&T
Yes	20%	0%	0%
No	80%	100%	100%

4.b.10

Only a minority of banks in Barbados felt that size was important in influencing banks' ability to meet official requirements. Commercial banks in Jamaica and Trinidad and Tobago thought it was irrelevant. It is observed that most banks in Jamaica and Trinidad and Tobago tend to be larger than in Barbados.

Table 4.b.10
Importance of size in meeting official requirements

Size as important in meeting requirements	*% of respondents*		
Country	*Bds*	*Jca*	*T&T*
Yes	20%	0%	0%
No	80%	100%	100%

4.c Responses on interest rate controls

Banks were unanimous in their views about the adverse effects of interest rate controls, but differed in identifying the major areas affected. Responses were very similar concerning the action which they would take to counteract adverse effects of interest rate controls. Remedies mentioned tended to be common across banks and across countries.

Table 4.c.1
Major difficulties arising from average or prime lending rate ceilings
(weighted by frequency mentioned)

Areas affected	*% weighted percent*		
Country	*Bds*	*Jca*	*T&T*
Costly monitoring	20%	-	-
Constraints on spreads	30%	50%	25%
Inability to price in relation to risk	50%	-	-
Restricts lending	-	25%	50%
Competition from non-banks	-	25%	25%

4.c.2

The responses from banks in Jamaica and Trinidad and Tobago placed a great deal of emphasis on competition from non-banks, suggesting that this was an important consideration in pricing. This compared with Barbados where this concern was not mentioned.

Table 4.c.2
Areas of banking activity first affected when prime or average lending rates are lowered

Areas first affected	*Weighted percent*		
Country	*Bds*	*Jca*	*T&T*
Control of spreads	40%	50%	50%
Adverse impact on profitability	20%	-	-
Difficulty in raising deposit levels	20%	-	-
Other	20%	50%	50%

4.c.3

All banks indicated that they attempted to lower deposit rates as soon as lending rates were cut, some immediately, others after monitoring deposit rate commitments. Banks in Jamaica and Trinidad and Tobago were inclined to cut rates irrespective of deposit commitments.

Table 4.c.3
Cut in deposit rates in response to reduction in lending rates

Cut in deposit rates	*% of respondents*		
Country	*Bds*	*Jca*	*T&T*
Immediate cut	83%	100%	100%
Cut after checking deposit	17%	-	-

commitments

4.c.4 and c.5

Most banks found that there was little scope for cutting other costs and indicated that increasing bank charges would be one of the last considerations.

Table 4.c.5
Scope in cost cutting/increasing bank charges

Scope for cost cutting/ increasing bank charges	% of respondents		
Country	Bds	Jca	T&T
Little scope for cutting costs	83%	100%	100%
Increased charges (least preferred)	100%	100%	100%

4.c.6

Most banks thought that a minimum rate on savings deposits was a major disadvantage, and that it did little to raise the level of deposits as savings deposits were interest inelastic.

Table 4.c.6
Disadvantage of minimum savings rate

Advantage/ disadvantage	% of respondents		
Country	Bds	Jca	T&T
Slight disadvantage	20%	50%	33%
Great disadvantage	80%	50%	66%
Advantage	0%	50%	-

Banks were asked to give their reasons for these conclusions. The following were the main reasons given.

A stipulated minimum savings rate:

   1. reduces the interest margin available when lending rates are falling.

280

2. does not allow for market forces to determine interest rates.
3. facilitates a higher interest rate regime for loans.
4. is an disadvantage if lending rates are controlled.
5. controls the margin between deposit and lending rates.
6. could make banks eliminate offering small savings accounts because of the inherent costs of servicing such accounts.

4.c.7

Most respondents felt that increases in the minimum savings rate had only a minimal effect on deposit growth. The responses are summarized below.

Table 4.c.7
Effect of increased minimum savings rate on deposit growth

Effect on volume of savings of a minimum savings rate	*% of respondents*		
Country	*Bds*	*Jca*	*T&T*
Helps a little	40%	33%	50%
Helps a lot	0%	-	-
Does not help	0%	66%	50%

4.c.8

Most respondents felt that competition for deposits was influenced more by changes in liquidity than by changes in interest rates. Commercial banks in Jamaica were undecided on the relative importance of liquidity or interest rate levels for competition.

Table 4.c.8
Competition for deposit: relative influence of interest rates or liquidity

Relative impact on competition	*% of respondents*		
Country	*Bds*	*Jca*	*T&T*
Interest rates	0%	-	0%
Liquidity	100%	-	100%

4.c.9

The sources of illiquidity were identified as follows:

1. Increases in reserve requirements.
2. Withdrawal of funds by a major customer.
3. High loan demand.
4. A combination of the above.

4.c.10

Although banks noted that the minimum savings rate had little impact on deposit growth the majority felt that interest rate controls impacted on liquidity in the banking system.

Table 4.c.10
Do interest rate controls impact on liquidity of the system?

Impact of interest controls on liquidity	% of respondents		
Country	Bds	Jca	T&T
Yes	33%	-	-
No	67%	-	-

4.d Responses on prudential requirements

There was a high level of non-response on many of the capital requirement questions by commercial banks in Barbados. Responses from banks in Jamaica and Trinidad and Tobago were much more explicit. This was attributed to the fact that most banks in Barbados are branches of foreign banks and are not directly affected by capital requirements as their global capital is used as a reference point. Banks were more forthcoming on other prudential guidelines. Generally, they saw capital requirements as restricting profitability, particularly risk weighted capital requirements, but thought they were necessary. They were very critical of the imposition of concentration ratios which limited lending to a single customer.

4.d.1 and d.2

Table 4.d.1
Adequacy of capital requirements

Minimum capital requirements	Adequacy of capital requirements, % of respondents		
Country	Bds	Jca	T&T
Adequate	60%	100%	100%
High	-	-	-
Low	-	-	-
No response	40%	-	-
Risk-based capital requirements			
Reasonable	40%	100%	-
Too-strict	20%	-	-
Not sure	0%	-	-

The wide range of responses probably reflects the uncertainty about risk-based capital since the methodology is not transparent to banks but depends on the assessment of auditors and bank supervisors.

4.d.3

Table 4.d.3
Are prudential requirements likely to affect the profitability of banks?

Affect on profitability	% of respondents		
Country	Bds	Jca	T&T
Yes	40%	-	-
No	40%	100%	100%
No response	20%	-	-

4.d.4

Most banks in Barbados who responded to the question of concentration guidelines commented that while it might affect short term profitability it was in the long term interest of banks. Responses from Trinidad and Tobago and Jamaica indicated greater concern about the impact of concentration guidelines on profitability. The lower level of concern in Barbados reflected the greater burden of customer concentration ratios on locally incorporated banks.

Table 4.d.4

Do customer concentration ratios on lending affect banks adversely?

Concentration ratios	*% of respondents*		
Country	*Bds*	*Jca*	*T&T*
Affect adversely	0%	100%	66%
Do not affect adversely	80%	-	-
No response	20%	-	33%

4.d.5 and d.6

All banks responding felt that capital adequacy provisions impacted favourably on liquidity and solvency but mostly adversely on profitability.

Table 4.d.6
Effect of capital adequacy provisions on liquidity, solvency and profitability

Response	*Liquidity responses (%)*			*Solvency responses(%)*			*Profitability responses(%)*		
Country	B	J	T	B	J	T	B	J	T
Favourable	100	50	-	100	-	0	20	-	66
Unfavourable	0	50	-	-	-	0	80	-	33
Not signif-icant	0	-	100	-	100	100	-	100	-

Bibliography

Agner, D. and Bryan W., 1971, 'A Model of Short Run Behaviour', *Quarterly Journal of Economics*, Vol. 85, pp. 97-118.

Akella, S.R. and Greenbaum, S.I., 1992, 'Innovations in Interest Rates, Duration Transformation, and Bank Stock Returns', *Journal of Money Credit and Banking*, 24(1), pp. 27-42.

Alejandro, D.,1983, 'Goodbye Financial Repression, Hello Financial Crash' Yale University Economic Growth Centre, Discussion Paper No.441.

Altman, E., 1968, 'Financial Ratios, Discriminant Analysis and the Prediction of Corporate Bankruptcy', *Journal of Finance,* 23(4), pp. 589-601.

Altman, E.I., 1984, 'The Success of Business Failure Prediction Model' *Journal of Banking and Finance,* Vol. 8, pp. 172-197.

Altman, E.I., Marco, G., Varetto, F., 1994, 'Corporate Distress Diagnosis of Companies Using Linear Discriminant Analysis and Neural Networks (the Italian Experience)', *Journal of Banking and Finance,* 18 (3), pp. 505-529.

Auman, R.J. and Shapley L.S., 1974, *The Value of Non-Atomic Games*, Princeton: Princeton University Press.

Averch, H. and Johnson, L.L., 1962, 'Behaviour of the Firm under Regulatory Constraint', *American Economic Review,* Vol. 52, pp. 1053-1069.

Bailey, E. and Baumol, W.J.,1984, 'Deregulation and the Theory of Contestable Markets', *Yale Journal on Regulation,* Vol. 1, pp. 111-137.

Bain, J.S., 1980, *Barriers to New Competition*, Cambridge, MA Harvard University Press.

Baltensperger, E., 1980, 'Alternative Approaches to the Theory of the Banking Firm', *Journal of Monetary Economics,* Vol. 6, pp. 1-37.

Bank of England, 1971, 'Competition and Credit Control', Bank of England

Quarterly Bulletin, June, September and December.

Bank of England, 1982, 'Techniques for Assessing Corporate Financial Strength', *Quarterly Bulletin,* 22(2), pp. 221-223.

Bank of England, 1991, 'Stability and Economic Policy', Speech delivered by the Governor of Bank of England at the Lord Mayor's dinner, Oct. 31, 1991.

Bank of England, 1992, 'Financial Regulation: What are we trying to do?', *Quarterly Bulletin*, 32(3), pp. 322-324.

Barclay, C.R., 1978, 'Competition and Financial Crises - Past and Present', in Revell, J., ed., *Competition and Regulation of Banks,* Cardiff: University of Wales Press, Bangor, Occasional Papers in Economics, Vol.14.

Barro, R.Y. and Santomero, A.,1972, 'Household Money Holdings and the Demand Deposit Rate', *Journal of Money, Credit and Banking*, 4(2), pp. 387-413.

Bassman, R. L., 1988, 'Causality Tests and Observationally Equivalent Representations of Econometric Models', *Journal of Econometrics,* Vol. 39, pp. 69-104.

Baumol, W., 1967, *Business Behaviour, Value and Growth,* New York: Harcourt, Brace and World.

Beckerman, P., 1988, 'The Consequences of Upward Financial Regression' *International Review of Applied Economics,* 2(1), pp. 233-249.

Beckford, G.,1972, *Persistent Poverty: Underdevelopment in the Plantation Regions of the World*, Oxford University Press.

Benavie, A. and Froyen, R.,1982, 'Monetary Policy: Fixed Versus Flexible Deposit Rates', *Southern Economic Journal,* 48(4), pp. 932-949.

Benston, G.J., 1972, 'Economies of Scale of Financial Institutions', *Journal of Money, Credit and Banking*, pp. 312-341.

Bera, A.K. and Jarque, C.M., 1980, 'Efficient Tests for Normality, and Serial Independence of Regression Residuals', *Economic Letters,* Vol. 6, pp. 255-259.

Berger, A.N., 1991, 'The Profit-concentration Relationship in Banking. Tests of Market Power and Efficient Structure Hypothesis, Implications for the Consequences of Bank Mergers', *Finance and Discussion Series,* Washington, 1991.

Berger, A.N. and Humphrey, D.B., 1991, 'The Dominance of Inefficiencies over Scale and Product Mix Economies in Banking', *Journal of Monetary Economics*, Vol. 28, pp. 117-148.

Berger, A.N., Hancock, D. and Humphrey, D., 1992, 'Bank Efficiency Derived from a Profit Function', *Finance and Economics Discussion Series*, No. 211, Federal Reserve Bank of Washington.

Bernanke, Ben. S. and Blinder, A.S.,1988, 'Credit, Money and Aggregate Demand', *American Economic Review*, 78, pp. 435-439.

Besanko, D. and Sappington, D.M.,1987, *Designing Regulatory Policy with Limited Information*, Chur, Switzerland: Harwood Academic Publishers.

Best, L.,1968, 'Outlines of a Model of Pure Plantation Economy', *Social and Economic Studies*, 17(3), pp. 283-326.

Bester, H.,1985, 'Screening and Credit Rationing in Credit Markets with Imperfect Information', *American Economic Review*, 75(4), pp. 850-855.

Binder, J.J., 1985, 'Measuring the Effects of Stock Price Data', *Rand Journal of Economics*, Vol.16, pp. 167-183.

Bird, G., 1982, 'Developing Countries Interests in Proposals for International Monetary Reform', in *Adjustment and Financing in the Developing World, the Role of the IMF*, ed., Killick. T., IMF in association with Overseas Development Institute, 1975, Washington D.C., pp. 198-232.

Black, F., 1975, 'Bank Funds Management in an Efficient Market', *Journal of Financial Economics*, Vol. 2, pp. 323-340.

Blackman, C.N., 1991, 'Some Critical Issues in Caribbean Economic Development', paper delivered at the University of the Netherland Antilles and reprinted in *Central Bank of Barbados Economic Review*, 9(3), 1982.

Blackman, C.N., 1991, 'Wage Price Policies for Increasing International Competitiveness in the Caribbean', in *Increasing the International Competitiveness of Exports from Caribbean Countries*, ed., Wen, Y. and Sengupta, J., Economic Development Institute of the World Bank., pp. 41-53.

Blinder, A.S., 1987, 'Credit Rationing and Effective Supply Failures', *Economic Journal*, Vol. 97, pp. 327-352.

Bork, R., 1966, 'The Rule of Reason and the per se Concept; Price Fixing Market Division', *Yale Law Journal*, Vol. 75, pp. 373-475.

Bös, D. and Tillman, G., 1983, 'Cost-axiomatic Regulatory Pricing', *Journal of Public Economics*, Vol. 22, pp. 243-256.

Bourke, P., 1988, 'International Comparisons of Bank Profitability', *Institute of European Finance*, Research in Banking and Finance, No. 7, North Wales, University College of North Wales.

Bourke, P.,1989, 'Concentration and Other Determinants of Bank Profitability in Europe, North America and Australia', *Journal of Banking and Finance*, Vol. 13, pp. 65-97.

Bourne, C., 1974, 'The Political Economy of Indigenous Commercial Banks in Guyana', *Social and Economic Studies*, 123 (1), pp. 97-126.

Bourne, C., 1977, *Commercial Bank Portfolio Behaviour in Jamaica*, Institute of Social and Economic Research, University of the West Indies, Jamaica.

Box, G.E.P. and Pierce, D.A., 1970, 'Distribution of Periodical Autocorrelations in Autoregressive Moving Average Models', *Journal of American Statistical Association*, Vol. 65, pp. 1509-1526.

Boyd, J. and Prescott, E., 1986, 'Financial Intermediary Coalitions', *Journal of Economic Theory*, Vol. 38, pp. 211-232.

Braeutigam, R. R., 1984, 'Socially Optimal Pricing with Rivalry and Economies of Scale', *Rand Journal of Economics*, Vol. 15, pp. 127-134.

Breusch, T.S. and Pagan, A.R., 1979, 'A Simple Test for Heteroskedasticity, and Random Coefficient Variation', *Econometrica*, Vol.47, pp. 1287-1294.

Brown, A., 1991, 'Jamaica's Transition from Direct to Indirect Instruments of Monetary Policy', in *The Evolving Role of Central Banks*, ed. Downes, P. and Reza, V., I.M.F. Washington D.C., pp. 326-340.

Brunner, K. and Meltzer, A., 1988, 'Money and Credit in the Monetary Transmission Process', *American Economic Review*, Vol. 78, pp. 446-451.

Buffie, E.F., 1984, 'Financial Repression, the New Structuralists and Stabilisation Policy in Semi-Industrial Economics', *Journal of Development Economics*, 14(3), pp. 305-322.

Burkett, P. and Dutt, A.K., 1991, 'Interest Rate Policy, Effective Demand and Growth in LDCs', *International Review of Applied Economics*, 5(2), pp. 127-154.

Buser, S.A., Chen, A.H. and Kane, E.J.,1981, 'Federal Deposit Insurance Regulatory Policy and Optimal Bank Capital', *Journal of Finance*, Vol. 36, pp. 51-60.

Caves, R.E., 1970, 'Uncertainty, Market Structure and Performance: Galbraith as Conventional Wisdom', in Markham, J. and Papenek,G., ed. *Industrial Organisation and Economic Development*, Houghton Mifflin.

Cavallo, D., 1977, 'Stagflationary Effects of Monetary Stabilisation Policies', PhD thesis, Harvard University, Cambridge, Mass.

Cho, Y.J., 1986, 'The Effects of Financial Liberalisation on the Development of Financial Markets and Credit to Corporate Sectors: the Korean Case', Washington, D.C., *World Bank*.

Cho, Y.J., 1986, 'Inefficiencies from Financial Liberalisation on the Efficiency of Credit Allocation', *Journal of Development Economics*, Vol. 29, pp. 101-10.

Cho, Y.J., 1988, 'The Effect of Financial Liberalisation on the Efficiency of Credit Allocation', *Journal of Development Economics*, Vol. 29, pp.101-110.

Cho, Y.J. and Chatkhate, D., 1990, 'Financial Liberalisation: Issues and Evidence', *Economic and Political Weekly*, May.

Chow, G.C., 1960, 'Tests of Equality between Sets of Coefficients in Two Linear Regressions', Econometrica, Vol. 28, pp. 591-605.

Clarke, L.C.,1986, 'Banking Distortions in the Financial Structure of Post War Economies', PhD thesis, University of the West Indies.

Coase, R.H., 1960, 'The Problem of Social Cost', *Journal of Law and Economics*, 3, pp. 1-44.

Cohen, J.,1968, 'Integrating the Real and Financial via the Linkage of Financial Flow', *Journal of Finance*, pp. 1-27.

Committee of Banking Regulation and Supervisory Practices, 1986, *Report on International Developments in Banking Supervision*, 5. Basle, Switzerland, Bank for International Settlements, September, 1986.

Cornett, H. and Tehrainian, H., 1990, 'Stock Market Reaction to the Depository Institutions Deregulation and Monetary Control Act of 1980', *Journal of Banking and Finance*, 15, pp. 81-100.

Courakis, A., 1984, 'Constraints on and Prices and Financial Repression in Developed Countries', *Oxford Bulletin of Economic and Statistics*, 46(4), pp. 341-370.

Cowling, K. and Waterson, M., 1976, 'Price-cost Margins and Market Structure', *Economica*, Vol. 43, pp. 267-274.

Craigwell,R., 1990, 'Interest Rate Policies and Economic Growth in Barbados, 1973 -1986', *Money Affairs*, 11(1), pp. 69-79.

Dann, L.Y., 1981, 'Common Stock Repurchases: An Analysis of Returns to Holders and Stock Holders', *Journal of Finance and Economics*, Vol. 15, pp. 119-152.

Dann, L.Y. and James, C., 1982, 'An Analysis of the Impact of Deposit Rate Ceilings on the Market Value of Thrift Institutions', *Journal of Finance*, Vol. 37, pp. 1259-1275.

De Ceco, M., ed., 1987, *Changing Money: Financial Innovation in Developed Countries*, Oxford, Blackwell.

Dermine, J., 1986, 'Deposit Rates, Credit Rates and Bank Capital: the Klein-Monti Model Revisited', *Journal of Banking and Finance*, 10, pp. 99-114.

Dermine, J. and Hillion, P., 1992, 'Deposit Rate Ceilings and the Market Value of Banks, the Case of France, 1971-1981', *Journal of Money Credit and Banking*, 24(2), pp.180-194.

Derthick, M. and Quirk, P.J., 1985, *The Politics of Deregulation*,

Washington, D.C.: Brookings Institution.

Dickey, D.A. and Fuller, W.A., 1981, 'The Likelihood Ratio Statistics for Auto regressive Time Series with a Unit Root', *Econometrica*, Vol. 49, pp. 1057-72.

Dixit, A.K., 1979, 'Quality and Quantity Competition', *Review of Economic Studies*, Vol. 46, pp. 587-600.

Dornbusch, R. and Park, Y.C., 1987, 'Korean Growth Policy', *Brookings Papers on Economic Activity*, No. 2, pp. 210-232.

Downs, A., 1985, 'Industrial Growth and Employment in a Small Developing Country, the case of Barbados 1955-80', PhD thesis, University of Manchester.

Downes, A., 1957, *An Economic Theory of Democracy*, New York; Harper and Row.

Ducca, J. and Vanhoose, D., 1990, 'Loan Commitments and Optimal Monetary Policy', *Journal of Money Credit and Banking*, 22(2), pp. 178-194.

Dutt, A., 1991, 'Interest Rate Policy in LDCs; a Post Keynesian View', *Journal of Post Keynesian Economics*, 13(2), pp. 210-232.

Earl, M.J. and Marais, D.A.J., 1979, 'The Prediction of Corporate Bankruptcy in the U.K. using Discriminant Analysis', Working Paper 79/5, Oxford Centre of Management Studies, Oxford.

Edwards, F.R. and Scott J.H., 1979, 'Regulating the Solvency of Depository Institutions: a Perspective for Deregulation', in Edwards, F.R., ed., *Issues in Financial Regulation*, New York: McGraw Hill, pp. 65-105.

Edwards, F.R., ed., 1979, *Issues in Financial Regulation*, New York: McGraw Hill.

Edwards, F.R., 1977, 'Managerial Objectives in Regulated Industries: Expense Preference Behaviour in Banking', *Journal of Political Economy*, Feb.

Ehrenberg, R.G.,1979, *The Regulatory Process and Labour Earnings*, New York: Academic Press.

Eisenbeis, R.A.,1983, 'New Investment Powers for S & L: Diversification in Specialisation', *Federal Reserve Bank of Atlanta, Economic Review*, 68, July 1983, pp. 53-62.

Eisenbeis, R.A., 1985, 'Economic Policy Issues Surrounding Regional and National Approaches to Interstate Banking', Havrilesky, T., Schweitzer, R. and Boorman, J., eds., *Dynamics of Banking*, Harlan Davidson, Arlington Heights, IL.

Englund, P., 1990, 'Financial deregulation in Sweden', *European Economic Review*, Vol.34, pp.385-393.

Engle, R.F. and Granger, C.W., 1987, 'Cointegration and Error Correction:

Representation, Estimation and Testing', *Econometrica*, Vol. 55, pp. 251-276.

Fama, E., 1980, 'Banking in a Theory of Finance', *Journal of Monetary Economics*, 6, pp. 39-57.

Fama, E., 1985, 'What's Different about Banks?', *Journal of Monetary Economics*, 15 (1), January, pp. 29-39.

Farrell, T.W., 1990, *Central Banking in a Developing Economy, a study of Trinidad and Tobago - 1964-1989*, Institute of Social and Economic Research, University of the West Indies, Mona.

Farrell, T.W., Najjar, A. and Marcelle, E., 1986, 'Corporate Financing and Use of Bank Credit in Trinidad and Tobago', *Social and Economic Studies*, 35(4), pp. 1-66.

Faulhaber, G.R. and Levinson, S.R., 1981, 'Subsidy-Free Prices and Anonymous Equity', *American Economic Review*, Vol. 71, pp. 1083-1091.

Fiorina, M.P. and Noll, R.G., 1978, 'Voters, Bureaucrats and Legislators: A Rational Choice Perspective on the Growth of Bureaucracy', *Journal of Public Economics*, Vol. 9, pp. 239-254.

Fischer, B., 1993, 'Financial Reforms in Developing Countries', in *Savings and Development*, Centre for Financial Assistance to African Countries, pp. 111-134.

Flannery, M. J.,1989, 'Capital Regulation and Insured Banks Choice of Individual Default Risks', *Journal of Monetary Economics*, Vol. 24, pp. 235-258.

Freidman, M., 1970, 'A Theoretical Framework for Monetary Analysis', *Journal Political Economy*, 78, March/April, pp. 193-238.

Friedman, D., 1984, 'Efficient Institutions for the Private Enforcement of Law', *Journal of Legal Studies*, Vol. 13, pp. 379-397.

Froyen, R.T., 1974, 'A Test of Endogeneity of Monetary Policy', *Journal of Econometrics*, 2(2), pp. 175-188.

Fry, M.J., 1988, *Money Interest and Banking in Economic Development*, John Hopkins University Press.

Galbraith, J.K., 1978, *The New Industrial Estate*, Houghton, Miffin Co.

Gibson, H. and Tsakalotos, E., 1994, 'The Scope and Limits of Financial Liberalisation in Developing Countries: A Critical Survey', *Journal of Development Studies*, pp. 578-628.

Gill, D., 1983, 'Financial System Development and Intermediation Costs', Cairo, Paper prepared for the International Conference on Capital Market Development, 17-19 May, 1983.

Giovanni, A., 1983, 'The Interest Elasticity of Savings in Developing Countries: The Existing Evidence', *World Development*, 11(7), pp. 601-607.

Glick, R. and Plaut, S.E., 1987, 'Off-balance Sheet Liquidity and Monetary Control', *Federal Reserve Bank of San Francisco*, Working Paper No. 87-12.

Goldsmith, R.W., 1969, *Financial Structure and Development*, New Haven, Yale University Press, 1969.

Gowland, D., 1990, *The Regulation of Financial Markets in the 1990s*, Edward Edgar Publishing Ltd.

Granger, C., 1980, 'Testing for Causality, a Personal Viewpoint', *Journal of Economic Dynamics and Control*, Vol. 2, pp. 329-352.

Granger, C.,1988, 'Some Developments in the Concept of Causality', *Journal of Econometrics*, Vol.39, pp. 199-211.

Grossman, S. and Hart, O.D., 1980, 'Disclosure Laws and Takeover Bids', *Journal of Finance*, Papers and Proceedings, Vol. 35, pp. 323-333.

Grove, M.,1974, 'On "Duration" and the Optimal Maturity Structure of the Balance Sheet', *Bell Journal of Economics and Management Science*, Vol.5, pp. 696-709.

Gupta, K.L., 1987, 'Aggregate Savings, Financial Intermediation and Interest Rates', *Review of Economics and Statistics*, Vol. 69, No. 2, pp. 303-311.

Gurley, J. and Shaw, E.,1960, *Money in a Theory of Finance*, The Brookings Institution Washington, D.C. 1960.

Hair, D.J., Anderson, R.E., Tatham,R.L. and Black,W., 1992, *Multivariate Data Analysis with Readings*, 3rd Edition, McMillan Publishing Co.

Halikias, D.J., 1978, *Money and Credit in a Developing Economy: the Greek Case*, New York University Press.

Hamburger, M. and Zwick,B., 1977, 'Instalment Credit Controls, Consumer Expenditure and the Allocation of Real Resources', *Journal of Finance*, 32(5), pp. 1559-1569.

Hancock, D., 1985, 'Bank Profitability, Interest Rates and Monetary Policy', *Journal of Money and Banking*, pp. 179-192.

Hancock, D., 1992, 'Testing for Subadditivity and Economics of Scope in Banking, Using the Profit Function', Working Papers, Board of Governors of the Federal Reserve System.

Hannan, T.H., 1991, 'Bank Commercial Loan Markets and the Role of Market Structure: Evidence from Surveys of Commercial Lending', *Journal of Banking and Finance*, Vol. 15(1), pp. 133-49.

Heggestad, A.A., 1979, 'Market Structure, Competition, and Performance in Financial Institutions: a Survey of Banking Studies', in Edwards, F.R., ed., *Issues in Financial Regulation*, New York: McGraw Hill, pp. 457-465.

Hicks, J.R., 1935, 'A Suggestion for Simplifying the Theory of Money', *Economica*, Vol.2, pp. 1-19.

Hirschman, A.,1958, *The Strategy of Economic Development*, New Haven,

Yale University Press.

Holland, D.W., 1986, 'Statistics and Causal Inference', *Journal of American Statistical Association*, Vol. 81, pp. 945-960.

Howard, D., 1982, 'The British Banking System Demand for Cash Reserves', *Journal of Monetary Economics*, pp. 21-41.

Howard, M., 1976, 'Interest rate Behaviour in an Open Economy: The Barbados Experience 1965-1976', *Central Bank of Barbados, Quarterly Report*, 3(4), pp. 24-50.

Hsaio, C.,1981, 'Autoregressive Modelling and Money Income Causality Detection', *Journal of Monetary Economics*, Vol. 7, pp. 85-106.

Humphrey, B.B., 1981, 'Intermediation and Cost Determinants of Large Bank Liability Composition', *Journal of Banking and Finance*, Vol. 5, pp. 167-185.

Hugguis, S.A. and Morgan, G.E., 1993, 'Regulatory Changes and Federal Mutual Thrift Behaviour: Evidence from the 1980s', *Journal of Money Credit and Banking*, 225(4), pp. 828-853.

Jarque, C.M. and Bera, A.K., 1980, 'Efficient Tests for Normality, Homoscedasticity and Serial Independence of Regression Residuals', *Economic Letters*, Vol. 6, pp. 255-259.

Johansen, S., 1988, 'Statistical Analysis of Cointegrating Vectors', *Journal of Economic Dynamics and Control*, Vol. 12, pp. 231-254.

Johansen, S. and Juselius, K., 1990, 'Maximum Likelihood Estimation and Inference on Cointegration with Application to the Demand for Money', *Oxford Bulletin of Economics and Statistics*, Vol. 52, pp. 169-210.

Kane, E.J., 1972, 'Proposals for Re-channelling Funds to Meet Social Priorities: Discussion', in *Policies for a More Competitive Financial System*, Conference Series No. 8, Federal Reserve Bank of Boston, pp. 190-198.

Kane, E.J., 1977, 'Good Intentions and Unintended Evil: the Case Against Selective Credit Allocation', *Journal of Money Credit and Banking*, pp. 55-69.

Kane, E.J., 1978, 'Getting Along Without Regulation Q: Testing the Standard View of Deposit-rate Competition during the "Wild Card" Experience', *Journal of Finance*, pp. 921-932.

Kane, E.J. and Unal, H., 1990, 'Modelling Structural and Temporal Variations in the Market of Banking Firms', *Journal of Finance*, Vol. 40, pp. 113-130.

Kapur, B.K., 1976, 'Alternative Stabilisation Processes for Less Developed Economies', *Journal of Political Economy*, 84 (4.i), pp. 777-795.

Kapur, B.K., 1983, 'Optimal Financial and Foreign Exchange Liberalisation of Less Developed Economies', *Journal of Political Economy*, 84(4.i), pp.

777-795.

Keynes, J.M., 1936, 'A Suggestion for Simplifying the Theory of Money', *Economica*, N.S.2, February 1935, pp. 1-19.

Keynes, J.M., *The General Theory of Employment, Interest and Money*, New York; Harcourt Brace.

Khatkhate, D.R. and Klaus-Walter, R., 1980, 'Multipurpose Banking: its Nature Scope and Relevance for less Developed Countries', *IMF Staff Papers*, 27(3), pp. 478-516.

Kim, M., 1985, 'Scale Economies in Banking: a Methodological Note', *Journal of Money Banking and Credit*, Vol.17, pp. 96-102.

Kim, Y.C. and Kwon, R.,1977, 'The Liberalisation of Capital and the Growth of Output in a Developing Country. The Case of South Korean Manufacturing', Journal of Development Economics, 4(3), pp. 255-278.

Kim, D. and Santomero, A., 1988, 'Risk in Banking and Capital Regulation', *Journal of Finance*, 43(5), pp. 1219-1233.

King, S., 1986, 'Monetary Transmission: Through Bank Loans or Bank Liabilities?', *Journal of Money Credit and Banking*, pp. 290-303.

Kiviet, J.F., 1985, 'Model Selection and Test Procedures in a Single Equation of a Dynamic Simultaneous System and their Deficits in Small Samples', *Journal of Economics*, 28, pp. 327-62.

Klein, M., 1971, 'A Theory of the Banking firm', *Journal of Money Credit and Banking*, pp. 205-218.

Koehn, M. and Santomero, A., 1980, 'Regulation of Bank Capital and Portfolio Risk', *Journal of Finance*, 35(5), pp.1235-1244.

Lane, C., 1993, 'Exchange Rates and the Effectiveness of Monetary Policy in Developing Countries', in *Monetary Policy in Developing Countries*, cd., Page, S., Routledge, London.

Leon, G., 1988, 'The Monetary Approach to the Balance of Payments', *Social and Economic Studies*, 37(4), pp. 1-31.

Lewis, A., 1954, 'Economic Development with Unlimited Supplies of Labour', *Manchester School of Economics*, 22(2), pp. 139-191.

Levine, M.S., 1977, 'Canonical Analysis and Factor Comparisons', Series: *Quantitative Applications in the Social Sciences*, Edited Uslaner, Sage Publications, London.

Lim, G., 1991, *Jamaica's Financial System: Its Historical Development*, Bank of Jamaica.

Litner, J., 1965, 'The Valuation of Risky Assets and the Selection of Risky Investments: Stock Portfolios and Capital Budgets', *Review of Economics and Statistics*, Vol. 47, pp. 13-37.

Looney, R.E.,1991, 'A Monetary Approach to Movements in Caribbean Balance of Payments', *Social and Economic Studies*, 40(1),1991, pp. 105-

294

132.
Long, M. and Vittas, D., 1992, 'Changing the Rules of the Game' in *Financial Regulation, Changing the Rules of the Game*, ed., Vittas, D., Economic Development Institute of the World Bank.

Mackinnon, J.G., 1990, Critical Values for Cointegration Tests', in *Long Run Economic Relationships: Readings in Cointegration*, ed., Eyle, R.F. and Granger, C.W., Clarendon Press, Oxford, pp. 267-276.

McCallum, B.T.,1987, 'The Case for Rules in the Conduct of Monetary Policy: a Concrete Example', *Weltwirtschaftliches*, Vol. 123, pp. 415-427.

McClean, A.W., 1975, *Money and Banking in the Eastern Caribbean Area*, Mona, Jamaica, UWI, Institute of Social and Economic Research.

Mckinnon, R., 1973, *Money and Capital in Economic Development*, Washington D.C., The Brookings Institution.

McKinnon, R., ed., 1976, *Economic Growth and Development*, Essays in Honour of Edward S. Shaw, Mercel Decker Inc.

Mackinnon, J.G., 1990, 'Critical Values for Cointegration Test', in *Long Run Economic Relationships; Readings in Cointegration*, ed., Engle, R.F. and Granger, C.W.J., Clarendon Press Oxford, pp. 267-276.

Melitz, J., 1990, 'Financial Deregulation in France', *European Economic Review*, Vol. 34, pp. 394-402.

Melnik, A.,1971, 'Short Run Determination of Commercial Bank Portfolio: an Empirical Analysis', *Journal of Finance*, Vol.25, pp. 639-649.

Meyer, R., 1980, 'The Regulated Firm', *Quarterly Review of Economics and Business*, 20(4).

Millon-Cornett, M.H. and Tehranian, H., 1989, 'Stock Market Reaction to the Depository Institution and Monetary Control Act of 1980', *Journal of Banking and Finance*, Vol.13, pp. 81-100.

Minford, P., 1990, 'Monetary Imperfection, Regulation and Discretion', *Journal of Monetary Economics*, Vol.26, pp. 316-325.

Mingo, J., 1978, 'The Effect of Deposit Rate Ceilings on Bank Risk', *Journal of Banking and Finance*, pp. 367-378.

Mingo, J. and Wolkowitz, B., 1977, *Journal of Finance*, 32(5), pp. 1605-1615.

Mitchell, W., 1986, 'Some Regulatory Determinants of Bank Risk Behaviour', *Journal of Money Credit and Banking*, Vol.18, pp. 374-382.

Mitnick, B.M., 1980, *The Political Economy of Regulation*, New York, N.Y., Columbia University Press.

Money and Credit: *The Report of the Commission on Money and Credit, their Influences on Jobs, Price and Growth*, Inglewood Cliffs, N.J.: Prentice Hall, 1961.

Monti, M., 1972, 'Deposit, Credit and Interest Rate Determination Under

Alternative Bank objective functions', in Shell, K. and Szego, G.P. eds., *Mathematical Methods in Investment and Finance*, Amsterdam: North Holland.

Moore, W.T.,1986, 'Asset Composition, Bankruptcy Costs and the Firm's Choice of Capital Structure', *Quarterly Review of Economics and Business*, 2(4), pp. 51-61.

Muellbauer, J. and Murphy, A., 1990, 'The UK Current Account', *Economic Policy*, pp. 347-395.

Mullineaux, D.J., 1978, 'Economies of Scale and Organisational Efficiency in Banking, a Profit Function Approach', *Journal of Finance*, Vol. 33, pp. 259-280.

Myrdal, G., 1951, *Utvecklingen mot Planekonomi: the Trend Toward the Planned Economy*, Tiden, Vol.43.

Nankervis, J.C. and Savin, N.E., 1987, 'Finite Sample Distributions of t and f Statistics in an AR (1) Model with an Exogenous Variable', *Econometric Theory*, Vol.3, pp.387-408.

Nissanke, M.,1990, 'Mobilising Domestic Resources for African Development and Diversification; Structural Impediments in the Formal Financial System', (mimeo), Oxford, June.

O'Brien, J.M, 1977, 'On the Incidence of Selective Credit and Related Policies in a Multi-asset Framework', *Journal of Finance*, 30(5), pp. 1539-1556.

Orden, D. and Fisher, L., 1993, 'Financial Deregulation and the Dynamics of Money, Prices and Output in New Zealand and Australia', *Journal of Money Credit and Banking*, 25(2) 25 No. 2.

Ordover, J. and Weiss A., 1981, 'Information and the Law: Evaluating Legal Restrictions on Competitive Contracts', *American Economic Review*, Vol. 71, pp.399-404.

Osborne D.K. and Zaher, T., 1992, 'Reserve Requirements, Bank Share Prices and the Consequences of Bank Loans', *Journal of Banking and Finance*, Vol. 16, 1992, pp. 799-812.

Osterwald-Lenuum, M., 1992, 'A Note with Quantiles of the Asymptotic Distribution of the Maximum Likelihood Cointegration Rank Test Statistics: Four Cases', *Oxford Bulletin of Economics and Statistics*, 54(3), 461-473.

Page, S., ed., 1993, *Monetary Policy in Developing Countries*, Routledge, London.

Pashigian, P.,1968, 'Limit Pricing and the Market Share of the Leading firm', *Journal of Industrial Economics*, Vol.16, pp. 165-177.

Pastré, O.,1981, *Multinationals: Bank and Corporation Relationships*, Greenwich, Connecticut: Jai Press.

Peltzman, S., 1976, 'Towards a More General Theory of Regulation',

Journal of Law and Economics, pp. 211-240.

Pierce, D.A. and Haugh, L.D., 1977, 'Causality in Temporal Systems: Characterization and a Survey', *Journal of Econometrics*, Vol. 5, pp. 265-293.

Pigou, A.C., 1970, *The Economics of Welfare London*, McMillan.

Polak, J., 1957, 'Monetary Analysis of Income Formation', IMF Staff Papers, November 1957, reprinted in Heller, H.R. and Rhomberg, R.R., eds., *The Monetary Approach to the Balance of Payments*, Washington, D.C. IMF, 1977.

Posner, R.A., 1974, 'Theories of Economic Regulation', *Bell Journal of Economics*, 5, pp. 335-358.

Price Waterhouse, 1992, *Barbados Banking Industry Statistics*.

Prebisch R., 1959, 'Commercial Policy in the Underdeveloped Countries' *American Economic Review*, 49, pp. 251-273.

Pyle, D.H., 1971, 'On the Theory of Financial Intermediation', *Journal of Finance*, Vol.26, pp. 737-749.

Ramakhrisnan, R.T. and Thakor, A., 1984, 'Information Reliability and a Theory of Financial Intermediation', *Review of Economic Studies*, Vol.51, pp. 415-432.

Ramsey, J.B., 1969, 'Tests for Specification Errors in Classical Linear Least Squares Regression Analysis', *Journal of Royal Statistical Society*, Vol.B31, pp. 350-71.

Ramkissoon, R., 'Commercial Bank Asset Portfolio Behaviour in Trinidad and Tobago', MSc Thesis, Department of Economics, University of the West Indies 1982.

Reuber, G., 1964, 'The Objectives of Canadian Monetary Policy 1949-61: Empirical Trade-offs and the Reaction Function of the Authorities', *Journal of Political Economy*, 72(2), pp. 109-132.

Revell, J., ed., 1978, *Competition and Regulation of Banks*, University of Wales Press, Bangor Occasional Papers in Economics.

Revell, J., 1980, 'Costs and Margins in Banking: An International Survey', Paris Organisation for Economic Cooperation and Development.

Rhodes, S.A. and Savage, D.T., 1981, 'Can Small Banks Compete?' *Bankers Magazine*, Jan/Feb.

Rocha, R de R., 1985, 'Cost of Intermediation in Developing Countries: A Preliminary Investigation', Washington D.C., *World Bank*.

Romer, D., 1985, 'Financial Intermediation, Reserve Requirements and Inside Money', *Journal of Monetary Economics*, Vol. 16, pp. 175-194.

Romer, T. and Rosenthal, H., 1985, 'Modern Political Economy and the State of Regulation', Carnegie-Mellon University, Graduate School of Industrial Administration, Working Papers.

297

Rolle, J., 1992, 'Bahamas, Bank Profitability and Monetary Policy (1985-1989)', Meeting of Technicians of Central Banks of the American Continent, Nov. 1992.

Santomero, A., 1984, 'The Banking Firm, a Survey', *Journal of Money, Credit and Banking*, Vol.16, pp. 576- 602.

Santomero, A., 1989, 'The Changing Structure of Financial Institutions', A Review Essay. *Journal of Monetary Economics*, Vol. 24, 1989, pp. 321-328.

Saunders, M. and Wood C., 1988, *Chronicle of Central Bank Policy*, Central Bank of Barbados.

Schreft, S.L., 1992, 'Welfare Improving Credit Controls', *Journal of Monetary Economics*, Vol.30, pp. 57-72.

Schwert, G., 1981, 'Using Financial Data to Measure Effects of Regulation', *Journal of Law and Economics*, Vol. 24.

Sealy, C.W., 1980, 'Deposit Rate-setting, Risk Aversion and the Theory of Depository Financial Intermediaries', *Journal of Finance*, Vol. 35, pp. 1339-1354.

Sealy, C.W. and Lindley, J.T., 1977, 'Inputs, Outputs and a Theory of Production and Cost, at Financial Institutions', *Journal of Finance*, Vol.32, pp. 1251-1266.

Sharpe, W.F., 1964, 'Capital Asset Prices: A Theory of Market Equilibrium under Conditions of Risk', *Journal of Finance*, Vol. 19, pp. 425-442.

Sharpe, W.F., 1978, 'Bank Capital Adequacy, Deposit Insurance and Security Laws', *Journal of Financial and Quantitative Analysis*, 13, pp. 701-718.

Sharpe, W.F., 1991, 'Capital Asset Prices With and Without Negative Holdings', *Journal of Finance*, 46(2), pp. 489-504.

Shaw E.S., 1973, *Financial Deepening in Economic Development*, New York: Oxford University Press.

Silber, W., 1973, 'Selective Credit Policies: a Survey', *Banco Nationale del Lavora*, Dec. 1973.

Silber, W., 1975, ed., *Financial Innovation*, Lexington Mass., Lexington books.

Slovin, M.B., Sushka, M. and Bendeck, M., 1990, 'The Market Valuation Effects of Reserve Regulations', *Journal of Monetary Economics*, Vol.25, pp. 3-19.

Smirlock, M., 1985, 'An Analysis of Bank Risk and Deposit Rate Ceilings, Evidence from Capital Markets', *Journal of Monetary Economics*, Vol. 13, pp. 195-210.

Smirlock, M., 1985, 'Evidence in the (Non) Relationship between Concentration and Profitability in Banking', *Journal of Money Credit and Banking*, 17(1), pp. 69-83.

Smirlock, M., Gilligan, T. and Marshall, W., 1984, 'Tobin's Q and the

Structure and Performance Relationships', *American Economic Review*, 74(5), Dec. 1984, pp. 1051-1060.

Sofianos, G., Watchel and Melnik, A., 1990, 'Loan Commitments and Monetary Policy', *Journal of Banking and Finance*, Vol.14, pp. 677-689.

Spiller, P.T. and Favaro, E., 1984, 'The Effects of Entry Regulation on Oligopolistic Interaction; the Urguayan Banking Sector', *Rand Journal of Economics*, 15(2).

Spulber, D.F., 1989, 'Regulation of Merkets', MIT Press, Cambridge, Massachusetts, London, England.

Stigler, G.J., 1971, 'The Theory of Economic Regulation', *Bell Journal of Economics*, 1971, pp. 3-21.

Stiglitz, J. and Weiss, A.,1981, 'Credit Rationing in Markets with Imperfect Information', *American Economic Review*, 77 (3), pp. 393-410.

Suppes, P.A, 1970, *A Probabilistic Theory of Causality*, Amsterdam, North Holland.

Taffler, R.J., 1982, 'Forecasting Company Failure in the U.K. Using Discriminant Analysis and Financial Ratio Data', *Journal of the Statistical Society*, Series, A45, part 3, pp. 342-358.

Taggart, R.A. and Greeenbaum, St.I.,1978, 'Bank Capital and Public Regulation', *Journal of Money Credit and Banking*, Vol. 10, pp. 158-169.

Taylor, L., 1983, *Structuralist Macroeconomics: Applicable Models for the Third World*, Basic Books Inc, N.Y.

Taylor, L.,1988, *Varieties of Stabilisation Experience: Toward Sensible Macro-economics of the Third World*, Oxford Clarendon Press.

Terrell, H.S.,1986, 'The Role of Foreign Banks in Domestic Banking Markets', *Financial Policy and Reform in Pacific Rim countries*, ed. by Hang-Cheng, Boulder, Colo: Westview Press, pp. 297-304.

Thomas, C.Y., 1974, *Dependence and Transformation: The Transition to Socialism*, N. Y. Monthly Review Press.

Timme, S.G. and Yang, W.K., 1991, 'On the Use of a Direct Measure of Efficiency in Testing Structure and Performance Relationships', Working Paper, Georgia State University, Atlanta, GA.

Tobin, J., 1963, 'Commercial Banks as Creators of Money' in D. Carson ed., *Banking and Monetary Studies*, Homewood, Ill: R. D. Irwin Inc.

Tobin, J., 1965, 'Money and Economic Growth', *Econometrica*, 33 (4), pp. 671-684.

Tobin, J., 1969, 'A General Equilibrium Approach to Monetary Theory', *Journal of Money Credit and Banking*, pp. 15-29.

Tobin, J., 1984, 'On the Efficiency of the Financial System', *Lloyds Bank Review*, (153), pp. 1-15.

Tullock, G., 1965, *The Politics of Bureaucracy*, Washington D.C. Public

Affairs Press.

Van Wijnbergen, S., 1983, 'Credit Policy and Growth in a Financially Repressed Economy', *Journal of Development Economics*, 13 (1-2), pp. 45-65.

Van Wijnbergen, S., 1983, 'Interest Rate Management in LDCs', *Journal of Monetary Economics*, 12(3), pp. 433-452.

Vittas, D., ed., 1992, *Financial Regulation: Changing the Rules of the Game*, Economic Development Institute, World Bank.

Vojta, G.J., 1973, 'Bank Capital Adequacy', New York: First National City Bank', privately circulated.

Warman, F. and Thirlwall, 1993, 'Interest Rates, Saving, Investment and Growth in Mexico, 1960-90: Tests of the Financial Liberalisation Hypothesis', *Journal of Development Studies*, 30(3), pp. 628-649.

White, L.J.,1981, *Reforming Regulation: Processes and Problems*, Englewood, Cliffs, N.J. Prentice Hall.

Williams, M., 1989, 'Regulation of Financial Institutions in the Caribbean and the Implications for Growth and Development', *Social and Economic Studies*, 38(4), pp. 181-199.

Williams, M., 1994, 'Domestic Debt in Barbados and the Implications for Economic Stabilisation', Paper presented at a Seminar Sponsored by the Centre for Caribbean and Latin American Studies, July 1994.

Williamson, S., 1986, 'Costly Monitoring, Financial Intermediation and Equilibrium Credit Rationing', *Journal of Monetary Economics*, Vol.18, pp. 159-179.

Wooler, J., 1980, 'Ratio Analysis as an Indicator of Financial Strength', *The Accountant*, pp. 220-221.

Wood, J.H.,1975, 'Monetary Theory and Monetary Policy: A Central Banker's View', *De Economist*, pp. 3-20.

Worrell, R.D., 1990, 'Finance and Investment in Barbados', *Central Bank of Barbados, Economic Review*, Vol. 17(2), pp.13-23.

Worrell, D. and Prescod, R., 1983, 'Development of the Financial Sector in Barbados', *Central Bank of Barbados , Economic Review*, 10 (2), pp. 9-26.

Zellner, A.,1979, 'Causality and Econometrics', in *Three Aspects of Policy and Policy Making: Knowledge, Data and Institutions*, ed., Meltzer, A.H. Carnegie Rochester Conference Series on Public Policy, Vol. 10, Amsterdam, North Holland.

Zellner, A.,1962, 'An Efficient Method of Estimating Seemingly Unrelated Regressions and Tests for Aggregation Bias', *Journal of American Statistical Association*, Vol.57, pp. 346-368.

Zellner, A., 1988, 'Causality and Causal Laws in Economics',

Econometrics, Vol.39, pp. 7-21.

Zephirin, M., 1990, 'Imperfect Information and Financial Liberalisation in LDCs'. PhD thesis, University of Warwick.

Index

anonymously equitable prices 4, 32, 158
Auman Shapley prices 158
accommodative pricing 2, 11, 106, 114, 115, 126, 136
    interest rate setting 158, 159
allocation
    credit 23, 35, 47
    portfolio 17
    prices 31
    savings 22
asymmetric information 35, 46
assets
    total 254
average lending rate 73, 76, 79, 86, 89, 101, 102, 109, 114, 129
autocorrelation 152

bank crises 2
bank evaluation 134
bank failure 83
bank performance 15, 30, 31, 41, 45, 50, 56, 57, 60, 61, 64, 92, 95, 96, 97, 99, 131, 132, 138, 139, 140, 143, 146, 149, 151, 152, 193, 207, 210, 214, 215, 219, 221, 223, 224, 225, 227, 229, 231, 232, 233

bank rates 175, 176, 197, 255
bank regulation 90, 213, 216, 217, 218, 225
Basle Committee 9, 14, 120
benchmark 223, 233
benefit-cost 31
British Caribbean Currency Board 100

camel rating 10, 14
canonical discriminant function 147, 213
capital
    accumulation 16
    bank 137, 258
    constraint 35
    criteria 223, 228
    decision 40
    requirements 229
    role of 193
    variable 164, 180
capital adequacy 1, 4, 5, 8, 9, 10, 14, 34, 36, 50, 51, 52, 53, 54, 55, 60, 82, 83, 115, 118, 120, 121, 122, 229
    minimum requirements 66
    physical 83
    requirements 65, 66, 88, 160
capitalization 121

causality tests 148, 151, 155, 176, 178, 201, 224, 225
   prima facie 148
central banks 65, 68, 69, 70, 71, 72, 73, 75, 77, 80, 82, 84, 89, 90, 91, 93, 94
conflicts of interest 6
cointegrating equation 152, 154, 156, 158,159, 161, 165, 166, 168, 169, 170, 172, 174, 176, 179, 180, 184, 189, 191, 197, 200
cointegrating vectors 202
cointegration 12, 143, 144, 151, 154, 165, 166
competitiveness 18
compliance 113, 114, 116, 129
   regulatory 34
composite
   index 127, 151
   regulation index 127
   bank performance index 127, 141
   performance score 131, 141, 146, 147
   regulation score 131, 141
concentration 160
   bank 60
   by customer 121, 130
   credit 81
   levels of 8
concentration ratios 4, 13, 60, 65, 81, 102, 121, 135, 136, 152, 160, 179, 181
consumer loans 111, 128
consumer protection 13
contingent liabilities 83
core deposits 47, 49
cost adjustments 109, 110, 111, 113, 114, 115, 116
cost-axiomatic 2, 54, 60, 106, 114, 115, 126, 136, 158, 159, 160, 172
costs 132, 133, 134
   information 134, 135
   insolvency 41, 132, 134, 135, 136
   liquidity 132, 134, 135, 136
   of credit 17
   resources 41, 134
credit availability 7, 17, 62
credit controls 17, 23, 24, 25, 26, 46, 68, 69, 70, 73, 77, 80, 90, 92, 101, 104, 111, 112, 113, 115, 116, 119, 120, 121, 125, 128, 155, 158, 159, 160, 170, 171, 172, 176, 180, 181, 184, 187, 193, 197, 199, 204, 207, 210, 225, 226, 229, 231, 233, 263, 264, 274-278
   selective 17, 113, 119, 128
credit ceilings 46, 47, 66, 81, 101, 102
credit rationing 22, 24, 46, 49, 63
   equilibrium 46
customer satisfaction 110

data
   base 139
   by bank 140
   constraints 131, 139, 150
   deficiencies 131
   differences 139
   generating process 150
   income and expenditure 140
   series 136, 137, 139
demand management 23, 24
deposit insurance 40, 50, 52, 54, 82, 83, 103
deposit maximising 18, 27
   deposit rates 20
deposit-taking 60
Depository Institutions

Deregulation and Monetary Control
   Act 58
deregulation 22, 101
devaluation 80, 102, 232
developing countries 88, 230
Dickey-Fuller 152, 153, 166, 167,
   171, 176
 augmented 152, 153, 159
direct controls 15, 27, 30
discount rate 110, 129
discriminant analysis 151, 210, 214
discriminatory pricing 2
discriminant score 146, 209, 210
diseconomy
 external 31
distribution sector 69, 136
domestic demand 23
domestic resource mobilisation 88
dummy variable 136, 143, 150
 seasonal 168
Durbin Watson 169

economic growth 15, 16, 17, 21,
   22, 62
efficiency frontier 54
efficiency hypothesis 55
efficiency studies 132
eigenvectors 145, 146
eigenvalues 145, 146, 201, 202,
   210
elasticities 168, 170, 199
 price 15, 59
 of loan demand 113
Engle-Granger two-step 154, 167,
   172
equity holders 45, 48, 60
error correction models, term 12,
   131, 143, 144, 145
event studies 44, 55, 57, 131
excess liquidity 119, 139, 184,
   185, 187, 193

exchange controls, regulations 74
exchange rates 65, 73, 77, 79, 80,
   83, 92, 102, 116, 118
 liberalisation 80
 two-tier 65, 80, 102, 175, 179,
   187, 199
exogenous controls 17, 37, 38
external balance 21

fiduciary responsibility 66
financial instability 231
financial intermediation 24,99
 costs 99
 ratios 64, 88, 90, 92, 99
financial liberalisation 16, 17, 22,
   23, 28, 35, 49, 62, 207
financial repression 16, 17, 24
financial regulation 137
financial risk 54
foreign exchange
 adequacy 69
 availability 13
 earnings 70
 markets 80
 reserves 65, 69, 70, 72, 74, 253
 sufficiency 69
floors
 interest rate 73, 74, 101
functional regulation 239

Galbraith-Caves hypothesis 181
globalisation 8, 13
government
 securities 45, 108, 109, 110,
   111, 115, 116, 120
 bonds 109, 110, 116, 128, 132
   134, 135
Granger causality 13, 137,148
gross margins 74
guarantee, guarantees 83, 103, 180

304

heteroscedasticity 139, 154, 156, 157, 161, 163, 169, 174, 179, 183, 184, 185, 186, 188, 189
Hicks, Hicksian 26
high risk customers 111, 113, 122

index
  of regulation 214, 216, 217, 218, 219, 220, 223, 225
  of performance 207, 210, 213, 214, 215, 216, 223, 224, 225, 227, 229, 231, 232, 233
infection 230, 233
IMF 129
insolvency 10
  costs 40, 48, 49, 50
  risks 51, 54, 61
  bounding 53, 54
inflation 18, 20, 27, 137
interest rates
  bidding up 106
  bunching of lending 130
  ceilings 16, 17, 22, 23, 24, 46, 47, 48, 73, 101, 102
  controls 17, 22, 23, 30, 46, 47, 50, 51, 61, 69, 73, 77, 80, 90, 99, 121, 122, 126, 128, 159, 169, 170, 171, 180, 187, 199, 201, 204, 207, 216, 227, 232
  freeing of 226
  interbank 109
  regulation of 201
  questionnaire on 265, 266, 278-282
  spreads 110, 113, 201, 207, 216, 229
intermediation 3, 16, 25, 28
international
  loan 130
  banks 138

investment broking 66

Jamaica Stock Exchange 140
Johansen (and Juselius) procedure 143, 144, 145

Keynesian 15, 16

Lagrange multipliers, solution 35, 234-236
least squares 131
leasing 101, 102
legislation 65, 66, 68, 72, 84, 88, 102
leverage, leveraging 35, 115, 129
  financial 52
  models 35, 60
liability management 38, 40
liberalisation 8, 21, 22, 80, 232, 233
  financial 17, 23, 28, 29, 35, 49, 62
  interest rate 21
licensing 66, 67,103
likelihood ratio tests 145
liquidity 1, 4, 7, 8, 10, 12, 14, 64, 69, 72, 74, 81, 85, 92, 115, 211, 227
  ratios 72, 100
loanable funds 7, 8
loan commitments 46, 113, 118, 119
loan deposit ratio 261
loan losses 137, 150
loan loss provisions 259
locally incorporated banks 83
long run model 151, 153, 155, 156, 158, 159, 161, 165
long term borrowing 114

macro-monetary regulation 4,7

macroeconomic outcomes 1, 4, 5, 13
macroeconomic stabilisation 7, 9, 32, 232
macro-financial 9
manufacturing sector 119, 227
marginal costs 31, 113
marginal productivity 28
market clearing
prices 20, 46, 55, 63, 126
market failure 1
market share 2, 4, 5, 7, 8, 10, 11, 13, 64, 92, 95, 96, 97, 99, 105, 112, 113, 123, 124, 125, 126, 127, 128, 138, 139, 140, 201, 203, 204, 205, 206, 207, 209, 211, 213, 223, 225, 226, 229, 255
material adverse clause 130
maximal eigenvalues 164, 201, 202
maximisation
deposit 27
profit 113
rate of interest 38
utility 40
wealth 62
maximum likelihood estimates, procedure 131, 145, 146, 151, 154, 165, 201
minimum down-payment 201
minimum savings rate 74, 76, 77, 101, 102, 120, 129, 132, 135
monetarist 16
monetary and prudential regulatory changes 237-252
monetary authorities 86, 103
monetary control, controls 1, 11, 12, 30, 35, 64, 68, 77, 79, 80, 230, 231, 232
tools 105, 113, 127
monetary measures 155, 188

monetary policy 64, 66, 68, 69, 72, 73, 77, 113, 127
monetary regulation 1, 2, 4, 7, 8, 13, 55, 115, 118, 121, 155, 164, 165, 179, 187, 193, 194, 199, 204, 207, 225, 229, 230, 231
monetary tools 101
money multipliers 28
money stock 16, 15, 28
mortgage rates 125, 132
multi-purpose banking 34

nationalisation 12
neoclassical view 7
neo-structuralist 17, 27, 30
nominal incomes 69
non-banks 2, 7, 10, 11, 12, 64, 66, 67, 68, 73, 78, 79, 84, 85, 86, 87, 88, 92, 102, 103, 110, 121, 123, 125, 127, 139, 140, 201, 204, 207, 223, 225, 226, 229
non-normalised scores 223
non-price rationing 61
non-priority sectors 106, 112, 120
non-regulatory variables 160, 175
non-stationarity 141

OECD 88
off-balance sheet liabilities 83
oligopoly, oligopolistic behaviour 2, 45, 160
operating costs 88
opportunity cost 41, 42, 43, 44, 105, 109, 110, 132, 134, 135, 136
overseas borrowing 129

pent-up demand 112, 113
performance score 221, 223, 233

personal sector
  loans 69, 71, 73, 78, 136
portfolio 46, 48, 50, 51, 53, 54,
  59
  allocation 17, 24, 35, 36, 41, 46
  asset 52
  risk 41, 48, 50, 51, 61
precautionary balances 115
prima facie causality 149
primary reserve requirements 69,
  70, 72, 103, 107, 116, 136
product moment matrices 202
profitability
  bank 31, 34, 35, 41, 42, 45, 46,
47, 49, 50, 51, 53, 55, 58, 60, 61,
105, 106, 109, 111, 112, 113,
114, 115, 116, 120, 121, 122,
123, 126, 127, 152, 154, 155,
156, 157, 158, 159, 160, 162,
165, 167, 168, 169, 170, 171,
172, 173, 174, 175, 176, 177,
179, 192, 211, 223, 225, 226, 227
profit
  function 132, 133, 134
  margins 126
  intertemporal 133
  maximisers 213
  maximising behaviour 231
  maximising objective 133
  variance 139
profits
  bank 134, 139, 140
Protection of Depositors Act 68
provisioning 138
prudential regulation 5, 6, 55, 64,
  80, 114, 118, 120, 122, 127,
  141, 197, 214, 225, 226, 230,
  231, 266, 267, 282, 283, 284
  variable 159

Questionnaires 105, 108, 111, 112,

114, 118, 119, 123, 138, 143,
158, 159, 160, 176

reaction function 151, 184
regulatory capture 3
regulatory changes 139
regulatory forbearance 135
Regulation Q 63
regulation of the firm 30
regulation score 222, 223, 224,
  233
regulatory resilience 166, 169
regulatory variables 137, 138, 140,
  141, 146, 151, 152, 155, 159,
  172, 175, 176, 199
repression
  financial 16, 17, 22, 24
return on assets 257
  abnormal 58
reserve accumulation 20
reverse causality 225
reserve deficiency 42, 43, 115
reserve requirements 1, 2, 4, 5, 8,
  17, 23, 27, 28, 30, 41, 42, 44,
  45, 56, 61, 69, 70, 72, 73, 74,
  75, 77, 78, 80, 83, 85, 86, 92,
  99, 100, 101, 105, 106, 108,
  109, 110, 111, 115, 116, 118,
  120, 121, 122, 123, 128,132,
  134, 135, 136, 151, 152, 155,
  159, 160, 165, 168, 169, 170,
  172, 175, 176, 178, 179, 180,
  184, 185, 187, 193, 197, 199,
  201, 203, 204, 207, 225, 227,
  229, 232, 262, 269,274
  cash 108
  growth maximising 226
  statutory 116
restricted sectors 116
restrictions 31, 46, 48, 50, 54
restructuring 84

retained earnings 9
risk,
  bank 2, 10, 48, 105, 118, 119, 120, 121, 127, 139, 140, 151, 179, 180, 181, 183, 211, 226, 227, 229
  financial 54
  of systemic failure 230
  portfolio 48, 180
  of default 47, 61
  weights 51
risk-based capital 14, 51, 55, 82, 83
risk-taking 4, 61, 181
risk-related capital 51

shareholder wealth, returns 56, 58, 131, 137, 138
scope economies 34, 35
secondary reserves 28, 70, 72, 74, 78, 79, 80, 85, 99, 100, 101, 103, 107, 108, 109, 112, 136
securities requirements 72
solvency 4, 40, 41, 46, 50, 51, 53, 57, 60, 61, 121, 122, 123, 132, 135, 139, 140, 151 193, 194, 195, 196, 197, 198, 199
  standards 54
soundness
  bank 35, 36, 37, 38, 53
stabilisation 7, 24, 25, 28
  macroeconomic 31
stability 77, 80, 83
staff expenses 135, 151, 152, 153, 159, 169, 170
Stand-by Programme
staff expenses 135, 137, 138
stationarity 131, 140, 142, 143, 145, 152, 169, 174, 175, 183, 191

tests 141, 142
sterilisation 25
stochastic matrix 164, 165
stock market 116
structuralists 7, 68, 231, 232
structural regulation 2, 4, 6, 7, 229
structure, structures 64, 65, 66, 100
  error 144
  of assets 132, 134, 135
  of liabilities 132, 134
  ownership 140
  production 69
  oligopolistic 81
  lag 149
students-t-distribution 141
supernormal profits 135, 160
supply side 17, 20, 21, 62
systemic failure 3

tax
  reserves as 27, 44, 56, 58, 61
technology 49, 230
transactions costs 74
transformation curve, function 132, 133
transmission 66
  mechanism 25, 46
treasury bill yields 86, 89, 106, 109, 111, 112, 128

utility maximisation 62

vector autoregressive model 143

wealth
  maximising 62
Wicksellian 17, 62

Z score, Zeta score 147, 214